Praise for Get Real, Get Gone

"Don't even think of buying a boat until you have read this book".

-**Tom Cunliffe**, legendary sailor and author of
The Complete Ocean Skipper

"Rick serves up hard-headed, unsentimental, and occasionally hilarious advice… More than a how-to manual for the would-be world traveller, *Get Real, Get Gone* also tells how to live life to the fullest, and make every day an adventure…You'll learn a lot, and laugh a lot, reading this book".

-**Marjorie Preston** *Good Old Boat* Magazine

"Free your mind and the rest will follow"

Practical Boat Owner Magazine

Before even mentioning sailing or the sea, [Rick] boots modern society on its keister, sending it scuttling across the floors of silent seas. But this isn't an attack or a rant; rather, it's a juxtaposition. Page holds up a mirror to the world we live and invites us on a voyage through that looking glass, into a world he has lived for many years. It's an invitation we should embrace.

Page's writing is confident, clear, and full of a voice many writers never manage to embrace. He does not hold back—he holds forth. The practical guide part of this book is evident in its structure. The author leads the reader through a checklist of essential sailing elements, from basic seamanship to "the fiery stinkbox" of an on-board engine to anticipating relationship challenges brought on by close quarters and rogue waves.

If the author treats some branches of the sailing world roughly, that's his prerogative. His honest tone might surprise some readers more used to a gentrified, 'kumbaya' approach to telling a story and sharing years of experience. But the ocean, Page reminds us, is indifferent to our needs and wants, our tender mercies. The ocean must be reckoned with, and luck is a poor choice of resource for a sailor.

Read this book not just for its practical advice about sailing; instead, read it for its underlying acknowledgement of the bigger forces at work in our lives. As Page reminds us near the end of the book, there is one vital truth to remember: It's just a boat. Like the material things that surround our consciousness, it too shall pass, revealing the real reason we sail: a quest for the things we cannot wrap our hands around.

Shawn Kerivan Sailor and Professor of Writing, Vermont

STAY REAL, STAY GONE

MORE TRANSFORMATIONAL TRICKS AND TRIPS FROM THE FRONT LINE OF SIMPLE LIVING AFLOAT

Copyright Rick Page 2021. All Rights Reserved

Photos by Rick Page except where mentioned. Additional photos by Caroline Molda, Fee Binnekade Terry Simons and Jasna Tuta.

ISBN:9798454218737

Licence Notes

This book is licensed for your personal enjoyment only and the author would be very grateful if you paid for it. It cannot be re-sold, reproduced electronically, stored electronically or re-printed in whole or in part without the authors' express permission in writing.

Disclaimer

While every effort has been taken to ensure that the advice given in this book is accurate, it is in no way definitive or claiming to be the ultimate word in seamanship. The purpose of this book is to help new sailors develop the right attitude to safety and sailing in general and should be considered the first step on the path to starting a life afloat, not the final one. As in all matters at sea, the skipper must use every resource at his disposal to decide upon the correct course of action. The authors accept no liability for any loss and/or damage howsoever caused that may arise from reliance on information contained in this book.

To Molly,

for keeping a light in the window.

CONTENTS

Preface and a quick "thank you"

PART ONE – STAYING REAL: More on the technical stuff

Introduction: A little motivational butt-kicking

Chapter 1. Staying Real about rudders and keels

Chapter 2. Staying Long: The wonderful world of the real sea-boat

Chapter 3. Staying Straight: Manoeuvring the longer-keeled boat

Chapter 4. Staying Single: What is wrong with multihulls again?

Chapter 5. Aluminium boats

Chapter 6. Staying Away from Disaster: 'Uncharted' reefs

Chapter 7. Staying Simple: Furling mainsails and other nonsense

Chapter 8. Getting Smart: More on buying.

Chapter 9. Staying Solvent: More money matters

Chapter 10. Staying Real about steel

Chapter 11. Staying Afloat: Hull Integrity

Chapter 12. Staying Real about Risk: Storms

Chapter 13.Getting Off: Running aground

PART TWO – STAYING GONE: Staying happy with your new life

Introduction: Perspective is everything.

Chapter 14. Staying Happy with your budget: Establishing new normals

Chapter 15. Staying Healthy: Do I need health insurance?

Chapter 16. Staying Covid-free

Chapter 17. Staying Sane: Taking a break

Chapter 18. Staying Solo: The joys of single-handing

Chapter 19. Staying Social: Finding good shipmates

Chapter 20. Not Staying Gone: Exit strategies

Chapter 21. Staying Strong: Ignoring the doubters and trolls

Afterword

Recommended Reading

Contacts

Preface and a quick "thank you"

Thanks for buying my second (and much longer) book. The overwhelmingly positive feedback from *Get Real, Get Gone* both delighted and surprised me.[1] I was amazed that the book was so successful, but even happier to find that there are so many kindred spirits in this world that share my desire for a simpler life (afloat or otherwise) and are prepared to take a stand against the avalanche of marketing nonsense that stands in the way of it.

A great deal has happened since 2015. I have made significant upgrades in both boat and partner, had another visit from the extremely likeable Ben Fogle for a new TV show (*NewLlives in the Wild Revisited*) and sailed many more nautical miles. I have explored many more gorgeous anchorages and, by the grace of Neptune, speared many more yummy fish to the point where my mercury levels are about the same as a cheap thermometer.

But what has made this period particularly memorable, is the great many readers who took the time to contact me personally either to seek advice or share their own plans to access the joys of this lifestyle and it has been my privilege to accompany them on their journey (albeit mostly by email). Several readers have even managed to catch up with me on their fantastic, simple, floating escape capsules and let

---

[1] This is the book you need to read before this one which is, most definitely, a follow-up. You will probably still be able to make sense of this book, but if you are struggling, then reading the first one may be the way to go.

me know how the book has positively impacted their lives, which has been very rewarding indeed (liver damage notwithstanding). My ever–expanding inbox suggests that these numbers will continue to grow as many dreamers dip their toes into the reality of this lifestyle. It looks as though I may not have to buy beer for a while.

So, thanks to everyone who bought the book and special thanks to everyone who wrote to me and made me an honoured guest in their great transition to blue nomad status – I have been delighted to be vicariously (and occasionally, actually) onboard!

There have also been a few trolls in the ointment that was previously reserved for flies, and it is great fun and quite illuminating to poke fun at them, so I am completely unable to resist doing so. Generally, they tend to fall into three categories:

- You are just thinking of yourself!
- Poor people are impinging on our exclusivity!
- I did not read the cover description and I am angry that this publication is not (like everything else in life) targeted toward the high-end consumer like me!

I mention this not just because it is fun to lampoon trolls (although, it definitely is) but also because this type of negativity has had quite an effect on the plans of many budding sea gypsies.

Maybe it is the rise of social media, but there seems to be growing numbers of very unhappy, very vocal people more than willing to rain on your parade. If you are thinking of abandoning your plans due to the words of trolls or guilt-tripping family members, then a quick read of chapter twenty-one, a pot of skin-thickening cream and a decent set of noise-cancelling headphones might constitute a good use of your time and money. If this trolling is tempting you to reconsider your plans, drop me a line and I will happily talk you back into them!

Admittedly, the trolls are just extreme examples, but to some degree, we all view the world through the lens of our pre-existing opinions and this can impact our ability to find satisfaction in the simpler life. In this book then, we will try and sort fact from opinion and look at how mistaking these two opposites can often stand in the way of our sailing happiness and even be dangerous. We will, once more, try and split the marketing from the reality and the mildly erroneous from the wildly apocryphal.

Of course, there will be more ninja-level practical advice on the tricks and techniques needed for living aboard on a skinny budget, but *attitude* is still the most important foundation upon whose shoulders our eventual satisfaction will stand and the (admittedly small) postbag of angry hate-mail I receive is a strong reminder of the fate that awaits those who have the wrong version of it.

So heartfelt thanks again to the 97% of people who responded in an overwhelmingly positive way – and genuine thanks to the other 3% who helped prove the point that money can only briefly help us on our universal human search for contentment.

⚓

Right, let's get cracking. One of the advantages of getting so much email from readers is that the first part of this book virtually wrote itself - or rather it was written as an answer to the more commonly asked questions that readers emailed me with. So thanks again to everybody who wrote to me and I hope this section will address those questions.

As always, I can be reached on sailingcalypso@gmail.com if further clarification is needed or any new questions pop up.

This book is much longer than the first one. To keep the book price as low as possible, the photographs have been reproduced in black and white. Colour versions of all the media in this book can be found on: www.sailingcalypso.com. Click on 'photos' and then enter the password 'neptune' when prompted.

Right, off we go then. But before we dive in, let us remind ourselves why we are here...

PART ONE

Staying on Message

Reality can be fun: Good friends can make even the boatyard jobs enjoyable.

INTRODUCTION

A Little Motivational Butt-Kicking

In this book, I will be answering the most often raised questions from readers and diving more deeply into some of the subjects that were merely skimmed in *Get Real Get Gone*. I will also be raising some completely new topics – both practical and psychological – that I hope will help you get the most out of this amazing lifestyle.

But you have to be in it to win it, and I know from the emails I get that the most common reason many budding nautical nomads never set sail is that fear of the unknown locks them into a never-ending cycle of superfluous research. Now, if you have read the first book, you will already know that I am the least likely person on earth to encourage anyone to set sail without proper preparation or on the wrong boat, but that is not what I mean.

I will try and explain what I mean with a joke. I will warn you now, it is not a very funny joke, so please don't feel under the slightest obligation to emit even the most delicate of polite giggles. The message it contains is quite interesting though and goes some way to explaining why, in certain situations, we should all be a little resistant to what can often sound like sensible advice from people who mean well. Even more confused now? Okay, let's get to the gag and we can talk later:

Two little boys are playing in a sand pit in a city park while the everyday business of urban life goes on around them. As the day wears on they notice a steady stream of men arriving at a particular house with a red door. The men would knock three times and an overly made-up woman would answer the door and engage the gentleman in a greeting ritual:

"Whaddya want?" the madam would ask. Whereupon the man would reply,

"You know what I want."

"Got any money?" the painted lady would retort.

"I've got $200" the guy would reply, brandishing a roll of notes. The door would then open the whole way and the man would enter, emerging some time later with a happy smile on his face.

This exact routine would repeat every few minutes, only with a different gentleman caller.

After a while, curiosity gets the better of the two boys and they rummage through their pockets to see how much money they have. They pool their change and find they have the princely sum of 65 cents. Clutching their combined wealth, they walk up to the door and knock three times. The madam answers and looks down at the two little boys and asks,

"Whaddya want?"

"You know what we want" the two boys reply in unison in their high-pitched voices.

"Got any money?" the madam growls suspiciously.

"We've got 65 cents" the boys proudly reply, holding out their cash.

The madam bends down, puts one hand on each side of their heads and smartly cracks them together, sending the boys tumbling into the street, bruised and bewildered.

Sitting in the dust and rubbing their heads, one kid says to the other,

"If that is what you get for 65 cents, I am glad we didn't have the $200!"

⚓

Okay, I did warn you that it was not particularly funny, but can you see where I am going with this?

There is a general consensus amongst reasonable people that you should, 'try before you buy' anything that takes your fancy before committing to it. Sounds terribly reasonable doesn't it? While this is probably advisable for consumer durables and arranged marriages, it is not such a good idea for fundamental lifestyle choices. There comes a point where simply 'dipping your toes' into a new lifestyle will produce an experience so fundamentally different from the full-blown, life-changing epiphanies experienced by those brave enough to jump in with both feet, that the two experiences are not even recognisable as versions of the same thing.

Here is another story, this time a true one. Again not funny though, so still no need to laugh.

In the nineties I had a lovely girlfriend who was horse-mad and an awesome rider. I liked horses too and had done some riding and played a bit of polo-cross, but nothing like she had. Anyway, her dream was to start a trail riding centre in Spain. She had her half of the necessary capital courtesy of her generous parents, but I had very little. So, not wanting to surrender my equality in any way, I worked hard to save my share. Eventually I managed to scrape together the minimum requirement and off we toddled to Spain with an old 4x4, towing a horse box that had everything in it except a horse. After many struggles with weird landlords, dishonest real estate agents and shotgun-wielding, alcoholic sheep farmers that could fill a much longer book, we had established a very marginal business and were just about getting by.

It was super-hard work with summers of 38°C (100°F) and snowy winters of -10°C (14°F) and no money for power tools or labourers. Within a fairly short time, my girlfriend had had enough. Having so many other options courtesy of her family money she (quite understandably in hindsight), found it hard to justify why she was moving horse shit around in the snow with a doofus like me when she could be skiing in the French alps with all her wealthy friends, her only worry being whether her new ski outfit made her bum look big (it did not).

And who can blame her? Unfortunately for me, I had everything I owned in this business, no money to buy my now ex-partner out, no trust fund, no supportive parents to fall back on and no option but to try to sell the place in order to raise some survival money for me and some ashram fees and ski passes for the ex.

Sipping a *cafe con leche* in our local village bar, I was explaining my plight to a friend who just so happened to work in the local bank. With a rather surprised expression he asked,

"Why have you not asked us for a loan to buy your partner out?"

I explained that it had never crossed my mind that a loan would be granted on such a marginal business so clearly in its infancy. However, with a couple of strokes of a pen on a napkin, he detailed the terms and conditions of the money (a fairly decent rate) and told me it would be available anytime I wanted it.

Well, you could have knocked me over with a sailor's wallet. I turned up on Monday morning with the required paperwork and an hour later, with what seemed like magic, I emerged blinking into the glorious sunshine of an Andalucian morning - the extremely happy, sole owner of my very own farm and business (albeit with a rather large mortgage to pay).

Now though, I had other problems to solve – the most pressing being that about half the horses my ex-partner had bequeathed me were useless. Having a background in dressage, she naturally had a tendency to favour beautiful horses with great confirmation whilst not paying enough attention to their feet and tendons (the most important feature of a working horse). My admiration for her riding skills overflowed into an inappropriate deference to her in these matters as well, and this now meant that half the horses were either lame or totally unsuitable for the work they were being asked to do - and I had very little money with which to replace them. With less than three months until the season was to kick-off again, I had to work harder than I had ever worked in my life. I spent the next eleven weeks scouring Andalucía for suitable, durable, working horses to buy and somewhere to offload my herd of fops and dandies. During this period, the need to stretch my body and budget to breaking point led to some amazing experiences:

I met (and partied with) every gypsy horse dealer in southern Spain (the horse biz in Andalucía is run by gypsies from a few extended families and negotiation requires serious drinking. The one who can hold out the longest, usually gets the best deal).

I have woken up with a massive hangover in a cave in Sacramonte with the most beautiful stallion tied to a beer barrel with my name scribbled in chalk on his butt (which I had bought for a song due to a combination of my desperation to get a bargain and enormous tolerance for alcohol).

I made a fantastic Mexican friend - a complete wild man who would help me ride the horses I had bought (or borrowed) impossible distances in order to save money on delivery. We even got into a bar fight with some Spanish racists. An actual bar fight! Those who have met me will know that I weigh 68 kilos soaking wet wearing sponge swimming shorts and am not disposed towards violence. But I had a cartoon bar fight alongside a mad Mexican in a cantina in Andalucía and we genuinely made our getaway on horseback galloping off into the sunset.

On one marathon ride, my wild Mexican friend was called away (I think it had come to his attention that there was a Spanish girl he had not yet slept with) and had to leave me with two young, green horses, which I now had to ride (ride one whilst leading the other two) up the twisting narrow mountain roads for 30 miles. It was while struggling with these two nervous neddies that I met a beautiful German dancer who was filming a music video in the mountains (with Sting no less!). She also loved horses and offered to help me get them home. This lead to the most mind-blowing erotic three months I had (up until then at least) ever experienced.

Impending penury and twenty-five mouths to feed continued to steer me towards the most bizarre adventures over the next few years until the business was up and running, and making a small profit as predictable as the next Coldplay album.

Now, I could go on about this period of my life forever (no, really, I could) but suffice it to say, that it was a real golden age that I still look back on and would struggle to believe had actually happened if I did not have the photos, a small collection of rather unattractive scars, a lower left rib that looks like the turn signal of a vintage car and an unresponsive eyebrow that makes strangers think that either I have taken Botox or the new Mr Bean doll is now in available in shops.

Now, imagine what my experiences would have been if I had decided to listen to the voices of caution and do the 'reasonable' thing by working on a horse farm in Spain for a couple of months to 'see if I liked it.'

The two experiences are incomparable. Eight weeks of shovelling horse shit and cleaning saddles for some old misanthropic battleaxe in jodhpurs and green gum boots is incomparable to the wild adventures I was forced into because I had jumped in with both feet, was fully committed to what I was doing and master of my own destiny.

This is true for many things and doubly so for the sea gypsy life. As the boys in the terrible joke at the beginning of this chapter discovered, the $200 option is not simply the 65c option magnified 308 times, it is a totally different experience altogether.

I am not saying one should launch straight into it without ever seeing a boat. But once you have the basics to keep you safe (as laid out to the point of madness in this book and the last one) then only jumping in with total commitment will give you the authentic experiences you seek.

In Miami I met a guy with safety pins holding his clothes together, a Marilyn Manson T shirt and black lipstick. I tend to gravitate towards the weirder people of the world and was soon talking to him. He explained that at the weekends he enjoyed 'being a punk'. When I asked what he did the rest of the time, I was uber-surprised to learn that he was a hedge fund manager for a (now defunct) merchant bank.

Now, I happened to grow up in London during the first punk movement and it was an incredibly exciting time, born of the hopeless desperation of kids like myself who felt (with some justification) that the whole of the UK was so moribund and sewn up with class distinctions, that they were powerless, irrelevant and inconspicuous. The noise they made was not so much about music (no great surprise there) but was a protest over the marginalisation of anyone without a private education or a sizeable trust fund. It certainly was not something you could do at the weekend.

Being a part-time punk is as 'real' as a billionaire banker donning denim overalls and singing the blues - and I am sure we would all agree that, "I just smashed up my Lexus and I am down to my last million bucks" would not really cut it as an authentic blues lyric anywhere within a thousand mile radius of Chicago. To play the blues you have to *live* the blues.

And so it is with the sea-gypsy life. Sometimes, just dipping your toes into something makes it far too easy to not be real - a real 'punk', a real blues singer, a real cowboy or indeed, a real sea gypsy. So buy yourself a 'real' boat, stick with it long enough to incorporate the more challenging aspects into your life (more on this in chapter 14) and become master of your own destiny - as this is an entirely different experience than weekend crewing at the yacht club simply scaled up to full time.[2]

Look before you leap
(but he who hesitates too long is lost).
Good research and good preparation is to be applauded and I will personally mud-wrestle anyone who says differently.

Unfortunately though, quite a few of the potential sea gypsies who email me get stuck here, paralyzed by indecision as to what boat to buy, which windvane to fit or what type of sails to buy. Or, if they

---

[2] Nothing wrong with crewing at the yacht club, but this is a book about the sea gypsy life.

already have a boat, when to leave or what supplies to take, which route to choose, etc.

By now, you know that I am not saying that you should leave half-cocked or simply 'just do it' as is so often the refrain of those attempting to appear cool from the sidelines. Every passage, every country, every sea condition will be unique and it is a fool that relegates research and preparation to the category of 'optional extras'. But waiting until you have controlled *all* the variables that the sea can present, is pretty much a synonym for staying at home.

This is equally applicable to whatever leap you are taking and while I certainly do not claim to be an expert in sailing, I can claim to be something of an authority on leaping. I tend to change lifestyle and/or geographical location quite often, which means abandoning the comfort of a world I am familiar with and becoming a nervous rookie again, and I can offer these two little gems of ersatz wisdom:

1. **You will always underestimate the problems that you will face in any new venture – and that is a good thing**.

Well, the good news is that, not only is it impossible to foresee all the problems you will face in any new venture, it would be quite counter-productive if you could. Anyone who could see all the problems in advance would most likely retreat in whole-hearted terror from the reality of *any* project. In short, without some degree of ignorance, we may never have the courage to embark on anything at all (I definitely include all marriages in this).

But don't let this foggy vision of your future freak you out too much because, although it is true that you can never predict all the challenges you will face, the second great truth is that:

2. **You are underestimating to an even greater degree, your ability to overcome them.**

This I have found to be true for everyone. The often heard refrain of, 'oh, it's okay for you but it's different for me,' is nonsense. The truth is actually quite simple: Those who successfully make the leap understand that they must prepare for the predictable and then accept that they will cope with further problems as they occur - rather than be paralysed by their own efforts to ascertain in advance what those further problems might be. This is why the process of simplifying (or 'getting real') is so important. The purpose of simplifying is not to join any 'purist' sailing club, but to narrow down the predictable failures so that you have the time and space to deal with whatever else crops up without being overwhelmed.

Again, I am not advising you to be any less than 100% diligent, but once you have the right boat, the right attitude and the right skills, you will have to be very vigilant that you are not procrastinating under the illusion that you can control *all* variables and risks. It cannot be done and even if you could narrow your adventure down to, 'occasional-clearly-defined-areas-of-uncertainty', I am not sure it would be any the better for it. (If this sounds like you, I would advise you to rip out the next page and stick it on your fridge).

So be bold my sea gypsy brothers and sisters! I hope the mental gymnastics and practical advice in this book help you STAY gone if you have already left, or GET gone if you are still teetering on the edge of this relatively safe, affordable and wonderfully accessible adventure.

⚓

The Sailor's Temperance Prayer

Neptune grant me the foresight to prepare for the things I can predict;

The fortitude to deal with the things I cannot;

And the wisdom to know the difference and get gone anyway.

CHAPTER ONE

Staying Real about Rudders and Keels

'Faced with the choice between changing one's mind and proving that there is no need to do so, almost everyone gets busy on the proof.'

JK Galbraith.

In *Get Real, Get Gone*, I covered the basic keel and rudder designs that are suitable for a safe voyaging vagabond boat. The gist of the message was that narrow, bolt-on fin keels and spade (unsupported/unprotected) rudders, despite being the most commonly found, were not suitable for a sea gypsy boat.

I did not go into the subject too deeply as the book was meant to be something of an introduction to the broader concepts of sustainable voyaging and I did not think delving into the structural analysis behind that claim was commensurate with such an approach. Basically, I didn't want the newly excited sailor to be as bored as a hermit's doorbell so early in her journey. Instead, I wanted to give her some sense of the reality that, with a few precautions and a dose of reality, she was trembling on the edge of a wonderful, accessible and relatively safe adventure - not signing up for a rather dull evening class on the biology of moss.

However, this has lead a lot of people to believe that my dislike of spade rudders and narrow fin keels is merely my 'preference' or 'personal opinion' and as such is no more valid than any other preference or opinion. This is a million miles from the truth. It may be a matter of opinion whether a glass is half full or half empty, but it is an engineering fact that the glass is twice as big as it needs to be for that volume of liquid. Engineering reality is about as different from opinion as it is possible to get. So I quickly want to expand on this and dip the smallest of toes into the murky waters of structural analysis in what I hope will be the final word on the subject. Even if you are already convinced, this little section will at least give you the knowledge to defend your position to the boat salesman who wants you to buy what he is selling - which is invariably a boat with a thin, bolted-on fin keel and an unprotected spade rudder, because nearly all modern boats are made this way (for reasons we will discuss later).

I have reproduced overleaf the diagram of keel and rudder arrangements from *Get Real, Get Gone* as I wish to comment further on it here without all that tiresome flicking between different books.

Keel and rudder arrangements

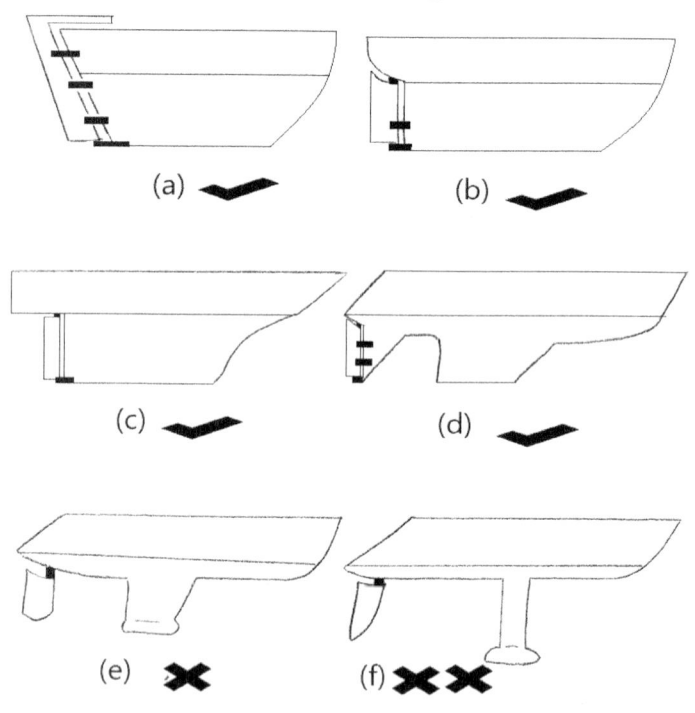

(a) (b)

(c) (d)

(e) (f)

I have exaggerated the diagrams (and omitted the propellers) in the interests of clarity, but you get the message – unsupported rudders are vulnerable to damage and loss, leaving you drifting helplessly or beam-on (sideways-on) to an angry sea. Keels that are not attached over a goodly portion of the hull can become separated from the hull leading to loss of boat and life (examples (e) and (f) above).

Much of why this occurs with such depressing regularity can be explained by looking at a simple bit of structural analysis on something called a 'cantilever' and why the considerations of accountants, not engineers, make them so popular. Let's do the engineering first:

Cantilevers

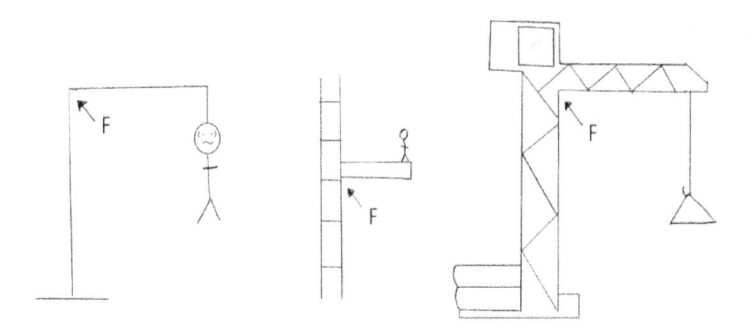

Figure 1. A gallows, a balcony and a crane are typical cantilevers. 'F' marks the likely failure point.

I am a qualified Disaster Engineer, which (before you say it) does not mean I engineer disasters – although if you have tried my home brew or have been my girlfriend for any length of time, you could easily be forgiven for thinking so. A disaster engineer specializes in analysing structures and predicting where they are going to fail and why. One of the most problematic, yet predictable types of structure to analyse is the simple cantilever.

What makes a cantilever quite vulnerable is that it is only supported at one end. This means that any loads placed on the free end are multiplied by the length of the cantilever. In short, the longer the cantilever the greater the stress at its only connection point for a given load. Here is how that works:

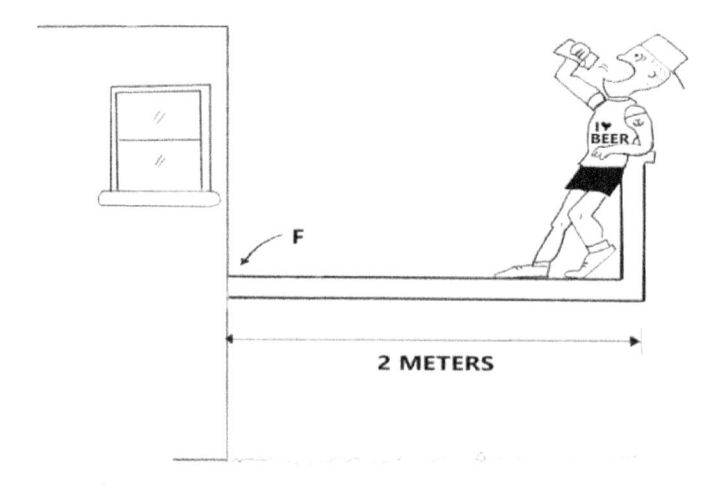

Figure 2: An 80kg guy enjoys a drink at the end of a 2 meter balcony. The stress at point F is the sum of his weight multiplied by the length of the balcony.

Fig 2 shows an 80kg (176lbs) chap drinking beer at the end of a 2 meter (6.6 feet) balcony. As the balcony is only connected at one point, all his weight is concentrated at that point, which we will call point F (for 'failure'). But it gets worse. As this is a cantilever, the drunk fella's weight is magnified by the length of the cantilever. So the stress at point F is actually his weight multiplied by the length of the balcony.

80 x 2 = 160. So there is actually 160 kilos of force at point F.

If we make the balcony longer, then the force at point F increases proportionally. Fig 3 shows our drunk friend again, this time on a 3 meter balcony:

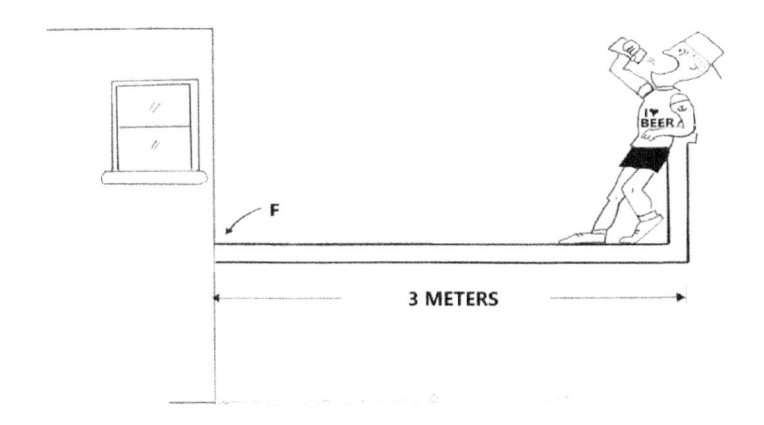

Figure 3: As the length of the balcony increases, so does the stress.

All his weight is now magnified by the 3 meter length of the balcony, resulting in a force at point F of:

80 x 3 = 240 kg.

What has this got to do with rudders? Well, quite simply, a spade rudder is a cantilever but upright, rather than horizontal like the balcony. Instead of a drunk fella providing the force in a downward direction, we have the waves providing the force from a sideways direction (fig 4). From an engineering point of view though, they are exactly

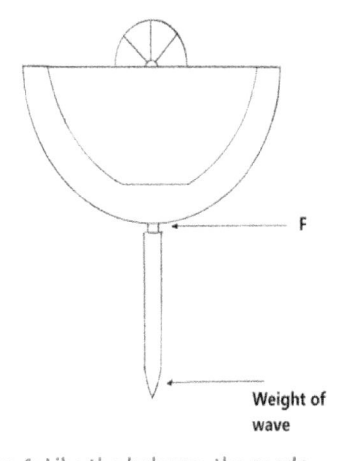

Figure 4: Like the balcony, the spade rudder is supported at just a single point (F) with the rudder acting like a giant lever to increase the stress at point F.

29

the same.

Just in case my rubbish sketching skills aren't cutting the mustard, here is a photograph of a typical spade rudder (fig 5).

If we assume the weight of the wave is the same 80kg as the drunk guy on the balcony and the rudder is 1.5 meters long, then you have a total force at point F of 120kg. In reality, the force of a wave (or a collision with a whale, or a grounding) can be a whole bunch more than 80 kilos, but you get the point.

Figure 5: Sticking out like a Scotsman at a charity gala, the spade rudder is a very vulnerable type of structure known to engineers as a 'cantilever'.

The take-away here is that with a cantilever, the forces at the connection point increase dramatically with the length of the cantilever.

Just to add more drama, spade rudders tend to be deeper and slimmer than supported rudders, further exacerbating the problem. As you can imagine, the shaft on the spade rudder (and the rudder bearing) are being asked to cope with enormous forces as the waves roll on past them - hour after hour, day after day, year after year. You would be easily forgiven for thinking that is reason enough to avoid them completely (and, incidentally, why you should resist the urge to join the dancing on the crowded balcony in Ibiza), but it gets even worse.

Work hardening on stainless steel

Pretty much most rudder shafts are made of stainless steel. Stainless steel is a much overrated material. One day I would like to own a boat without a single structural scrap of it. The problem with stainless is that it is brittle, it corrodes in unusual ways and it fails catastrophically. Furthermore, stainless can often give no visible signs of imminent failure. This means that visual inspections are of very limited value from an engineering point of view, (but they keep the insurance people happy by providing more meaningless paperwork, so there's that). Stainless is also particularly vulnerable to a process called 'work hardening'.

Work hardening

We have all experienced work hardening in other areas of our lives. This is the process that allows us to break certain materials by repeated bending. Take a paper clip and straighten it out. Now bend it backwards and forwards. Pretty soon the paper clip will break at the point where you have been bending it. This is not because it has got softer, but because the point where all the flexing or 'work' was being done actually got *harder*, and therefore more brittle and no longer able to bend as efficiently.

As is often the case in so many areas of life – nature has a way of breaking that which cannot bend.

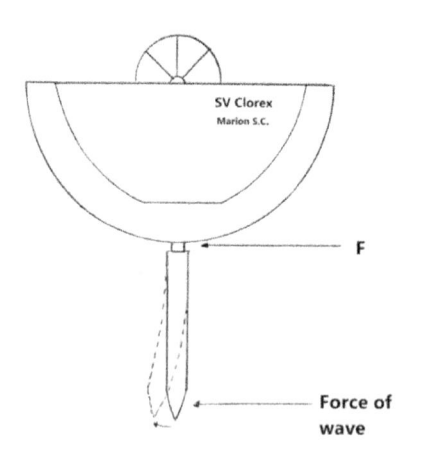

Figure 6: As the waves roll past, the force they produce is magnified by the length of the rudder causing the shaft to flex at point F. Wave after wave, hour after hour, day after day.

All rudders have to absorb large forces from the sea - that is a given. The problem the spade rudder has (being supported only at point F) is that each time a wave rolls across it, the shaft flexes from one side to the other - just like the paper clip you were just bending – with the most 'work' being done where the shaft of the rudder exits the hull (Fig 6). Can you guess what happens when an already quite brittle metal becomes more brittle? You got it – work hardening at that point. Then failure.

Funnily enough, I was just explaining this very process to a potential sea gypsy who had contacted me by email when I heard that a boat had been towed into the local yard with rudder problems.

Being fantastically nosey about this kind of thing, I rowed over (all of 500 meters) to find out what had happened. I think the pictures tell the story. As you can see in Fig 7, the rudder has gone (what you can see under the boat is an oil drum).

Figure 7: Oops, where is my rudder?

Figure 8

The whole thing is now sleeping with the Krakens five kilometres under the surface of the Pacific Ocean just south of Vitu Levu and will cost several thousand dollars to replace because it 'aint coming back.

In Fig 8, (we are standing where the rudder should be and looking directly up) you can see the shaft has snapped at precisely the place that the principal of work hardening would predict (point F on the diagram in Fig 6).

This poor sailor is also facing a bill of US$7000 for the tow into Fiji and a couple of thousand for the boatyard. Had he been further offshore, the tow could have cost several times that. If he had been offshore in bad weather, he may have paid the ultimate price (and I don't mean being forced to listen to Jimmy Buffet on loop).

33

False diagnosis

Another thing that can affect the stainless shaft is anodic corrosion. This is where two different metals (referred to as an 'anode' and a 'cathode' for reasons we will discuss later) in a warm salty solution, set up a kind of low-tech battery.

Did you ever make a potato battery in your science class at school? If, like me, you were too busy gazing out the window and trying to work out how to sit next to Susan Reading, then Fig 9 will be a quick reminder. All you need is two dissimilar metals in a salty wet environment (in this case a humble spud) and voila, the bulb lights up! Seemed like magic when I was kid. (Still does actually).

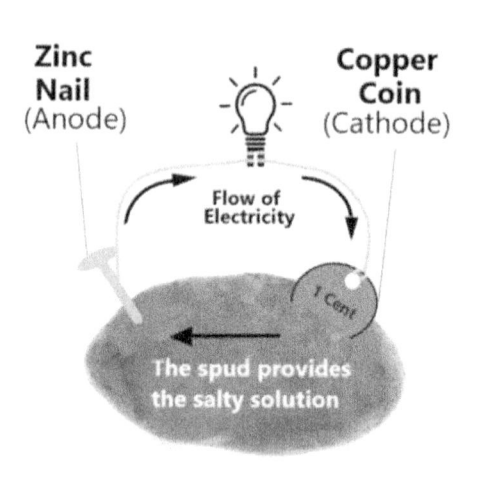

Figure 9: Any two dissimilar metals in a salty solution will produce an electric current.

Anyway, what is not shown in the diagram is that over time, the zinc nail (the 'anode') will get eaten away by a process unimaginatively called, 'anodic corrosion'. Not a big deal in a potato which will go mushy well before then, but quite a pain in the spuds when it happens on a boat because it means something is corroding - and corrosion never sleeps.

A boat can have quite a few dissimilar metals in a warm salty solution (seawater this time) and while there are things you can do to mitigate anodic corrosion (more on this later) it is not unusual for there to be a little bit of it on many rudder shafts. So, when a spade rudder snaps off and a little anodic corrosion is discovered, the cause of failure can often be misdiagnosed as anodic corrosion, instead of the more obvious and far more likely, 'work hardening due to bad design'. Furthermore, work hardening will often cause little surface cracks – the ideal breeding ground for another type of corrosion in stainless steel known as 'crevice corrosion', which I will not go into today because I can already feel you nodding off and looking longingly at the Play Station. But you see what I mean? A lot of little problems, all starting to hold hands.

Now let's look what happens when we support the rudder on the bottom by attaching it to the back of the keel or on a good skeg. Here is our drunk geezer on the balcony again, only this time, we have added a support under his little alcoholic butt.

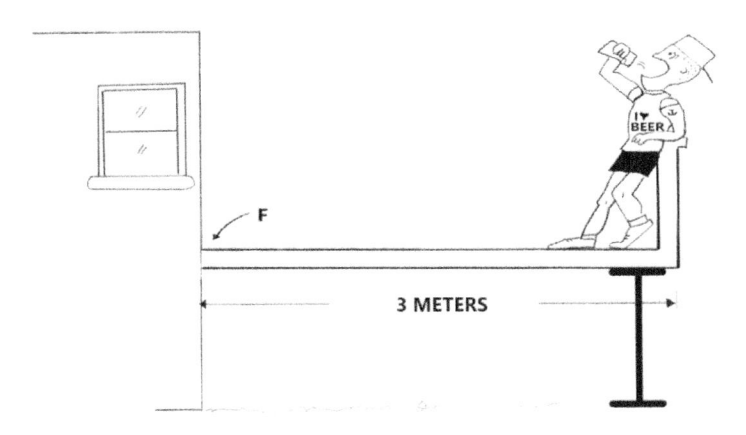

Figure 10: Adding a support reduces the stress at point F to a fraction of its previous levels.

As this structure is no longer simply supported at one end, it is no longer a cantilever and the stresses are not calculated in the same way. As our lounge lizard is now standing directly above the support, the strain of his weight is being taken directly down onto the ground and is not multiplied by the distance from point F.

So let us look at how that translates to rudders:

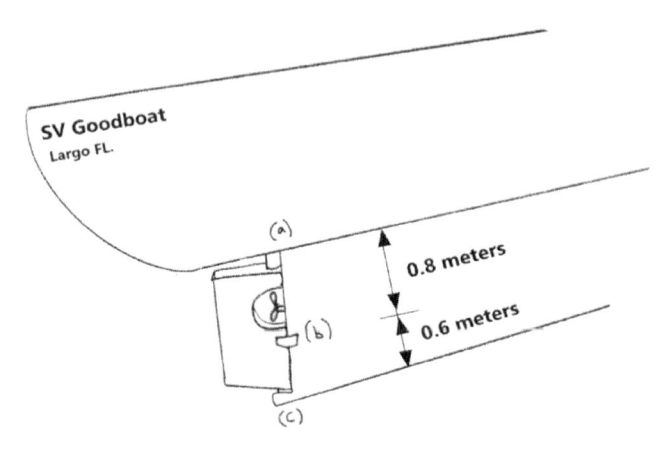

Figure 11: A rudder supported at several points (a, b and c in this example) is under many times less stress than the cantilevered spade rudder as the forces of the sea are divided by the number of supports, not magnified by the cantilever effect.

The above is based on the rudder of *Calypso* which is supported at three points. The advantages of having three supports are even greater than putting the single support under the drunk guy on the balcony because when our 80 kilo wave rolls over this rudder, rather than being magnified by the length of a cantilever to insane levels, the force is *divided* between these three points and reduced to a fraction of that of the cantilevered spade[3]. I think we have done quite enough calculations today already, so let's not do any more, but it is fairly obvious that any structure supported in several places is many times less problematic than a cantilever.

Furthermore, having the rudder supported by the keel or skeg also allows for only a fraction of the flexing of the cantilevered spade rudder and thereby all but eliminates the problem of work hardening and the crevice/anodic corrosion failures that can often be mistakenly attributed to it.

Also, if you glance again at Fig 11, you can see that if the shaft on a properly supported rudder did snap where it enters the hull (although I have never heard of this happening) then the rudder will not be lost to the mermaids as it will still be held in place by the other connections, leaving many options for jury rigging a temporary steering system.

Calypso II has an ingenious little modification that the rather awesome people at the Island Packet Yacht Company put on most of their boats: A 25mm hole drilled on the top of the trailing edge (and reinforced there too) allows a line to be fed through and led back to the cockpit via turning blocks so that steering is still possible should the worst happen.

---

[3] The calculation is a little more complex, but not so much that it changes the point even slightly. I don't really want to bore you with the actual calculations unnecessarily. Those who want to get nerdy can drop me a line.

The well-made spade

So why not simply make spade rudders stronger? Well, apart from the fact that the popularity of spade rudders is largely due to their cheapness to make (which would rather defeat the object of making a better one – more on this later) a stronger spade rudder introduces another problem.

Let me explain:

When analysing simple structures, it always pays to keep in mind that forces are

Calypso II has a 25mm reinforced hole in the trailing edge of her supported rudder to facilitate jury rigging. One of many signs that the IP yachts are designed by actual voyaging sailors.

never lost, just transferred elsewhere or converted into something else. As soon as the energy cannot 'pass the parcel' somewhere else, you can be pretty sure something is about to come under a bit of stress. When you kick a football, the energy from your leg gets transferred to the ball, is then turned into motion and dissipates that energy by flying into the back of the goal. If you miss the ball and kick the ground, the whole planet cannot fly off to dissipate the energy, so the energy is dissipated by breaking your toe and making you look a bit of a dick. In short, forces are always going somewhere until they can be dissipated by movement, by breaking something or being transferred elsewhere and it pays the self-sufficient sailor to start developing a bit of an eye for this process in order to predict (more or less) the outcome of each input of energy.

So, if we now have a super-tough spade rudder with a large, strong shaft, it may not break when it collides with a piece of ocean debris, but because it cannot dissipate the energy by bending or breaking, that force will have to be transferred somewhere. In the case of my friends on *SV Ciao* (who own a Sweden Yachts 45 with a very well- made spade rudder) the rudder did not break and therefore transferred the entire force of the impact (multiplied by the cantilever) into the hull of the boat causing it to be holed mid-Atlantic. The boat sank in minutes. Fortunately they were sailing in company and were picked up. You can see what happened to them here:

https://www.youtube.com/watch?v=jIZvq9sRKvo

All the same forces that rudders are subject to (and more) are also imposed upon the keel. The difference here being that if your keel drops off you are toast, whereas if your rudder drops off, hopefully all you have to put up with is a large bill and a chorus of, "well what did you expect?" from structural analysts like me whilst you are bobbing around mid-Atlantic with a sheepish grin on your face.

So, although keel failure is less common than spade rudder failure, the repercussions are far more severe and therefore demand our attention and respect.

Keels

Keels are the most important part of any boat and the least considered when buying one. For example, if you log on to any of the big boat brokerage websites, you can search for your boat based on criteria like length, price, number of cabins, colour etc, but I have yet to see a site that allows you to sort by keel (or rudder) type, despite these being the things most critical to safe boat design. Nevertheless, any sailor concerned with the fundamentals of safety cannot afford to be so blasé, so let's have a more in-depth look at them here.

Structurally, keels fall into two main categories:

- Integral
- Bolt-on.

Now, it would be far too easy to condemn all bolt-on keels to hell (and I confess that I am sorely tempted), but it is not that simple.

Not all bolt-on keels are created equal, so I would like to take the second category of 'bolt-on' and split it into two.

So our three keel categories are now:

- Integral
- Acceptable bolt-on
- Unacceptable bolt-on

So let's have a look at them in order:

Integral keels

Integral keels don't need much time spent on them as they are the most reliable and the strongest, so are the best choice for the long-term voyager. As you can see in Fig 12, the integral keel is part of the overall structure of the boat which means that any forces from impact or general sea conditions are spread evenly over the whole structure of the boat and therefore, easier to absorb. The ballast (the best is still lead) at the bottom of the keel is usually (and ideally) 'encapsulated' which means it is fibre-glassed over to provide a watertight barrier between the top of the ballast material and the inside of the boat. Should you knock a hole in the keel, the water will not enter the boat. Pretty much all long-keel boats have integral keels as do many medium-keel boats.

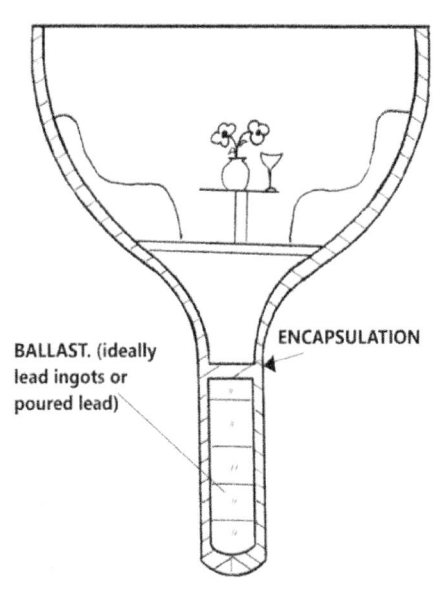

Figure 12: Cutaway of hull with integral keel and encapsulated ballast. The encapsulation isolates the keel from the rest of the boat which means if you hit a reef and knock a hole in the keel, you only need to apologise to the environmental protection people, rather than meet Davy Jones in person.

BALLAST. (ideally lead ingots or poured lead)

ENCAPSULATION

There is not much more to say about integral keels really. If the boat you are interested in has one, then you are probably good to go as I don't know any designer who makes a good integral keel and then ruins all that good work with an unprotected spade rudder (although feel free to drop me a line if you are unsure).

Acceptable bolt-on keels

I must say that, given the advantages of an integral keel, I sometimes wonder why anyone would want to introduce another possible point of failure (and maintenance) by having a bolt-on keel at all, but that would force us to overlook a lot of excellent designs. Bolt-on keels boats when engineered correctly with a substantial margin of safety, and combined with a good skeg to protect the rudder (example (d) in the keel diagram on page 26) can be a great recipe for a fast, seaworthy voyaging boat. It is important to remember that a keel (like a spade rudder) is a cantilever and can concentrate great stresses on the keel bolts. Anyone buying a boat that is prepared to overlook this in favour of a marble counter-top may not live to regret it.

Nevertheless, some great classics like the Sparkman and Stephens 34 and the Pearson 36 have very well-engineered bolt-on keels and have proved their mettle in the big tank far too consistently to be ignored. Having said all that, the important phrase here regarding bolt-on keels is, 'well engineered' and many are most certainly not.

The best way to make a strong bolt-on keel is with a good-sized keel 'stub' (a strengthened, properly bonded part of the hull) which you then bolt the keel to using a goodly amount of properly sized bolts with large steel backing plates. Snug and strong (Fig 13).

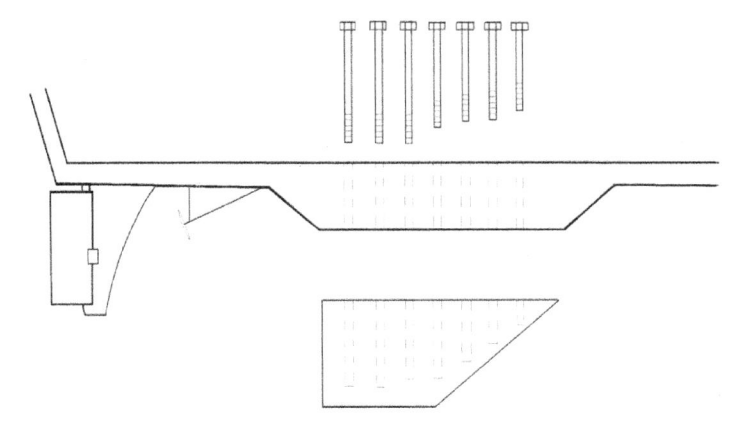

Figure 13: A properly engineered bolt-on keel viewed from the side. Please note the accompanying, properly supported, skeg-hung rudder.

If we cut the boat across its width (about amidships), the well-engineered bolt-on keel will look something like Fig 14.

You will still have to pull the keel bolts occasionally to check for corrosion (not all at once, obviously!), but this type of design is entirely acceptable and can be found on many great cruising boats.

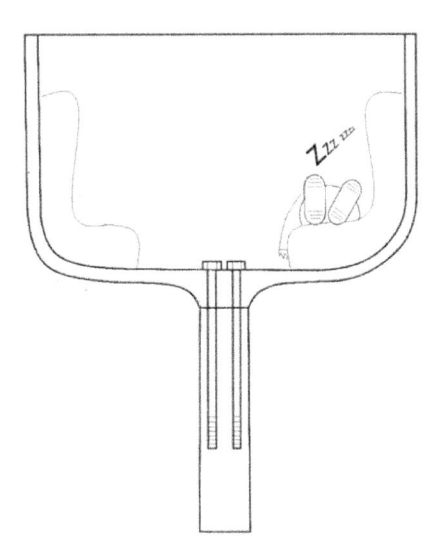

Figure 14: A drunken sailor sleeps happily in the knowledge that his bolt-on keel is as likely to move as a sex addict who lives next door to a brothel.

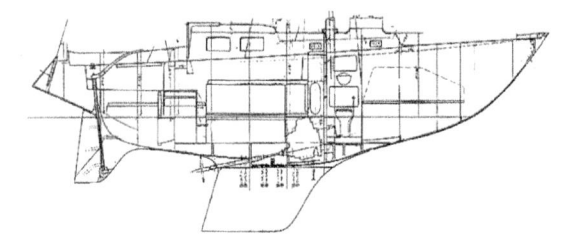

Figure 15: The S&S 34 has a well-bolted keel and a skeg-hung rudder. Jessica Watson (the youngest person ever to circumnavigate non-stop) did so in this boat as did the previous holder of that title, fellow Australian Jesse Martin. They make simple, sea-gypsy boats and are capable of some impressive passage times.

Unacceptable bolt-on keels

Unfortunately, not all designers are as savvy as Bill Shaw and Olin Stephens. Under increasing pressure to build to a price, many designers and builders are installing keels that are very close to the edge of what is acceptable and then spending the money they save on flashy cabins and gel coats that are more likely to attract new sailors or sailors with less engineering literacy.

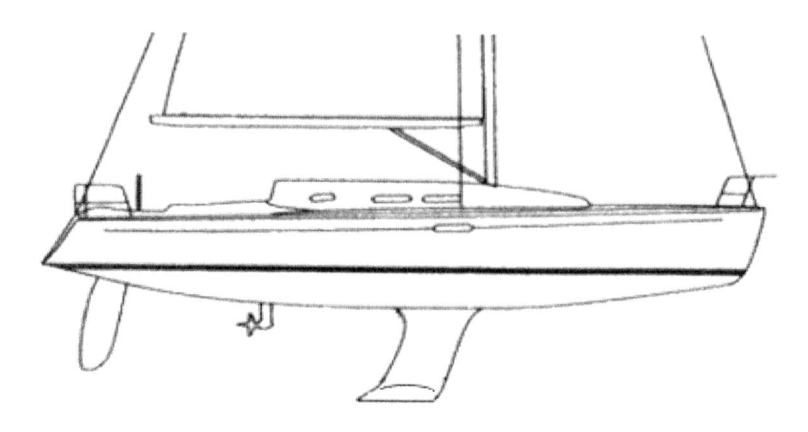

Figure 16: A modern production boat

Fig 16 is a drawing of popular production yacht cleared for 'blue water' use.[4]

The keel is attached to a very small portion of the hull by a single line of bolts and there is no keel stub. As the keel is so narrow, there is not enough room to fit sufficient ballast, so it has to be made deeper (and have a lead bulb hung off the bottom of it) in order to provide enough weight to counteract the heeling forces of the sails. Now, you will remember what weight and distance did to a cantilever in the example of the spade rudder and the drunk guy on the balcony? All the same concepts are at play here. The big weight at the end of the keel gets added to the force of the waves, multiplied by the length of the keel and then all that force gets focused on the tiny area where the keel meets the hull. Would you feel happy about that?

Unfortunately, the four sailors on *SV Cheeky Rafiki* did not consider that too much of a risk.

The Cheeky Rafiki story

Four sailors were lost when *Cheeky Rafiki* – a boat of precisely the design shown in Fig 16 – parted company with her keel and rolled over.

---

[4] I cannot write the model of the boat for fear of litigation, but it is not really important as it is the general modern design concept that is flawed, not any particular manufacturer (although some are worse than others). Having said that, good luck suing me as I only have a small boat, chlamydia and a collection of rather awesome Hawaiian shirts - all of which anybody can share with me if they only but ask.

The Marine Accident Investigation Board (MAIB) had this to say about the incident:

"On 16 May 2014 the UK registered yacht Cheeki Rafiki and its crew were lost. Despite an extensive search that found the upturned hull of the yacht, the four crew remain missing. The hull was not recovered and is assumed to have sunk. In the absence of survivors and material evidence, the causes of the accident remain a matter of some speculation. However, it is concluded that the yacht capsized and inverted following a detachment of its keel."

Figure 17. The upturned hull of SV Cheeky Rafiki clearly shows that the keel has parted company with the hull causing the boat to roll over. There were no survivors.

Picture courtesy of the US Coast Guard.

As you can see from Fig 17, there is no keel stub, and the heavy keel was held on by a single line of bolts over a very small area. Given what we have been discussing about forces on a cantilever, perhaps the only mystery here is that it held on as long as it did. When the news first broke I was of course, outraged by the totally unnecessary deaths of my fellow sailors but at least hoped that their tragedy would highlight the increasingly prevalent scandal of inadequately designed boats. Strangely enough though, the court found the design not to be at fault because the boat had not been immediately removed from the water and checked after a light grounding (when the keel touches the bottom) as specified by the manufacturers. Excellent loophole, but who can even do that? What if you touch bottom going into a Pacific atoll without anywhere to haul out? Remember, this is a boat that is cleared for blue water duty and any boat cleared for that surely must be able to survive a bump with a whale or touch bottom (a hundred times!) without the need to haul out, and pretending otherwise is an absolute scandal.

To their credit though, the MAIB in its findings made several recommendations which were thinly veiled criticisms of yacht designers, but did not go anywhere near far enough in its condemnation of this type of accountant-driven yacht design.

Figure 18: A similar 'blue water' yacht to *Cheeky Rafiki* being salvaged after a routine grounding knocked the keel clean off. Are we getting the message yet? (Photo courtesy of Mike Kahr of Death's Door Marine).

Further disadvantages of the fin and spade.

A life without the odd grounding is practically impossible. Nor is it desirable. Even if you have the insane levels of hubris it would take to imagine you will be the first sailor to never touch bottom accidentally, there are times when deliberately touching the dirt is actually to your advantage.

Calypso II awaits cyclone Harold tied up in a cobweb of lines and anchors, deep in the mangroves of Viti Levu. (Pic courtesy of Jose on www.sailingseabbatical.com)

On your wanderings around the saltier parts of the planet, you will eventually need to pass a cyclone season somewhere[5].

---

[5] I appreciate that some people do the whole Pacific in one season, but this is a book for people in less of a hurry and without the resources to burn through at that rate. Even if you have those kind of resources, repairs, illness, border closures (that caught a lot of people out this year in the Pacific) and a thousand other things make spending cyclone season somewhere almost inevitable. It was never my intention to spend a cyclone season anywhere, yet I have been through six now and counting. This may be because once you have experienced the sea gypsy 'cyclone party' you may not have enough brain cells left to make rational decisions.

While that sounds quite dangerous (and it can be, but not nearly as dangerous as we are often led to believe by a sensationalist media) nature often provides a fantastic resource for sailors needing to hide from cyclones. I am, of course, referring to the wonderful sanctuary of that little natural marvel, the mangrove.

Mangroves offer surprisingly effective protection from the strong winds and waves of cyclones as well as virtually limitless strong points onto which you can attach your boat.

There is only one problem: Mangroves can be quite shallow – particularly if you want to snug up really close to them where all the really good protection is.

In the picture on the previous page, you can see that *Calypso II* is happily tied to both sides of the mangrove with several lines (I also have three anchors out just to be sure).

All well and good, and snug as a weevil in a damp flour bag. Time to go below and binge watch *Downton Abbey* while cyclone Harold does its worst and then sail off again into the glorious dawn of another Fijian sunrise with another great story to tell once the whole thing has run its course. Cool eh?

Well, not for everyone.

The shallowness of most mangroves means that you can often only get your boat into position at high tide. When the tide goes out, this happens:

Now, as those who have seen my website will know, all my boats have had goodly keels which can take the ground well - which is a bloody good thing because I was in this mangrove for 4 days on this occasion. With two tides a day, that is 8 light groundings. And that is assuming one's pride and joy is lowered gently to the bottom – a huge assumption in a cyclone. What is more likely is that, as the tide drops and your keel or rudder first touch bottom, a surge from the cyclone will roll up the mangrove, lifting you off the bottom and then dropping you back down again. And again. And again until she has settled into the mud. The whole process repeats itself when the tide returns.

With her long keel and protected rudder, *Calypso II* takes the ground without issue

With the narrow fin and spade, this can cause serious damage to the keel structure and/or rudder, as much of the weight of the boat is now pressing into that tiny patch where the keel is attached or cantilevering the spade rudder shaft like a banana. It is certainly not a configuration I would like to own, because when the cyclone has passed, there is no way I want to haul out, inspect the keel/rudder and make all those repairs that the UK court deemed essential for bolt-on fin keeled boats after any type of grounding.[6] It is also fairly likely that those services will not be available in the aftermath of a cyclone. We nautical nomads may be okay tucked up in the mangroves, generating our own electricity, binge-watching *Battlestar Gallactica* and wondering if the harbour master is secretly a Cylon, but the rest of the country might be devastated and in a state for shock for some time, and the last thing it needs is some rich (to them) foreigner taking engineers away from the relief efforts to fix the mistake he made when he prioritized aft cabin size over keel integrity. Even if you never plan to sail anywhere that has a cyclone season or anywhere that has reefs or sandbanks (although I am not entirely sure where that place is) it still pays to be able to take the ground.

In 2010 I sailed my little steel Van de Stadt into Coff's Harbour (Australia). A couple of days later a tsunami warning came through and as it was too late to get out of the little harbour there, I sealed up the boat as best as I could and retreated to higher ground to watch the wave come in.[7] Well, it wasn't so bad – only a tiddler. But just before the baby tsunami came in, most of the water ran *out* of the harbour, dropping all the boats on their sides. All in a day's work

---

[6] The owner of Cheeky Rafiki (who was not aboard) was charged with manslaughter because he did not haul out and inspect the keel after a minor grounding and this is where the court decided to lay the blame for the loss of the boat and the four souls aboard, rather than at the feet of the designer. I think we need more engineers in the high courts and less lawyers

[7] Interestingly, while sitting up on the cliff waiting for the tsunami wave, I looked out to sea and saw several people in the water also waiting for the wave. On surfboards. Say what you like about Australians, but you have to admire their panache.

for the long-keeled *Marutji*, but not so good for a great many owners of thin fin and spade boats. The boatyard was busy for a while after that!

The guy in the picture below is Terry. Terry was going to buy a modern fin and spade boat but after reading *Get Real Get Gone*, he took less than half the money and bought *Buenasea* – a sturdy little Tom Colvin designed aluminium ketch with a long keel and fully supported/protected rudder that I would be happy to take anywhere in the world (she also has the most pleasant lines I have seen for a long time on any boat).

Terry then caught up with me and bought me a beer. A few weeks later, we were both lashed up in the mangroves escaping the wrath of Cyclone Harold. *Buenasea* was grounded many times with no damage at all. (Terry was fine too).

Reef encounters

East of Savusavu in Fiji, the Danish yacht SV *Tico-Tico* struck the well-charted Duff Reef in broad daylight, knocking off her bolt-on keel and capsizing instantly. Fortunately, the three souls on board were found two days later drifting in their liferaft by the Australian frigate HMAS *Newcastle* which was (rather

Be smart. Be like Terry

fortuitously) on exercise in the area, so they lived to tell the tale. Others have not been so lucky.

Again, thanks to the nature of marketing and human psychology, it is easy to forget the lost souls as we tend to only hear from the survivors. Had they not been picked up, their fate (like that of so many others) may never have been known. It is not entirely difficult to understand why so many commentators were quick to point out how their liferaft saved them. Unfortunately, it always seems to be means of salvation that gets the attention rather than what caused them to need it (see *Dead men don't write blogs,* below).

So, let us try and re-set the balance a bit here and have a quick look at what happens when a bolt-on thin fin bumps an obstruction compared to what happens when a full-keeled boat with integral keel and encapsulated ballast does the same.

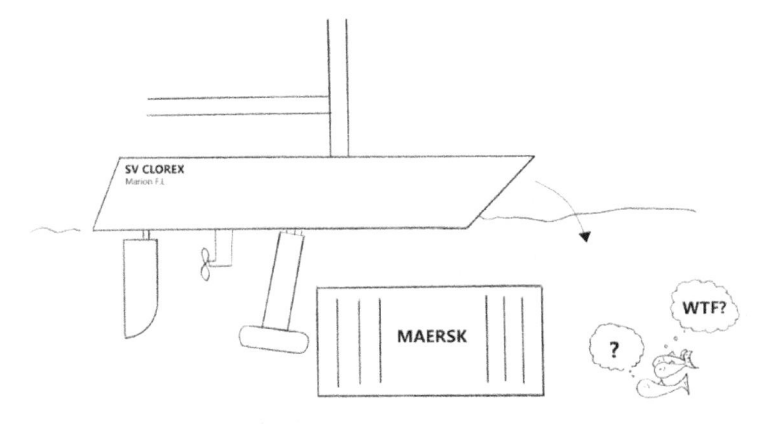

Figure 19: A supposedly 'blue water' design similar to Sv *Cheeky Rafiji* and *Tico-Tico* colliding with a submerged object. The diagram shows a container, but it could easily be a log, reef, sleeping whale or the bloated corpse of Robert Maxwell.

As you can see in Fig 19, the impact on the bolt-on fin keel 'trips' the boat and tries to push the bow downwards. For a well-bolted keel, attached to a 'wine glass' hull with a strong keel stub, this would hopefully be enough to dissipate the energy. For the extremely buoyant modern production boat with a flat bottom and a marginally attached fin keel, the impact can cantilever the bolts out of the hull, often taking a large section of the boat with it, causing her to capsize and sink immediately.

Rolling with the punches

If, like me, you are a bit of a boxing fan then the name Floyd Mayweather will need no explanation. For those who do not share my enthusiasm for the sweet science, Floyd Mayweather is the greatest defensive boxer of all time. His secret is to roll with everything. When an opponent takes a swing at him, he is already rolling his shoulder up and turning his head away. Hopefully that is enough to avoid contact, but if contact is made the blow is 'glancing' and not a full frontal, brain-juddering impact. In other words, he is dissipating the energy of the impact by moving with it and spreading the impact over a greater area as the punch rolls over his shoulder and around a third of the surface area of his head, rather than taking it square on the chin and hitting the canvas like Vincent Van Gogh. When a boat with a gently sloping long keel bumps a submerged object, it behaves like Floyd Mayweather by making contact *gradually* and spreading the impact over a wider area as she tries to rise above the obstacle or push the obstacle down, or a bit of both.

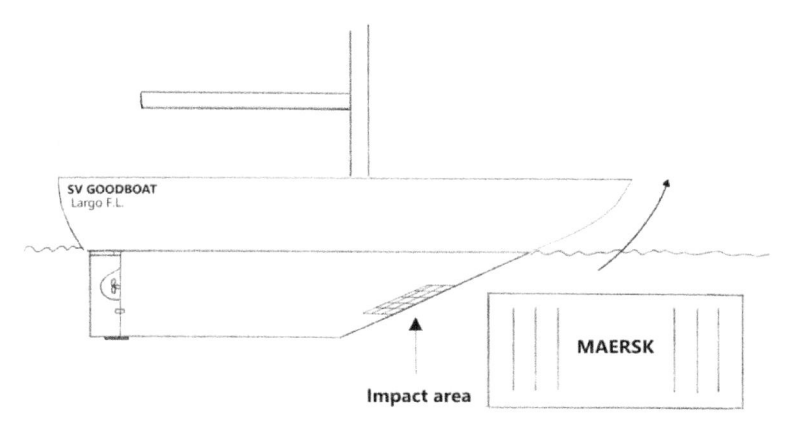

Figure 20: A longer, sloping keel will dissipate the energy of an impact over a wider area.

As the keel is a part of the boat, not bolted on to it, what is left of the force will be spread evenly throughout the hull, rather than concentrated in one small spot. Depending on any number of factors, the obstruction may still puncture the keel, but as the ballast is encapsulated (sealed off from the rest of the boat) no water will enter the boat if the keel is holed. A quick inspection with a snorkel will determine whether you need to haul out or leave the repair until the next scheduled antifouling.

Obviously a direct impact at full tilt with a submerged object can sink any boat if you hit it with enough venom, but you are much more likely to survive it with a heavily laid-up hull, an integral, gently sloping keel of moderate draft because it can 'roll with punches' and dissipate the energy of the collision over a wider area. Furthermore, as longer-keeled boats do not need to be as deep (because the ballast can be spread fore and aft) you may even completely miss an obstruction a deeper fin keel would smack full in the chops. It is also important to remember that the type of boat with a thin keel and spade rudder has been built this way to get a little extra speed (and a little extra profit - more on that later). So it is safe to assume that the boat least likely to survive an impact will also be the boat to have that impact at a higher speed. It all adds up.

So, when the occupants of a liferaft are fished out of the water after a keel detachment, the question we should be asking is not whether this is evidence that liferafts should be compulsory but whether manufacturers have a duty to stop calling these types of boat 'blue water' boats (or implying it by giving them names like 'Oceanator' or 'Sea Master') and then hiding behind technicalities in almost impossible to follow maintenance schedules when they turn out to be anything but.

Staying off lines

Another consideration (and why I often speak of keel/rudder configurations in the same breath) are fishing lines, crab pots and other ropey things. These do not loom as large in the hierarchy of danger in most people's psychology because they are normally coastal phenomena and we all, perhaps erroneously, feel more comfortable closer to shore. But coastal waters can just as easily highlight the inadequacy of the fin and spade combo as ocean conditions do - as the owners of SV *Duckbill*[8] found out recently.

Last year I sailed from the delightful little town of Savusavu in Vanua Levu to the French territory of Wallis and Futuna. I didn't really fancy the trip as the weather is pretty unpredictable and the wind and wave action seem to be always on the nose, but I had to go because I needed to renew *Calypso II's* visa.

---

[8] Not her real name

When you sail into another country you are allowed to temporarily import your boat into that country for a given period without incurring import duty. In Tonga you get one year, in Mexico it is ten years. When you come to the end of your allotted time, you are required to leave (and check into another country) or pay the duty.

In Fiji you get 18 months and part of the reason I got *Calypso II* for such a good price is that she needed to leave or cough up the duty.[9] I could have paid the duty and imported her permanently into Fiji (and quite frankly it is worth considering because Fiji is utterly, utterly fantastic) but that would have generated a bill of about US$10,000. I am disappointed to report that sailing books (even best-selling ones) don't sell in anything like the same numbers as books about pre-pubescent children attending wizard university, so it was off to Wallis and Futuna for me!

The trip took about four days and was about as pleasant as being smacked in the face every two minutes with a wet fish whilst being sleep deprived and spat-at on a roller coaster, but eventually I arrived at Futuna at 2am on a rolly sea. It was a dark, rainy night with no stars or moonlight, but the island of Futuna was doing a decent enough job of keeping the worst of the swell down so, in the interests of good seamanship, I hove-to, lit the boat up and went below to rest. In the morning I sailed into the small bay and dropped anchor with reefs on both sides of *Calypso II*.

Having checked in to Futuna, the weather forecast immediately sent me scurrying back into the customs office to check out again. A fairly

---

[9] Fiji has since extended its welcome to 5 years

decent blow was due from the west (quite rare for these parts) which would have blown directly into the little, rocky harbour and turned it into a bit of a washing machine. So, pausing briefly to buy as much French cheese as my arteries could cope with, I weighed anchor and headed out to sea again.

About 20 minutes out of the small bay, I passed a smart little yellow boat on her way in. I later found out that despite having arrived in good daylight (like any responsible skipper should when entering an unknown anchorage) *Duckbill* had picked up a line in her propeller and the engine had come to a sudden, jarring stop. As the anchorage was well protected, raising the sails again made very little difference and before they knew it, she had gone aground on the reef damaging her spade rudder and fin keel. *Duckbill* had taken the same line into the anchorage as me, yet I had no problems.

The fin and spade set-up leaves not just the rudder exposed, but also the propeller. With a decent keel and rudder arrangement, lines are pushed down by the keel and exit harmlessly past the rudder pretty much most of the time. It is still possible to pick up a line even with the long keel arrangement, but far less likely – and that is the essence of disaster management, not producing certainties (which cannot be done) but reducing *likelihood.*

I am pleased to say that *Duckbill* was not too badly damaged and was able to limp back to Fiji for repairs. But remember, these were pretty benign conditions – if she had arrived a few hours later when the wind was up, *Duckbill* could easily have been lost and maybe her crew injured.

So why are so many yachts built this way?

I had a very angry message from a reader whose general defence of spade rudders and unacceptable bolt-on keels was not based in engineering reality but blind faith in business law.

"If they were dangerous", he wrote in capital letters, "all the boat builders would be in jail!"

Like everyone who sells tobacco products or junk food I suppose.

Touchingly naive though that statement is, it does highlight how much faith many people have in the free market when a decent dose of cynicism would probably steer them closer to the winds of truth.

Most modern production yachts have five things in common:

- Spade Rudder
- Bolt-on thin fin keel
- Flat bottom without keel stub (sometimes called, 'a hard turn of the bilge')
- Saildrive or exposed shaft drive and propeller
- Light construction

The only *sailing* advantage to any of these is that they give a little more speed in light winds and a few more degrees to windward - which is not really an advantage for the ocean-going sailor because light construction also means the last thing you want to do is hit a piece of debris at speed. Furthermore, heading into the swell when the weather is less than ideal, a heavier boat can often be faster as it develops more momentum and is not stopped dead in its tracks by every little wave. It is certainly more comfortable than a 'corky' light boat! Anyway, like me, I imagine you bought a boat to spend time on the sea. Risking my life with a thin bolt-on keel and a spade rudder is simply not worth the extra few hours I can knock off the very thing I came to do – spend time on the sea.

Furthermore, the flat bottom is truly horrible going to windward in a decent seaway as it pounds so hard that it shakes the boat and the crew half to death. I know one owner of such a boat who refuses to go offshore anymore as she is tired of having to re-bed all the portholes after every bit of rough weather.

The saildrive transmission offers no nautical advantage at all. It is higher maintenance, creates more drag and is far more vulnerable to collision and corrosion than the traditional transmission. It also introduces an unnecessary large hole into your boat which is never good.

"So", I can already hear you saying with understandable exasperation, "stop waffling Rick and get to the bloody point. Why are so many boats built this way?"

Well, strangely enough, those five things all share one common feature:

They are cheap.

They are cheap to fabricate, they are cheap to assemble and they are cheap to ship.

A flat-bottomed production boat will sit easily in a single shipping container (or on the back of a truck) with its keel, rudder, mast, saildrive transmission and engine crated up next to it and can be shipped anywhere in the world for assembly by the local dealer. Boat builders have to survive on the narrowest of margins and are one of the most vulnerable businesses in the world. As discussed in *Get Real, Get Gone,* the new boat market is driven by the charter industry and by the first-time, inexperienced boat buyer with very little engineering literacy or ocean experience[10]. The boat builder who does not respond to that is at a competitive disadvantage. This type of boat owes its popularity not to any nautical reason, but to the fact that it is cheap to make and transport and feels much more manageable to the novice sailor in calm waters outside the marina (where the test sail takes place) and whilst docking.

No second chances

As the robot so famously said when climbing off the dumpster, "hey, we all make mistakes". I do, you do, every sailor does. The question then, is how do you want to be punished for them? Like me, I imagine you would prefer a little slap on the wrist and feeling like a bit of a doofus over dying in an upturned boat in the cold grey waters of the Atlantic. How about a small reduction in rum rations, rather than a mid-ocean rescue and the honour of paying some licensed bandit with a clapped-out tugboat more money than he has ever seen in his life?

---

[10] The charter market is also a brutally competitive industry and would probably not be viable without cheap boats with large cabins. As the charter industry mainly deals with coastal sailing in selected waters, this type of boat is less of an issue. Every boat is good for something. As always, my issue with these types of boat is not that they are lightly built, but that they are marketed as blue water ocean-bashers.

To proceed with choosing a boat on the assumption that you can avoid going aground or making a howling mistake is totally unreasonable. We are all idiots and we all do dumb things. Those who know it, accept it and plan for it are at a great advantage.

Dead men don't write blogs

99% of all species that ever lived are extinct – often through no fault of their own. A sudden shift in temperature or failure of a species below them in the food chain that they relied on for survival can scupper their chances, however good at hunting they are. It is important to remember that the seemingly myriad forms of life we see around us (or via David Attenborough) today is not the culmination of biological diversity, but the 1% that is left. When you look at the impressive array included in that 1% – from birds of paradise, to whales the size of apartment buildings - it is sometimes hard to remember this.

But nevertheless, these are the facts, counter intuitive though they may be.

The same logic can be successfully applied to sailing. When you watch a vlog of somebody claiming that flimsy fin keels and spade rudders are perfectly okay, it simply means that this person did not have a problem on their year or two out sailing. What we have to remember is that dead men don't write blogs and all those who drowned at sea because their keels *did* fall off, tend not to make good YouTube bikini click-bait. When we watch a vlog, we are not seeing the culmination of data, but the faces of those that are left. Of course their stories are going to be positive – just as everyone you are likely to be talking to today will have a 'near miss' driving story rather than a tale of a fatal accident.

I often think the best job in the world would be a liferaft salesman. If the bloody thing opens and doesn't immediately deflate, the purchaser is rescued and the life raft praised to the heavens. If it fails to open or pops a seam soon after, then the client is silenced forever. A perfect system for guaranteed five-star reviews but as reliable as a source of information as allowing Basil Fawlty to write his own reviews on Trip Advisor.

Everybody knows somebody who has smoked two packs of cigarettes for 60 years and is happily puffing away in their 80s. Does this mean that smoking is good for you? Of course not. For every happy octogenarian smoker, there are a thousand ghosts of people who died in their middle years of lung cancer, only we don't meet any of them as they are holding up the lawn in a forgotten corner of an overgrown graveyard somewhere instead of claiming the dangers of tobacco are overblown on daytime TV.

Anyway, the point is that we must always remember that anecdotal evidence is 100% skewed in favour of the survivors with those less fortunate being horribly under-represented.

Meeting somebody on the dock who has just circumnavigated in a boat with a marginally attached keel and flimsy unprotected rudder does not mean that it is a good idea to do so any more than the occasional cancer resistant pensioner is evidence that the dangers of smoking are all hype. In short, when speaking in engineering terms we must always keep the following in mind:

The plural of 'anecdote' is not 'fact'.

A final word

Well, I hope that this little re-visiting of keels and rudders has helped put some numbers and engineering theory on what often feels intuitive to many and has given you enough evidence to hold your ground against the overwhelming barrage of marketing from the industry and the echo chamber of the competitive or novice yachtsman. It really is the most important consideration for the sea gypsy life and I need you all to be safe, catch up with me and claim your free glass of Chardonnay[11].

However, for those still not on message, I will leave this chapter with the following, rather chilling, statistics:

100% of keel detachments occur on boats with bolt-on keels. Nearly 100% of rudder detachments occur on spade rudders[12].

Well, that was all a bit technical and slightly intense, so let's move on to something really positive....

---

[11] No conditions apply.

[12] I am only using the caveat 'nearly' because I am sure somebody out there knows of a rudder detachment that occurred on a non-spade rudder. I have never heard of, nor do I know of anyone who has heard of, a properly supported rudder becoming detached. If you know of one, then the statistic is 99.99% (or 'nearly' 100%) and does not disprove the rule.

CHAPTER TWO

Staying Long:
The wonderful world of the real sea boat.

The good news is that all the reasons not to buy a thin fin and spade boat with a flat bottom are also all the great reasons to buy a long keel (or long-ish fin and skeg) boat. And what wonderful things they are! Yet, talking to many readers on their way to becoming salty sea bums, I have noticed that there is an awful lot of misinformation out there and I thought it might be useful to nip some of that in the bud. So here we go – all the common misconceptions about longer-keeled boats in one easy to swallow package:

They are hard to manoeuvre in marinas

Not really, no. It is certainly easier to park a Mini than a Lexus, but we are all capable of learning the new skills required to park a Lexus when we upgrade from a smaller car. The myth that it is not possible to manoeuvre a long keel boat comes mainly from fin and spade boat owners who tried it once using the techniques they learned on that type of boat, found those techniques to be less effective on longer-keeled boats and immediately gave up. Admittedly, you need to learn a new technique, but once learnt, one never gives it another thought. I bring the full-keeled *Calypso II* into the dock in all weathers – forwards, backwards and sideways. I can turn her in a little over her own length - and I am a shocking parker at the best of times, have terrible depth perception and wear glasses as thick as a dolphin burrito. I will go into more detail about manoeuvring longer-keeled boats in close quarters in chapter three, but for now let us give some thought as to why the criticism of being difficult to manoeuvre is actually a very positive attribute indeed.

Directional stability.

Listening to the media, you would be forgiven for thinking that the *only* reason that well-made sea boats have longer keels is to make them more difficult to park, but that is possibly because they have not been offshore in one.[13] The reason that a good sea boat has a longer keel is that a long keel makes a boat more 'directionally stable'. This means she will hold her course with less effort from the steering (as well as being a little more forgiving of less than perfect sail trim). In turn, this gives windvanes and autopilots (which is what you will be using most of the time if you are not racing) far less work to do, thereby reducing the risk of failure as well as ensuring that you sail a shorter distance compared to a less directionally stable boat that is constantly wandering off course and being corrected by an over-worked autopilot or windvane.

But perhaps the biggest disadvantage of the thin fin keel (other than the minor issue of falling off and killing everyone on board, of course) was bought home to me when I delivered a 60 foot sloop with this configuration from Tahiti to Fiji.[14]

---

[13] I have often been called a 'traditionalist' or a 'purist' for preferring properly made boats. I am not sure what that means, but if it means that I am a person who wants to live, then I'm that.

[14] To be fair, the problem was a combination of thin fin and huge, flat, aft sections, but as most fin and spade boats are built this way, it generally holds true.

I was unfortunate on that passage to have 10 days of bad weather. 35-40 knots with stronger gusts the whole way. When you have this kind of weather over a long time, the swell, wind and waves all tend to line up in the same direction, producing some pretty steep curves. 40 knots is no big deal for an aluminium 60 footer weighing in at 40 tonnes, but it is not a breeze either.

I only had one crew and there was no windvane self-steering, so we were using the powerful electric autopilot to keep us on track. All the systems on board were controlled by a very complicated hydraulic/electric hybrid arrangement, managed by two computers and (as is pretty much guaranteed with tech on boats) eventually it failed. I got my crew to hand steer while I was investigating and within 10 minutes she was exhausted (and this was a strong woman who can usually steer all day in most conditions). When I took the wheel, I could see why. Arnold Schwarzenegger could not have held it for as long as Jasna did!

Now, this was not because we were hard pressed or had too much sail out as we were broad reaching (sailing nearly directly downwind) and therefore unaffected by weather helm. We had only a small amount of headsail out to keep us straight and maintain a sensible speed. The problem was that every time a wave from behind lifted us, the super-buoyant aft section (designed to get the double 'island' bed and en-suite bathroom in) would rise like a cork, forcing the (far less buoyant) nose of the boat down into the wave. The flat-bottomed aft part of the boat, with no keel or skeg to grip the water, now wanted to go skipping merrily sideways down the face of the wave faster than the dug-in forward section, and try to overtake it.

Now, if there had been a longer, more directionally stable keel under the boat, this would have provided resistance to that sideways movement. But there wasn't, so the boat happily pivoted around its skinny keel while its flat bottom skidded over the surface of the wave and only Jasna's super-human efforts at the wheel were keeping us from broaching and possibly being rolled. Wow. Somebody paid nearly $2million for this!

Eventually, I got the electrical problem solved and the powerful autopilot went back to masking the shortcomings of the keel/hull/rudder configuration.

After the boat was safely delivered, I flew back to Tahiti and picked up *Calypso* and made the same journey again with the same crew in more or less the same conditions, using the same sail configuration. Apart from the fact that *Calypso* is only a quarter of the displacement (weight) of the delivery boat, she was far more comfortable, manageable and finger-light on the helm the whole way, which made it easy for the windvane to do all the work and would have made hand-steering a breeze had we encountered a breakdown - which in turn was less likely because of the simplicity of mechanical self-steering over the type of electric autopilots required to mask a bad-mannered boat[15].

---

[15] See how these things all affect one another? A mechanical self steering will struggle with a directionally unstable boat in certain conditions. So you will have to rely on complicated electronics, which will need hydraulics to develop the power, generators for overnight, large battery banks to store the power... and on it goes, swallowing the spider to catch the fly. Best not to swallow the fly.

This is usually what is behind the claim, often made by fin and spade boat owners, that windvane steering is not accurate. It may also be what lies behind the claim that heaving-to does not work, as it requires the same directional stability that helps windvane steering do its job to the best of its ability, as part of the boat's innate design.

All these lovely advantages you get with a nice long or long-ish keel and the only price you have to pay is that you have to read chapter three, *Maneuvering the Longer-keeled Boat* and spend a few afternoons practicing the techniques on an empty dock somewhere. Honestly, even if it *were* difficult to park a longer-keeled boat, it is utter madness to prioritise ease of parking over safety, directional stability in big seas, ability to take the ground or any of the other benefits that such a configuration bestows (particularly because us budget sailors tend to live at anchor and hardly ever visit the marina anyway).

If you can't hand-steer in big seas, what will you do when your autopilot craps out (which is far more likely if it is being overworked by a directionally unstable boat)? Sailing is supposed to be fun! I suppose you could do what the owner of the 60 footer was doing; sail your boat in calm waters and then pay some doofus like me who needs the money to do the ocean stuff. That would work too.

They are old fashioned

The sea is a great testing ground and not all innovation survives it. Yes, the fin and spade looks modern, but this is an innovation based on market forces and the endless need for recognition that some racing sailors seem afflicted with, not on the demands of the sea which have not changed one bit. See *Get Real, Get Gone* for the full story, but if you can't be bugged to read that, never forget the yachting industry is primarily focussed on wealthier weekend sailors, not us ocean bashers and sea gypsies to whom seaworthiness and general ruggedness are more important than appearing modern, wealthy or winning races.

But it is not really fair to blame the yachting industry for everything. The builders have to respond to the largest area of demand – that is just good business. What is perhaps less forgivable is that rather than re-design their boats to produce a proper 'blue water' version for the minority of sailors like us who take their boats offshore, they attempt to convince us that what they are already making for the regatta and charter market is also appropriate for the blue water sailor. It is just a fact of business that it will always be more economical to try and sell what you are already producing to a new market than to re-tool and produce something entirely new that is better suited to that market (particularly if that market is small).

Innovation can be a great thing – one only has to look at the advances in winches, rigging, solar panels, marine diesels, marine cordage etc, but the movement to thin, bolt-on fin keels is not driven by the needs of sailors like us. Let other people be the beta-testers of the latest fads. It is important to remember that while the early bird does occasionally catch the worm, it is always the second mouse who gets the cheese.

They are slow.

This is the most common worry people have about longer-keeled boats (for the purposes of clarity, I will use the phrase 'longer-keeled boats' to include full keels and long fin and skeg boats). While it is true that a longer-keeled boat creates more drag (resistance to moving forward) by dint of having more actual boat in the water and will be slightly slower in calm conditions than a thin fin and spade boat if all other things are equal, it is also important to remember that other things are seldom equal!

Firstly, the whole argument is a little spurious because one cannot compare a Land Rover to a Ferrari. Yes the Ferrari is faster, but it would not last 5 minutes off-road and the Land Rover would certainly clock a better time across the Gobi Desert than the Ferrari. As watery wanderers, we are <u>absolutely</u> looking for a boat that can stand up to a bit of punishment. We are looking for an off-road vehicle.

A fairer comparison would be between two boats that were actually built for the ocean, rather than comparing ocean-going boats with regatta boats that are *marketed* as ocean-going boats, but what the hell, let's do it anyway:

The need for speed

Speed is a factor of many things – wind strength/direction, sea conditions, sail area, displacement, drag, condition of sails, experience of crew, sail trim, etc. But the granddaddy of them all is waterline length.

As a (monohull) boat moves forward through the water it creates a standing wave at the bow and the stern. As the speed of the boat increases, the standing waves get bigger and impede the progress of the boat – they kind of 'suck' the boat down into themselves. The faster the boat goes, the stronger the suck. This process continues until the boat reaches a certain speed, after which, the sucking effect of the standing waves becomes so strong that it would take an enormous input of energy to get the boat to go any faster. A motorboat can overcome this obstacle by stepping on the gas, but we sailors rarely get a chance to exceed this point.

Now, this 'certain speed' that we cannot exceed is different for every boat and is entirely dependent on the length of the part of the boat that is in the water – its 'waterline length'. Basically, the more waterline length you have, the greater the speed you can achieve before you come up against this virtually impassable barrier.

It is fairly easy to work out where that point is for any boat. Below is a diagram based on the great Robert Perry design, the Hans Christian 36.

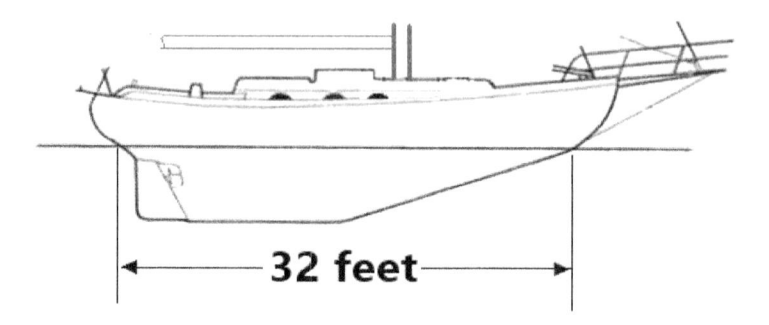

Figure 21: The HC 36 is 36 feet on deck, but only 32 feet of her are in the water

This boat with her long keel and protected rudder is 36 foot on deck (which is what most designers mean when they say, "this is a 36ft boat") but only 32 feet of her are in the water. So, now we know the waterline length we can find the boat's top speed (the speed it can attain before being terminally impeded by its own standing waves) by plugging the numbers into this simple formula:

Max Boat Speed = 1.34 x the square root of the waterline length in feet.

Now, I am hopeless at mental arithmetic, so if you are similarly afflicted with the doofus gene, do what I did and simply Google 'square root of 32' and we get this:

Max Hull Speed = 1.34 x 5.657

Therefore: **Max Hull Speed = 7.58 Knots (nautical miles per hour).**

Now, there are lot of other forces to overcome to achieve this hull speed and we will need wind to do it, but as *Calypso* was a Hans Christian 36, I can say with some confidence that this point is reached at about 15 knots in a beam reach (wind coming from the side of the boat).

Now let us look at the figures for a thin fin and spade boat of about the same length. I have chosen the enormously popular Beneteau 36.7. When you perform the same calculation for the Beneteau, you get a max hull speed of 7.37 knots – slightly less than the full-keeled *Calypso*.

However, the Beneteau is much more lightly built and has less keel in the water which means less drag, so the Beneteau will reach hull speed with a few knots less wind than the 15 knots needed by *Calypso*. But once the wind reaches 15 knots (the point at which the forces on the sails are great enough to achieve full hull speed) then *Calypso* will overtake the Beneteau.

Even the slight advantage the Beneteau has in drag can be significantly mitigated by clever designers like Bob Perry. Knowing that a long keel will create more drag, the Hans Christian has a bowsprit which, apart from looking super-salty and giving the birds somewhere to land, means that *Calypso* can fly an impressive 850 sq feet of working sail compared to the Beneteau's more conservative 655 sq feet, allowing us to somewhat compensate for the increased drag of our super-safe, super directionally stable long keel.

Furthermore, the performance figures given for modern boats are based on an empty boat. Studies show that modern flat–bottomed boats are far more sensitive to overloading than the more 'wine glass' sections of traditional, longer keel designs. As practically everyone who is living aboard will be carrying all their worldly goods, spare parts, provisions, extra diesel, backpackers, and several copies of both my books to give as gifts, it is a fairly safe bet that those with more traditional boats will be less affected by overloading for a given weight, further closing the gap in light air performance.

Displacement (weight) also has a direct mathematical influence on what you can put in your boat. The more you exceed the design displacement, the greater the effect on speed. This is a very simple concept to understand as it is purely mathematical – if you have a 5 ton boat and you put a ton of gear in it, you have increased its displacement by 20%. If you put a ton of weight in a 10 ton boat, you have only increased its design displacement by 10%.

The point I am making is that it is entirely possible to have a boat that is solidly built and has light air performance. You just need a bit more sail area, the right sails and a clean bottom. On the left is a picture of *Calypso* sailing on a flat calm Sea of Cortez with a huge, light wind sail called a 'drifter'.

The wind is wafting at 6-7 knots and *Calypso* is ticking along nicely at a respectable 3.5 - 4 knots. A lovely Texan couple who I buddy-boated with for a while always used to say that when they saw *Calypso's* big sail come out, they knew it was time to start their engine (despite having a much lighter boat with a longer waterline).

Have your cake and eat it - get a well made boat and some light wind sails. Thanks to SV Wendaway for the picture.

So, in the real world where we must all live, the slight extra speed advantage of thin fin and spade boats is diminished even further when you start loading them up, and even that gap can be further closed by the owner of the longer-keeled boat by keeping her bottom clean, maintaining good sail trim and by being the type of sailor that prefers getting the most out of light airs over the noise of the fiery stinkbox.

And always keep in mind that the slight speed advantage only applies to boats of the same waterline length, in the same wind speeds – and only then up until the point that the hull speed is reached and drag is no longer the limiting factor.

If you have a traditional longer-keeled boat with a longer waterline, it will usually be faster than a lightly built fin a spade of a shorter waterline. The same is also true if you plan your journey in favourable winds and not on calendar dates (here we see more evidence of the importance of attitude). A dead horse with a bed sheet for a sail will move faster in 15 knots than the lightest-built race boat will in 1 knot, so picking your departure on weather (rather than date) can often have more effect on your speed than all the design concepts combined. In short then, if you want to go faster you can:

- Keep your bottom clean
- Get a folding prop to cut down drag
- Get some light wind sails
- Get the right attitude and wait until the winds are more favourable.
- Get a boat with a longer waterline.
- Stay light by not overloading her too much.

In fact, do anything at all – put a 'go faster' stripe on the side, write the word 'turbo' on the stern if you have to *but under no circumstances accept a design that has sacrificed strength in the keel and rudder*. These are non-negotiable items! The lighter boat may arrive a few hours before you, but the risk isn't worth it. Plus you and your crew will be in a lot better shape and still on speaking terms.

I saw a documentary recently about a race across the Australian Desert. Two teams faced off against each other. On one team were the hard-as-nails Australian Special Forces – all dripping in ripped muscle and steroid rage. On the other side were a motley looking mob of Aboriginals whose ancestors had been crossing that desert for nearly 40,000 years.

The race got underway and the Special Forces team went at it with all the vim and vigour you might imagine and soon developed an early lead. Then the Aboriginals did an odd thing. They insisted that the camera stopped filming and the film crew were blindfolded.

"Ahh" thought I, "they obviously know a faster route that they want to keep secret".

I was only half right. What they had was not a faster route, but a *better* one. When the crew were allowed to film again, they were in an oasis that looked like an unrealistic Hollywood set – all waterfalls and beautiful Aboriginal girls frolicking in idyllic tropical pools while fresh kangaroo meat (bloody delicious and very good for you by the way) roasted on the fire.

They continued in this vein, blindfolding the crew for sections of the journey and then allowing them to film only when they had arrived at another amazing oasis. Finally, the Aboriginal team rocked up at the finish line a couple of days behind the special forces who had achieved a marvellous time, but looked half-dead with serious heatstroke, cancerous lips and god-knows-what kind of dehydration issues and tissue damage.

What really impressed me though, was that the Aboriginal group could not understand why they had not won the competition. Their way was obviously the best way! They had feasted, loved, laughed and were in exactly the same condition as when they left (a bit fatter and a bit happier, if anything). The slight increase in time it took was irrelevant to them.

That left a great impression on me and the more I think about it, the more I don't know why the Aboriginal team did not win either. Why do we value those that can do something unpleasant quickly over those that can do something enjoyable for longer? Beats me. Imagine if we approached sex like this.

Once more, we see how attitude is everything and the endless self-created problems that await those with the wrong version of it.

A final word

If you ask any sailor who was the greatest Sea Gypsy of them all, you will hear names like Bernard Moitessier, Joshua Slocum, Larry and Lyn Pardey, Eric and Sue Hiscock, Robin Knox Johnson etc. One name you will probably not hear is Jon Sanders. Which is a pity because it could easily be argued that he is the rightful owner of that particular title. Certainly he has achieved far more than any other nautical nomad and I was lucky enough to meet him recently whilst in quarantine in Port Bundaberg Marina, Australia. He was 81 years old and had just returned from his 11th circumnavigation.

Just look at the stats:

Despite having never set out to beat a world record, Sanders holds 12 of them, has several honours including an OBE from the Queen and the Order of Australia. Best of all, he has a road named after him in his home town of Perth.

He was the first person ever to double-circumnavigate the globe alone and non-stop. Shortly after, he became the first person to sail solo and continuously *three* times around the world – covering more than 71,000 miles on this trip alone. This still stands as the longest period alone at sea during a continuous voyage (419 days: 22 hours: 10 minutes) and is duly credited in the *Guinness Book of Records*.

Nor did he pick the easy routes. In 1981 he was the first person to complete a double circumnavigation of Antarctica – battling freezing winds and enormous seas.

Finally – and this is what seals the deal for me – his most recent circumnavigation was undertaken to highlight the appalling plastic pollution in the ocean. Like any good sea gypsy, Jon has compassion and love for the medium in which he travels, rather than seeing it simply as a problem to overcome in the shortest possible time.

None of his journeys were undertaken to beat a record or achieve a fast time and most of them were made in the same Sparkman and Stephens designed boat, *Perie Banou II* that he bought used in 1971. She is a 39 foot well laid-up fibreglass boat with traditional wine-glass sections, a well attached medium keel and the rudder mounted on a strong skeg – kind of like a stretched out version of the Sparkman and Stephens 34 shown in Fig 15 in the previous chapter. This is what he has to say about modern boats:

"Modern boats are built different. They are wider, higher and the bottom is flatter," Sanders says.

"The modern boats bang every single wave. I wouldn't be able to do some of the things I've done in the past with a modern boat".

Jon also has the right attitude, which he describes as "over-cautious". He is certainly not full of A-type-personality hubris, flying at full speed in the dead of night, glued to a chart plotter, trying to knock a second off the Pacific crossing time in a shiny coastal boat with a spade rudder and inadequately fixed keel in the highly dubious belief that his ability to purchase expensive things will trump any collision with reality.

I could go on about this (really I could) and continue to produce more evidence, but I don't want to bore

Jon Sanders, probably the greatest nautical nomad of them all, arrives in Australia at the end of his 11th circumnavigation at 81 years young. Photo courtesy of Emma Dolzadelli /Minderoo Foundation.

everyone more than is strictly necessary. So we will leave that there.

I will say this though. As an engineer, I deal with physical facts. I do not hold a 'personal opinion' about keels and rudders any more than I hold a personal opinion about gravity. As I do not sell boats, I have no particular axe to grind or vested interest in what boat you buy. As a writer of books about the transformational nature of safe budget sailing though, I most fervently hope that you allow the evidence to guide you on this first and most important decision of your new and wondrous adventure. If you still don't get it, I am afraid you will have to take it up with Jon Sanders.

And Sir Robin Knox Johnson.

And Sir Francis Chichester.

And Bernard Moitessier, Larry Pardey, Lyn Pardey, Eric Hiscock, Tom Cunliffe, Joshua Slocum, Annie Hill, Webb Chiles, James Baldwin, Pete Hill, Trevor Robertson, James Baldwin, Nick Skeats, etc., etc. In fact, pretty much all of the great nautical nomads whose knowledge and experience have made (and continue to make) this wonderful way of life so much more attainable to us mere mortals. If my dislike of spade rudders and badly attached fin keels is mere opinion then, by Neptune, I am in some good company!

CHAPTER THREE

Staying Straight:
How to manoeuvre the longer-keeled boat in close quarters

....if you judge a fish on its ability to climb a tree, it will spend its whole life thinking it is stupid.

Albert Einstein

Don't push your weaknesses, play to your strengths.

J-Lo

When I was trying to visualize the broader picture of this adventure – a position you probably find yourself in now - I found it very difficult to find any information on manoeuvring the longer-keeled boat in close quarters under power. A brief surf down the greatly improved information highway confirms that nothing much has changed. Nearly every source of information – from published books by respected authors to YouTube chancers, offers the same advice and pretty much all of it assumes you own a boat with a fin keel and a spade rudder. In fact, the most common advice I heard in marinas and yacht clubs all those years ago when I was looking to get gone, was to avoid longer-keeled boats on the grounds that they didn't steer well in close quarters. I was almost beginning to believe that directional stability was a curse, rather than a blessing for a blue water boat. But what do people actually mean when they say a longer-keeled boat does not steer well?

To steer a boat under power, you must introduce drag from the rudder to throw it off course. Looking at it from this perspective is much more illuminating. A boat that has a longer keel is not so easily thrown off course, and that is a good thing for all the reasons given in the last chapter. Does this make them difficult to handle in close quarters? The answer to this is yes, if you play to your weaknesses and no if you play to your strengths. Let me explain.

1. The strength of a thin fin and spade boat is that its flat bottom and narrow fin keel allows it to be easily knocked off course. A great disadvantage at sea, but this does mean she can easily pivot around her narrow keel. This is the strength you play to when manoeuvring this type of boat and you develop your technique accordingly.

2. The strength of a longer-keeled boat (overlooking for now the overwhelming benefits of staying attached to the boat) is that it is not easily knocked off course and does not easily pivot around its long keel. This is the strength you play to when manoeuvring this type of boat and you develop your technique accordingly.

Overwhelmingly what I am finding is this: People who have learnt the techniques needed to park the boats described in paragraph 1 are attempting to apply those techniques to the boats described in paragraph 2. They then throw their hands in the air and claim that "longer-keeled boats cannot be manoeuvred in close quarters" when in reality, they have simply been applying the wrong set of skills and playing to the wrong strengths.

The right set of skills

I don't intend to waste too much time describing how to park the fin and spade boats described in paragraph 1, but as many people considering a boat for the sea gypsy life may have only experienced this type of boat in the past, we do need to know how longer-keeled boats differ from the boats you may have chartered on holiday if we wish to trade on our strengths rather than our weaknesses and learn to chuck our lovely long-keeled, directionally stable, solid sea boats around like they were dinghies. (You may wish to buy a pipe at this point). These differences are:

More inertia and momentum. Having more inertia means that it takes more energy to get her moving. Having more momentum means that it takes more energy to stop her moving. Both these qualities can be used to our advantage.

Less responsive to the rudder in reverse. This is often portrayed as a weakness but, as we will see later, is in fact a super-power when you know how to use it.

Better course stability. We have already covered why this is essential at sea, but having better course stability whilst docking means that the longer-keeled boat is not so easy to blow off course by a sudden gust when approaching a berth or a mooring buoy. It also means that longer-keeled boats are generally less affected by a phenomenon called 'prop walk'. Prop walk is the tendency for boats under power in reverse to have their stern dragged in the direction the prop rotates. Some props rotate counter-clockwise in reverse (in which case the stern will be dragged to port) and others rotate clockwise, dragging the stern to starboard. Prop walk can be useful as we will see, but is not to be confused with our next super-power which, for longer-keeled boats, is an absolute gift from Neptune. I am referring to the action of 'prop wash'.

Better prop wash. Understanding prop wash is fundamental to our technique, so I fear another one of my crappy diagrams is about to hove into view.

Prop wash is the way we use forward thrust from the engine to turn the boat. In the diagram on the left, we are looking at our boat from underneath. As you can see, when the rudder is hard over and the engine is given a healthy burst, a goodly proportion of that burst gets deflected out to the side creating a turning motion (with a little forward motion too). Used in conjunction with backwards momentum, we can create a turning motion without moving forwards, but I am jumping ahead. Prop wash is a force available to all boats, but is particularly useful on longer-keeled boats because the

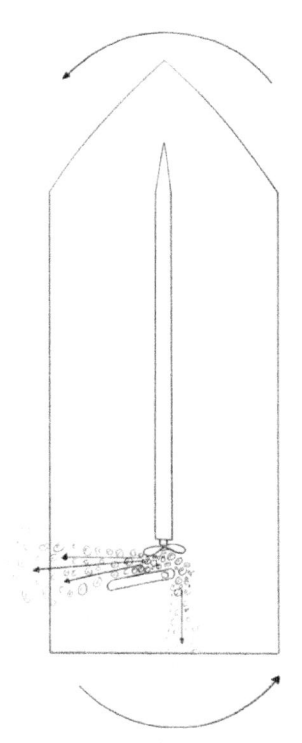

Figure 22: Looking at a long-keeled boat from underneath. The rudder is hard over which deflects some of the forward thrust out to the side, introducing a turning force. This is known as "prop wash."

rudders tend to be so much closer to the propeller resulting in a larger proportion of the forward thrust being converted into a turning motion.

Putting it all together

So, now that we have an inventory of all our strengths, let us look at how we combine them to be a real smarty-pants.

The secret to close quarters manoeuvring under power has three components:

- Turning slowly in small spaces
- Turning quickly in slightly larger spaces
- Moving accurately in reverse

Master these three things and you can combine the techniques to park your boat anywhere. Let us take them in order.

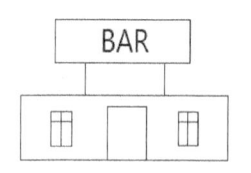

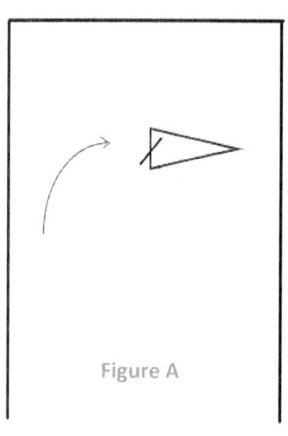

Turning slowly in small spaces. This technique will rely on using prop wash, momentum and the fact that the rudder has very little effect in reverse at slow speeds (see, I told you that was a super-power, not a handicap).

Fig A shows your lovely sea boat with its super directionally-stable keel with land on three sides. Perhaps you came into a marina only to find the bar closed and thought (quite justifiably) there was little

Figure A

point paying for a berth, so you are going to skedaddle. You turn your helm but there is not enough space to go around. So what to do, what to do?

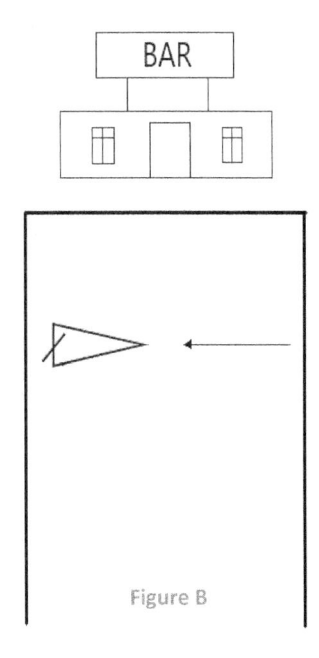

Firstly, give your boat a good burst in reverse to stop her dead in the water. Then, leaving the helm exactly where it is and with as little power as you can, get her moving *slowly* backwards until your stern is approaching the dock on the other side as in fig B. (This instruction will seem strange to those accustomed to fin and spade boats. Because the position of the helm matters greatly in reverse on that type of boat, the captain of such a vessel would now have to spin the helm to the other side. A long-keeler in slow reverse avoids all this confusion as helm position is not usually enough to overcome the directional stability of the longer keel).

Figure B

Now, slip her into neutral and while the boat is still drifting backwards, put the engine into forward and give her a hearty burst of power. As the helm was already in the correct position, this will divert the stream of water you have produced, past the rudder and out to starboard, causing the stern to swing to port and that means the bow must turn right. What we are also doing is using the superior momentum of the longer-keeled yacht to our advantage here because as we were still moving in reverse when you gave her a hearty burst in forward, the forward component of that burst will be used up stopping the backward momentum of the boat (rather than pushing her forward). This means that all your forward burst gets converted into a nice, tight turning motion without forward movement (fig C).

As soon as you find yourself moving forward and turning (rather than simply turning) you have a choice. If you have enough space (as if often the case if you get it right) you can simply drop the revs a bit, leave the helm where it is, produce your curly pipe, complete the rest of the turn and be on your way.

If you don't have enough space, you may have to repeat the procedure several times, like a three point turn in the car. This is where the fact that the rudder is fairly ineffective in reverse becomes even more of a help rather than a hindrance. Let me explain:

Imagine that we have performed our lovely turn as in Fig C and are reaching into our pocket for our ironic curly pipe only to find that an enormous catamaran has moored in

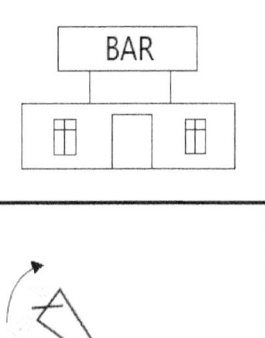

Figure C

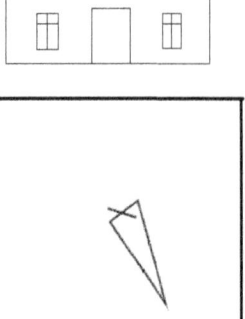

Figure D

a position that prevents us from completing the turn and leaving the marina (fig D).

The pipe gets returned to the pocket, a few words as to the parental lineage of catamaran owners are muttered and then we simply reverse slowly away, again leaving the helm where it is.

Now, a less directionally stable fin and spade boat would follow the helm and her stern would swing to starboard as she reversed, undoing all the good work you have just done.

Therefore, skippers of fin and spade boats would be furiously spinning the helm backwards and forwards during this manoeuvre, but as this does not apply to us, we can repeat this process as often as necessary without trying to get our head around where the helm should be at any particular time (and simplicity always leads to less mistakes). Simply leave the helm where it is (in the correct position for the upcoming burst in forward) and slowly reverse more or less directly backwards without putting down your tea. See Fig E.

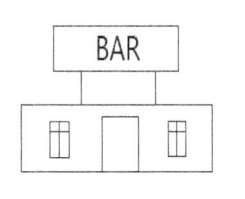

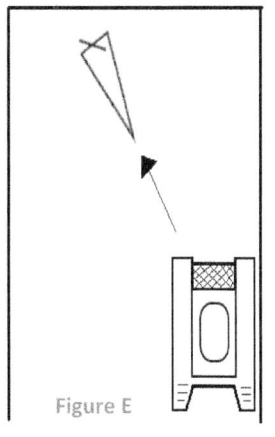

As our stern approaches the opposite bank/pontoon we again give her a good blast in forward to arrest our backward progress and turn the boat as before (fig F). Repeat as necessary – all the while leaving the helm where it is – until you have given yourself enough space to exit.

Figure E

89

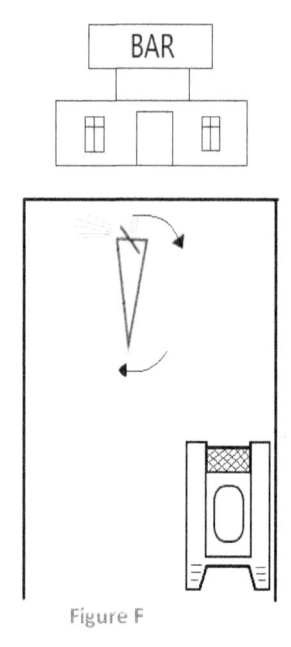

You can now re-light your pipe.

TIP: When you get really good at this, you can increase your speed in reverse which will then require a stronger blast of engine in forward to arrest your backward momentum and produce a tighter turn. But for now, slowly does it until you get the knack. When increasing your speed in reverse be aware that at a certain speed (all boats differ, but usually around 2.5- 3 knots) the position of the helm may start having a slight effect, so it is up to you to work out where that speed is on your boat and keep it under that to avoid all that undignified, panicky swinging of the helm from side to side and the inevitable confusion it causes trying to remember which way the rudder is facing. You don't really want to be doing 3 knots anyway in a marina full of expensive toys, with the following exception.

Figure F

Turning quickly in slightly larger spaces. This technique is used when you have a little more space than in the previous example and uses a combination of momentum and prop walk (not prop wash). Prop walk is not nearly as effective as prop wash, but can still be useful. Firstly of course, it might pay to discover which way your prop turns in reverse so that you don't get it completely wrong and look like an utter doofus. On a calm day in tide-less water, centre your helm and give your boat a strong burst in reverse. (If you learnt on fin and spade boats, this may need to be a stronger burst than you are accustomed to due to the directional stability of the longer keel. At slow reverse, many long-keelers demonstrate very little prop walk). Make a note of which way the stern swings out. You can also stick your head in the engine room to confirm the direction your prop shaft is turning (mind your digits!). Let's assume you have done this and have discovered that your prop is turning counter-clockwise and swinging your stern to port. Make a mental note of that and add it to your growing inventory of new super-powers. So, let's see how we can combine this newly acquired super-power with the knowledge that heavier displacement boats (which is pretty much all longer-keeled boats) have more momentum than modern production boats.

The "cut and fill" turn.

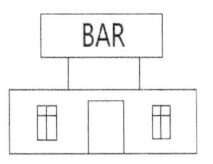

So, we have been busy chatting with our squeeze and have completely motored past our allocated berth and need to turn around.

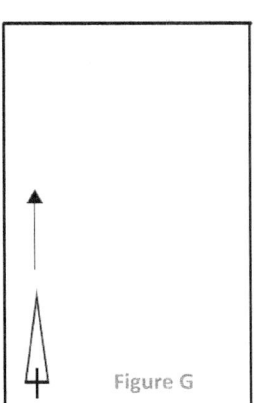

The channel is fairly wide, but not wide enough to simply turn the wheel and motor around without taking out a few thousand dollars worth of shiny white plastic and seeing yourself on YouTube 'fail' videos for the rest of eternity.

As we now know that the stern will swing to port as we give her a hard burst in reverse,

Figure G

we position ourselves close to the port side of the channel (Fig G). Maintain a good speed (more on this later). Slip the engine into neutral and immediately swing the helm over to starboard (wheel to the starboard, tiller to port). As the boat is about half way through the turn, engage reverse and give her a sustained, healthy blast (Fig H).

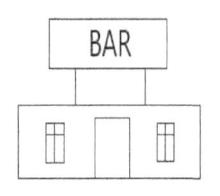

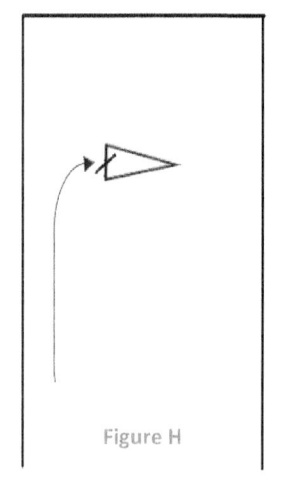

Because you started this turn with good speed, this will not stop you. What it will do is introduce your prop walk (which you will remember, drags your stern to port whilst *slowing* the forward motion and making the turn tighter. To get the full tightness of turn, leave your engine blasting in reverse until you just start moving backwards. This will probably produce a tight enough turn to get you around (I can turn *Calypso* in about one and a half times her length using this technique) but if it does not, then you simply use the technique for turning slowly in small spaces that we learnt it the last section to get you the rest of the way around. Generally speaking, this technique should narrow your turn as shown in Fig J.

Figure H

TIP: It certainly pays to practice this in open water on a calm day before unveiling your new superpowers to nervous marina residents.

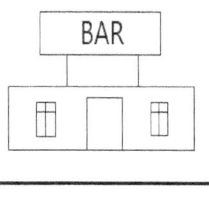

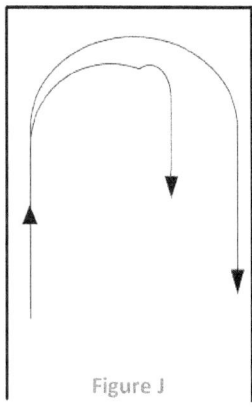

This trick is more effective when performed at a decent speed, as the more momentum you generate, the more reverse it takes to stop that momentum and therefore, the more prop walk you introduce – which of course makes the turn tighter. But how much speed is enough? Ha ha! I wish I could tell you because every boat is different (which is half the fun of it). However, *Calypso* with her full keel needs at least 2.5 knots of momentum for this to have any real effect, whereas *Calypso II* (with her cutaway forefoot) can get by on less. So practice somewhere safe until you get the heft of your own boat.

Figure J

However, if you don't have total confidence in your drive train, then you may find yourself turning at 3 knots in a marina with no way of arresting your (previously considered as a superpower) awesome momentum and picking which superyacht owner looks the least litigious. While that is indeed a risk, it is mitigated somewhat by the fact that marine transmissions tend to fail in forward rather than reverse (because it gets used all the time) so it is much more likely to stop you from creating the momentum than prevent you arresting it. However, consider yourself duly warned!

Prop walk can also be useful when docking. If you know that you have port prop walk, then when you are approaching a port side berth you can come in at a little at a bit of an angle and slightly faster, as you know that the slightly stronger burst of reverse needed to stop her will walk the stern of the boat in nicely.[16] (See figure K).

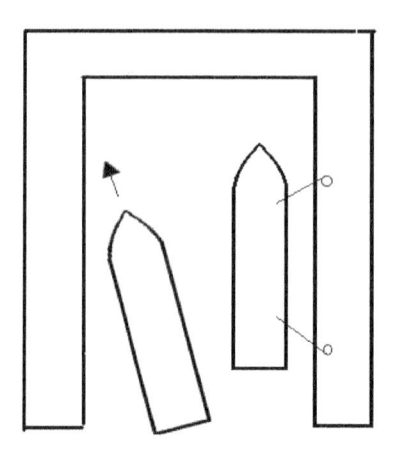

Figure K: Forearmed with the knowledge that your stern walks to port in reverse, you can enter this dock a fraction faster and at a slight angle in the knowledge that......

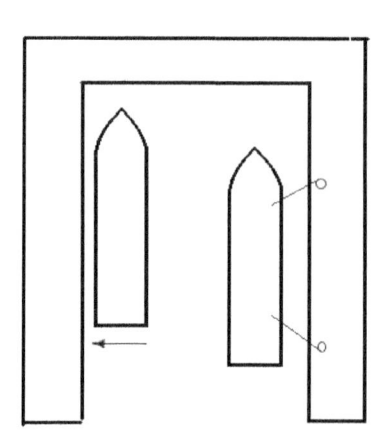

...the extra burst of reverse needed to halt your forward momentum will also walk your stern nicely on to the dock. Save the curly pipe until you have secured the dock lines though as there are few things quite as embarrassing as celebrating early and then making a complete doofus of yourself. Nobody likes a smart arse.

---

[16] "Cut and Fill" is the technique that Kurt Russel's stunt man uses in the awesome sailing comedy, Captain Ron to bring the long-keeled CT51 ketch into an impossibly tight marina berth.

Conversely, if you are approaching a starboard berth in the same boat (with port prop walk) at s similar angle and then use a strong burst of reverse to stop you, this can happen: (Fig L).

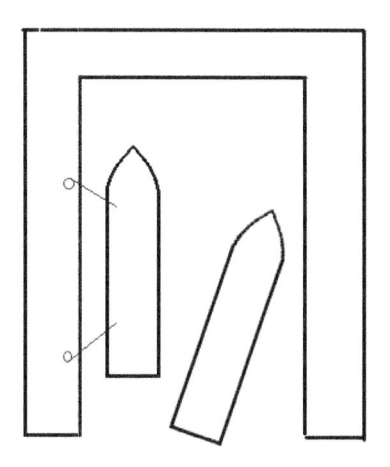

Figure L. The trick only works if you remember in which direction your prop walk acts. This poor skipper has forgotten that his boat walks to port in reverse and is approaching a starboard dock with undeserved optimism...

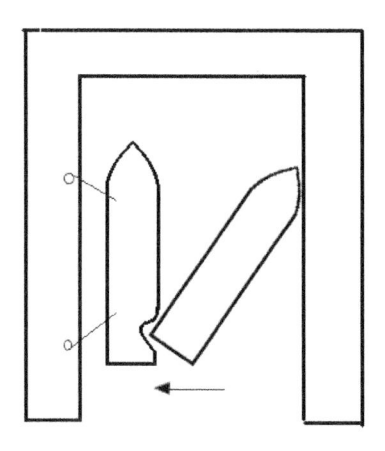

...only to find that the hard burst in reverse to arrest his forward movement does not tuck his stern nicely into the dock, but drags it into the neighbouring boat and his chances of being the star of a YouTube 'fail' video have increased exponentially in line with his insurance premium.

So, approaching a starboard berth in a boat with port prop walk, I would favour lining up to enter straight and using your momentum to just drift slowly into the dock in a straight line so that very little (or no) reverse burst is needed to stop you. If current or high wind prevents you from just drifting in like this, fear not! You can still use your prop walk to your advantage:

Look again at figure L. You know that the prop walk is going to drag your stern to the left (port) so now would be a good time to throw your helm over port quite aggressively whilst giving a strong burst in reverse, knowing that the aggressive steering (which will throw your stern to starboard) will be mitigated by the opposite action of the port prop walk, whilst the faster forward motion will be arrested by the reverse thrust. Every boat is different and you will have to practice this on an empty dock, but once you have got it, pat yourself on the back and add it to your increasing arsenal of super powers.

TIP: If you have been sailing in charter boats, you will be surprised how much momentum a heavier boat has. Once lined up at a berth, *Calypso II* can keep moving forward at half a knot without power seemingly forever. To this day, I still underestimate her momentum so, as with all things, practice somewhere safe and away from litigious people with gin palaces and good legal representation.

Moving accurately in reverse. Up until now we have used reverse to make super-slow backwards progress, as a means to stop us whilst inducing prop walk or as a way to create backwards momentum in order counteract the forward component of our prop wash. We have also relied on the fact that in slow reverse, our rudder has little effect. So how can we steer accurately astern down a long channel given the lack of response of our rudder?

Well, again, it is just a matter of knowing the techniques. If you have just done a sailing course, you will have learnt that it is best to face backwards and steer the helm in the direction you wish the stern to follow (facing forwards and looking over your shoulder is very much like trying to pat your head and rub your stomach at the same time). This is good advice for the fin and spade production boats used by most sailing schools but rarely works for long-keeled boats.[17] Due to various design factors, some longer-keeled boats do semi-respond to the rudder going astern, but generally speaking, if you learnt how to drive your boat backwards on the sailing school boat, you will need to forget what you have learnt and learn the following technique.

All astern!

The technique used to go astern down say, a long channel, utilizes pretty much the same skills that we discussed earlier in the section *turning slowly in small spaces* to transform our momentum and prop wash into a powerful aft 'bow thruster'[18]

---

[17] Sailing schools use this type of boat because they do not need to go offshore and the voluminous accommodation means they can fit more students aboard per dollar of boat cost. It certainly should not be seen as an endorsement for buying this type of boat as vagabond ocean basher.

[18] A bow thruster is a device fitted to the bow of a boat below the waterline to help push the bow around in close quarters. While undoubtedly useful, they are also expensive, problematic and introduce another hole into your hull at the most likely collision point.

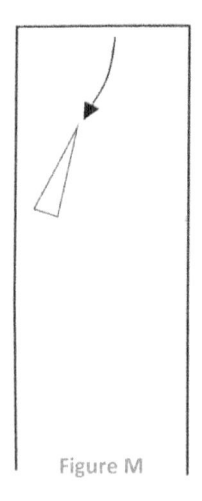

So, let's get cracking. Imagine you have to reverse down a long channel. As your long-keeled boat is (to a greater or lesser extent depending on design) relatively unresponsive to the helm in slow reverse, it is fairly safe to assume that sooner or later you will begin to drift off course (normally in the direction of your prop walk, but not always) and end up in a position like that shown in Fig M.

Figure M

Just as we used our aft momentum and a blast in forward to ramp up the effect of prop wash, we will now use it to turn our stern the way we want to go. So, with the boat still drifting backwards, slip the engine into fwd and turn the helm fully to port (yes, port, this is not a typo) and give the engine a good blast. This will have two effects. The forward component of the blast will arrest our backwards progress and bring us to a stop. The port component of the blast (the prop wash) will push the stern to starboard, lining it up in the direction we want to go. (See Fig N)

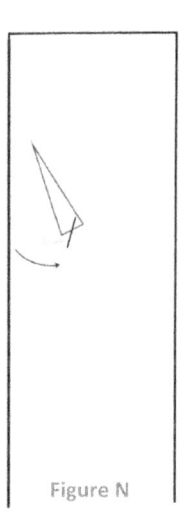

Now, slowly motor in reverse in that direction until you find yourself approaching the opposite bank (Fig P) and repeat the process again, but the opposite way (wheel to starboard, tiller to port) with a nice big blast in forward to arrest your

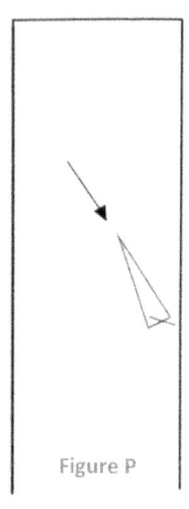

Figure N

Figure P

98

backwards progress and to spin your stern towards the centre of the channel again. (Fig R). Repeat as required.

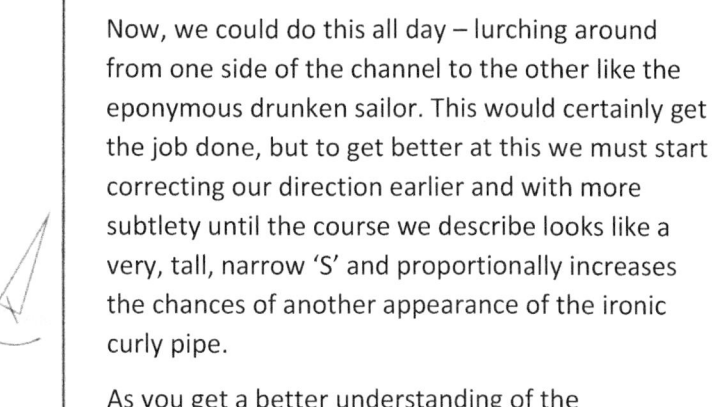

Now, we could do this all day – lurching around from one side of the channel to the other like the eponymous drunken sailor. This would certainly get the job done, but to get better at this we must start correcting our direction earlier and with more subtlety until the course we describe looks like a very, tall, narrow 'S' and proportionally increases the chances of another appearance of the ironic curly pipe.

As you get a better understanding of the characteristics of your boat, you will be able to reduce the zig-zagging to a *very* stretched out 'S' curve. (Fig S).

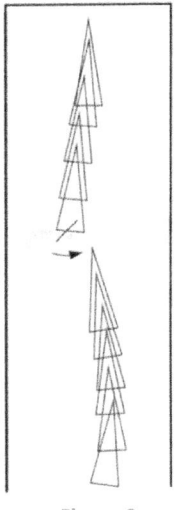

Figure R

TIP: Have another look at Fig S. As you are reversing slowly down the channel, the prop walk may tend to pull the boat off course more dramatically in one direction than the other (this effect will increase with speed). We can use this to our advantage by over-compensating in the opposite direction of the prop walk. With a boat that has counter-clockwise prop walk (that 'walks' the stern to port in reverse) any deviation to port should be corrected early, whereas any deviation to starboard can wait as the prop walk will probably make that correction on its own (if it does not, try increasing the revs a bit).

Figure S

Obviously, you will to need invert this technique if you have starboard prop walk.

Another TIP: As you get your confidence you will be able to use your forward engine bursts more sparingly, thus never completely stopping the boat and making faster (as well as straighter) progress.

A final word and a word of warning.

These three techniques will serve you well and make many people think you must have a bow thruster.[19] In the real world of course, wind, tide and current will all contrive to undo your best efforts and all need to be taken into consideration. Wind has a relatively greater effect on light displacement boats than on long-keelers, and tide/current effects long-keelers more than light displacement boats, so it is good to bear that in mind and, as always, play to your strengths. Taken altogether, it is too much to learn all at once without exploding your brain, so I suggest that you be as reductionist as you can. Pick a day with no wind and a place with no current or tide and practice, practice, practice. Then later, when you have to incorporate a strong wind or current into your thinking, you are not overloaded with information or still wrestling with first principles. I appreciate it all sounds a bit complicated, but if you take it one step

---

19 I have been asked several times and at least one sailor has accused me of lying about not having a bow thruster – such is the simplicity and efficacy of these techniques. Anyone is free to dive on my boat and check for themselves, but must wager a bottle of wine in advance.

at a time it will all come together much more easily than you would imagine once you start practicing.

A word of warning though: Every single source of information I could find on this subject – from published books to random YouTube commentators - is based on the fin and spade boat and will be of limited value. So carry a large pinch of salt with you. Your own personal practice will be far more valuable than random advice.

Good luck and when you have mastered it, you can buy a *really* curly pipe here: https://www.tabaccheriatoto13.com/en/4671-aldo-velani-churchwarden-very-curly-black-rustic-pipe.html

CHAPTER FOUR

Staying Single:
So, what is so wrong with multihulls again?

I get asked this quite a lot. I understand entirely what is attractive about catamarans and if I were to come into a bit of money and retire to a single area (such as the wonderful Whitsunday Islands where I am writing this), I would have one in a heartbeat. I love the stable platform, the safety of having two engines (plus the manoeuvring possibilities they provide) and the deck space for toys and general goofing off. But, as always, I am concerned with those new to sailing and specifically new to blue water sailing on a tight budget. As such, there are some very good reasons why I would not advise any blue water novice on a budget to consider a catamaran as their first offshore boat, some of which I covered in the last book, but there are more, such as:

Seaworthiness per dollar.

There is no doubt that catamarans cost more to buy than mono-hulls for the same level of build quality. It can often be a bit of a challenge for some budget buccaneers to find even a monohull of sufficient quality for voyaging, so looking for a suitable cat could simply scupper their dreams right there. Even if you were lucky enough to find an affordable catamaran, you can always find a better quality monohull for the same price. I am not saying it is impossible, but in all my years of looking at boats for myself and others, I have never seen a multi in seagoing condition that is as good value in a 'seaworthiness per dollar' sense as its mono counterpart.

Sure, all that space is nice, but people like us on a skinny budget should concern ourselves with quality and sea-kindliness, not space and luxury. Furthermore, even if you never visit a marina (which of course, you will) there are other extra costs. You will still need the boatyard – also very expensive for catamarans. And two engines do not live as cheaply as one. Catamaran owners also tend to use quite a lot of fuel due to their limited windward ability.

There is a fairly iron-clad rule of thumb that it pays to bear in mind when choosing a boat:

Whatever boat you buy, you can choose two of the following three things, but never all three.

1. Size

2. Quality

3. Economy

Now, assuming you are on a bit of a budget, you have already chosen economy, so the only thing left to decide is whether you want quality or size as your second choice, which to me (as you have probably guessed by now) is a no-brainer, assuming you like breathing air.

Sailing with kids
Yet I also get quite a bit of email from people on a budget, who have a big pile of kids in tow, wondering what can be done.

So, if you are hoping to set sail on the type of budget that most of my readers have, plus you also have five kids who you are (mysteriously) not prepared to sell into slavery, you may feel this fairly iron-clad rule rather dissolves your dreams.

Silver linings.

But before you despair, there is hope here. As I have said, my books are aimed at people without much money who want to get sailing and explore the world. With this assumption as my point of departure, a good quality boat is much more important than a large one. That is why I encourage my readers to choose quality with their side order of economy as part of the 'getting real' process.

For example, I started off in a 10 meter Van de Stadt. Nothing to look at all. But she was custom made to a very high spec and only 4 years old. For the same price I could have bought a shiny 50 ft production boat with 4 cabins which would have impressed the bikini off anyone who passed by. In short, 'getting real' for me was spending my dollars on quality and forgoing size (as it is for much of my readership).

Your five kids mean you have a different path to 'getting real' because size is essential for you. If you really want a boat with space for all your ankle-biters to have their own cabin and are on a budget, then the only real option is to forgo quality to some extent.

Now, this may at first seem like dangerous advice and completely at odds with the rest of the book, but remember - my advice to go for quality over size is based on people who want to sail oceans.

Budget catamarans and large production boats are not really suitable for ocean bashing (yes, I am aware that some people get away with it, but I cannot recommend it) but they are just about within spec for coastal hopping in the Greek Islands or the Caribbean. In short, if economy and size are not negotiable, then your bit of 'getting real' is to tailor your sailing to the quality of your boat and not let others who have taken stupid risks by crossing the Atlantic in a low-quality production boat convince you that, 'it will be okay' simply because they got away with it (plenty did not, but they tend not offer their unsolicited opinions in marinas). Again, it is vitally important to 'get real' in terms of personal change rather than try and manipulate reality because it is inconvenient or getting in the way of your immediate gratification.

There is a ton of beautiful sailing in the Med, the Caribbean, the Fiji Islands, Mexico, the Whitsundays, etc that would take several lifetimes to explore without making huge ocean passages and if you need to buy a cheap, large volume production boat or a (less-cheap) production catamaran to fit your nippers in, then that is what you should do. Horses for courses! Young kids are going to enjoy going ashore every day much more than enduring sea-sickness and boredom on a long passage anyway. [20]

---

[20] I tend not to write about things I have no idea about, so that is all I will say about sailing with kids. For a really in-depth look at this subject, see Recommended Reading at the end of this book or check out www.sailingcalypso.com

Safety

Even if you have more cash than my usual reader there are still a lot of good reasons, other than financial, to reject a catamaran as your first offshore command.

The great sailor and boat builder Larry Pardey said that to describe a sailing vessel as seaworthy, it must be able to beat off a lee shore under sail alone and recover from a knockdown (when the boat is rolled flat or all the way over). No multihull can do both these things. Most can do neither and therefore, by Pardey's definition at least, none of them are actually seaworthy. While I wouldn't go quite that far, the only reason I do not fully support Mr Pardey's argument, is that a very experienced sailor can mitigate the risk of being capsized quite significantly. But a novice cannot.

Catamaran aficionados often say,

"It is better to be upside down on the surface than the right way up on the bottom", but this is a common logical fallacy called a 'false dichotomy' or a 'black and white fallacy' which is often used to sound smart through being merely epigrammatic. The statement is misleading because it asks us to believe that only two choices exist:

- To be upside down on the surface, or
- The right way up on the sea bed.

When of course what we would all prefer is to be the right way up on the surface – which is a position you are far more likely to find yourself in if you own a monohull with a well-attached keel and have remembered to shut the hatches.

Even in normal sailing, it is much easier to judge when a monohull is too hard pressed and when it is time to reef because she gives such obvious signals. In short, monohulls are much more forgiving - a quality important for all sailors, but absolutely vital for new sea gypsies.

Plenty of people circumnavigate in catamarans, but too many writers are pretending it is risk-free (because they got away with it). You will definitely make mistakes, that is normal, healthy and to be expected. Again, the only question is how severely do you want to be punished for them?

Heaving -to
Catamarans do not heave-to nearly as well as the long and long-ish keel boats I recommend in my books. It is hard to explain how important this is to anyone who has not half lost their mind through fear in a big storm that lasts a few days (where large amounts of accurate hand steering, drogue towing etc are only really possible with large, experienced crews – and quite often, not even then).

Heaving-to is the defensive sailor's ace in the hole. (See chapter 12). Even now, I would find it very hard to give up this awesome superpower for a bit of extra deck space. It would be like swapping invisibility for the ability to make soup.

If you are only planning coastal hops, then it matters less what boat you buy, but if you have plans to travel further, I hope that you will consider a small, seaworthy mono as your first offshore command. She will teach you a lot and not punish you so harshly for your inevitable mistakes. She will also help you develop the skills you will need in order to avoid calamity and ruin if you later decide to mortgage the farm and buy a catamaran.

If you absolutely must have a cat as your first offshore boat, then you should try and find those cats with properly supported/protected rudders. The Privilege models (most of them anyway, so check) have mini keels, with properly supported rudders and at least *some* windward ability. They also have shaft drive rather than saildrive (saildrives offer nothing to a blue water sailor except hassle) thus, they avoid having unprotected props as well as the (cross yourself when you say it) dreaded spade rudders.

The Wharram designs also avoid the 'saildrive and spade' configuration and are very seaworthy indeed, but not everybody's cup of tea. Remember though, that the cats most likely to be affordable to the budget sailor are probably not up to the job of ocean bashing and be careful not to convince yourself otherwise with wishful thinking as the moment you realise the truth of this, there may be very little you can do about it.

CHAPTER FIVE

Aluminium Boats

I deliberately did not address the subject of aluminium boats in the last book because I thought they would be a bit too expensive for the reader I had in mind. Having gone to great lengths to assure readers that yachting does not have to be the exclusive domain of the rich, I was worried that the price of aluminium boats may immediately contradict my own position and give ammunition to those of a contrary nature.

In hindsight, that may have been a mistake. Not only because this omission seems to have given the erroneous impression that I have something against aluminium as a boat building material, but also because, on at least two occasions now (that I know of), readers have actually been able to find reasonably priced aluminium boats for the sea gypsy life. So, just to set the record straight here is my answer to the often asked question...

What have you got against aluminium?
Put simply, nothing at all. In many ways, unpainted aluminium is hard to beat as a boat-building material. It is certainly the lowest maintenance material and that always leads to savings and more time on the water. They are also several times stronger than fibreglass (though not quite as strong as steel) and they do not rust or get osmosis. The only hull painting they ever require is antifouling below the waterline and there are seldom any leaks in the welded deck-to-hull joint. The fabulous Ovnis with their lifting keels can be

beached for maintenance – thus avoiding the boatyard for many simple repairs.

Yet, there is never such a thing as a free lunch in engineering and aluminium for all its general excellence, comes with its own set of unique challenges. I have touched on some of them below.

Electrolysis and galvanic corrosion

Remember the potato battery in chapter one? When you put two dissimilar metals in a salty solution (the 'electrolyte') you effectively create a little battery that produces a small electrical current. What is not clear in the spud diagram is that during this process one of the metals in the spud will corrode to nothing.

Now, it is important to know that all metals are not created equal and that in any pair (or group) of different metals (in an 'electrolyte' like seawater or spud juice), there is a very strict and predictable hierarchy as to which one corrodes first. This hierarchy (and I suspect a bit of British snobbery at work here) is called the 'order of nobility'. On the top of the table are the most 'noble' metals. These will corrode last. On the bottom of the table are the least noble metals. These will corrode first.

The most important thing to remember though (and something which will be to our great advantage later on) is that the more 'noble' metals will not start to corrode until the less 'noble' metals are almost completely gone. Take a look at the chart below:

Nobility of Metals

Most Noble
- Titanium
- 316 Stainless Steel
- Bronze
- Copper
- Copper-Nickel
- Brass
- Lead
- Tin
- Iron
- Steel
- Aluminum
- Zinc

Least Noble

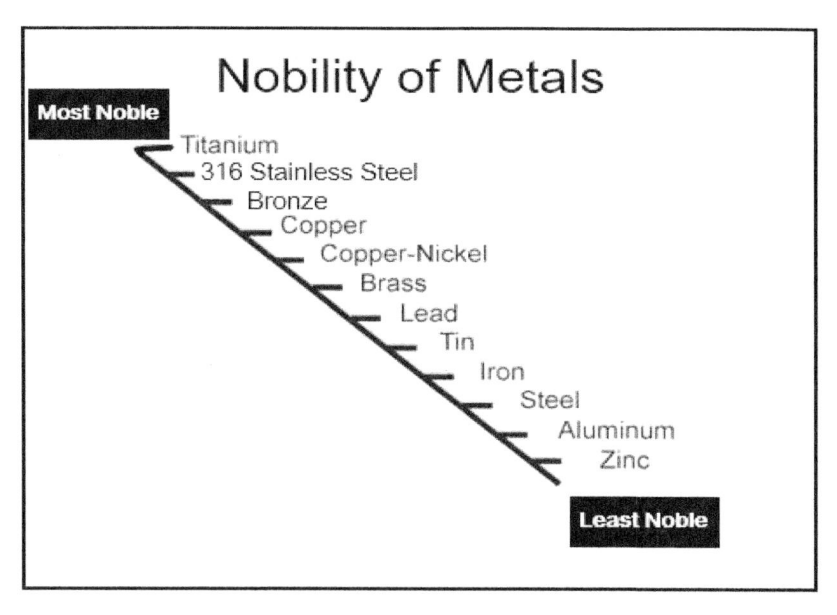

So, keeping in mind that this is a strict hierarchy, imagine you had a boat with a rudder shaft made out of stainless steel and propeller made out of brass. These two dissimilar metals are both in a salty solution effectively creating a battery. Being the least noble of the two, all the corrosion would be focused on your poor old brass propeller which would start to disintegrate and give you quite a nasty surprise when you fire up your engine to get you out of trouble, only to find that it drives the boat forward with about as much vigour as a depressed pilchard with asthma.

Now take a look at the table again – particularly the level of nobility for aluminium. See the problem? Virtually all metals are more noble than aluminium and this can be a serious issue for an aluminium boat which is basically a floating anode looking to team up with virtually any other metal so it can begin disintegrating and turning itself into powder.

Hurrah for zinc

Zinc is way too soft to be useful as a structural boat building material but being the least noble of the metals (except for magnesium which is truly, epically useless), it pays to introduce it somewhere so it can heroically sacrifice itself to protect the more important metals of your boat that are being used to steer her, push her along or generally keep the water out. This is why, when we bolt a few lumps of zinc onto our boats, we call them 'sacrificial anodes'.

SV Marutji being re-launched. The arrow shows one of several sacrificial pieces of zinc attached to her hull. (Yes, she is rather fair for a steely, I agree).

Sacrificial zinc anodes are important on all boats, but absolutely vital on aluminium boats as galvanic corrosion is the 'Achilles' heel' of this material. An aluminium boat will most likely have a stainless propshaft (among other things) under the waterline looking for another metal to team up with to form a battery. The zinc will be its first choice of partner and in normal circumstances, the sacrificial anodes generally take a year to disappear before the stainless propshaft goes looking for another partner. This new romance will be with your hull, so, needless to say, it pays to keep an eye on your sacrificial anodes.

Nor can you simply change them on your yearly haul out and then forget all about them until the next time. It pays to keep a constant eye on them as they can act as a real 'canary in the coal mine' by disintegrating a great deal earlier. If you find that they are falling to pieces faster than the British Royal Family, then you have to suspect the other great threat to aluminium boats.

Stray electrical currents (electrolysis).
One advantage that fibreglass has over aluminium is that it does not conduct electricity. If a stray electrical wire comes in contact with a fibreglass hull, there is usually no harm done. Not so with aluminium. If a stray current finds its way onto your unpainted aluminium hull, then this will super-charge the corrosion process. Your sacrificial anodes will be throwing themselves under the bus far more quickly than usual and this is your first and last warning sign before your boat starts disintegrating.

If you park your boat in a marina then you have a bunch of other threats to deal with as well. Firstly, if you are plugged into shore power, you will be connected to a common ground with all the other boats. Now, this is not good for some entirely dull and technical reasons, but can be dealt with by fitting a 'galvanic isolator' when attached to shore power. They cost about five hundred bucks and most aluminium boats will already have one, so you just need to remember to use it.

Another marina problem can occur when you have been given a berth next to a steel boat. This sets up the battery again as steel is higher in 'nobility' than aluminium which means your pride and joy can become a sacrificial anode for another boat the moment your zincs disappear (which will not be long). Admittedly for this to occur, the steel boat will have to have a section of paint missing below the waterline, but have you considered the structure of the pontoons themselves? Many of them are steel and have not been painted in years.

The problem here is further exacerbated because it is not really safe or advisable to go diving under your boat in a marina to check – particularly if you suspect a stray electrical current in the water. People with pacemakers should be particularly wary about entering the water in a marina as many have low-level electrical currents that can seriously ruin your day.

The above are another couple of reasons (as if more were needed) to set your boat up to be self-sufficient and live at anchor rather than in the crowded, expensive marina with all those dissimilar metals and stray currents.

Don't spend a penny.

You will also have to be super careful about dropping even a coin in your aluminium boat, as dissimilar metals start to corrode on contact - with aluminium always coming off worse (unless the metal dropped is magnesium, which is pretty unlikely). Even those few strands of copper wire that flew off when you fitted your new speakers are going to cause problems. One French sailor I know won't let anybody on board his gorgeous, aluminium Ovni 43 who has loose change in their pockets and keeps several plastic cases by the companionway to store his guests' coins until they leave. This is much more a problem for aluminium than steel, not only because steel is higher in nobility, but also because steel is always painted which provides a break in the electrical circuit.

Aluminium and chlorine

If you are building a boat out of aluminium, it makes a lot of sense to also build the tankage (water and fuel) out of aluminium, rather than stainless steel (as is often the case in fibreglass and steel boats). Not only will you already be set up to use these materials, but making aluminium tankage avoids the 'dissimilar metals' issues as discussed above. And this is indeed what most builders do. Fuel tanks seem to do quite well, but water tanks can begin to deteriorate due to the significant amounts of chlorine that is added to much of the world's tap water.

If you fill your aluminium water tank with tap (chlorinated) water, you will start to notice small, sandy pebbles in your water filters. Most people take this as a sign that their beach activities have been a bit extreme and they need to clean out their tank, but what they are actually seeing here is their tank being eaten away by chlorine. Those 'pebbles' were once part of your tank. This is such a misunderstood process that I would strongly advise you to check out the water filters of any boat that has an aluminium water tank to see if the owner has been blissfully unaware of it.

Fortunately, chlorine can be easily removed from tap water by passing it through a carbon filter on its way to the tank, but if the previous owner has not done this, then the water tank may well be about to become problematic which, depending on location, is either a big, expensive pain in the neck or a massive, expensive pain in the neck.

The caveats above notwithstanding, unpainted aluminium has so many overall advantages in terms of strength, weight, oxidation (rust) maintenance, etc., that with a bit of careful management there is a very good case for unpainted aluminium being possibly the best boat material available if (and this is a biggie) the following conditions are met:

Marine grade aluminium is used. Not all aluminium is created equal and you will have to make sure that the boat you are considering has been built with the right stuff.

The highest standards of electrical wiring are adhered to. For all the above reasons. Stray current is such an issue for aluminium, it has to be wired in a totally different way than a fibreglass boat.

The weld quality is top-shelf. Most aluminium boats are built by professional aluminium boat builders with published practices. This is important because it is far easier to screw up when welding aluminium than steel. Any air bubbles in the weld are going to come back to haunt you. As many home builders tend to choose steel or aluminium as their hull material, it becomes even more important to get a surveyor who is a specialist in these materials if you are buying from an amateur builder. In fact, weld quality is so critical, I would (at the risk of upsetting the hundreds of home builders who do an excellent job) be super-cautious when buying an aluminium boat that was not professionally built.

Without doubt, the French builders like Alubat and Allures are the world heavyweight champions of aluminium yacht construction and have been at it long enough to make excellent boats that have been tested in the big tank. They use skilled welders/electricians and marine grade aluminium which is partly why they are so expensive (and why I chose to ignore the subject previously). But if you can find one that ticks all the boxes at a good price, then you will have an excellent, low maintenance boat as long as you follow good practices, don't do anything silly like paint it (it just falls off) or bring anything containing muriatic acid aboard as this eats aluminium like a beaver chewing pencils.

CHAPTER SIX

Staying Away from Disaster
(Avoiding the 'uncharted' reefs!)

There is a tendency amongst journalists to polarize and simplify any complicated issue in the belief that sacrificing reasoned argument on the altar of sensationalism will appeal to a wider audience. I hoped to avoid exactly this tendency when I wrote what I thought was a fairly well-balanced article about navigation for a well-known cruising magazine. In the article, I tried to make the point that both electronic and traditional navigation methods have a role to play for today's seafarers. But the media, being what it is, re-titled the article,

"GPS v Sextant – which is best?"

Thus turning the discussion of electronic charts into the very 'us v them' well-bloodied gladiatorial arena I was hoping to avoid and leaving readers with the impression that you were either in one camp or the other.

Although I would most definitely rather sail a boat, ride a horse, spear a fish, climb a tree or do virtually anything other than sit in front of a screen, I am not anti-electronic charts at all. In fact, it seems a little churlish to me not to use these things as they are a great help. On the other hand (and this is a very large hand indeed with many calluses and warts) it is absolute madness to utterly rely upon them as they have not achieved anything like the accuracy of paper charts and, regardless of this being the modern age of nano technology, hipsters and Instagram, water and electricity still don't mix (more on this later in the chapter).

The point I was attempting to make in the article is that to use electronic charts safely, one must be aware of their limitations.

The problem with electronic charts.
Currently it seems like not a month can pass without another story of a poor unfortunate yachtsman, through no fault of his own, coming to grief on some kind of 'uncharted' reef in the back and beyond of nowhere. The press currently seems to be overflowing with such stories. I can't blame anyone for being put off this lifestyle after reading these horror stories. In fact if you have been deterred from your dreams by such a story, you have my complete sympathies – they are enough to frighten Donald Trump half out of a porn star. The impression these articles leave us with is that of an ocean practically littered with uncharted perils. But is there any truth in it?

When I was learning to skydive, I would study accident reports in the hope of learning from other people's mistakes, as becoming a little British meat patty was not particularly high on my wish list.

What I learnt is that the press, in their seemingly limitless enthusiasm to underestimate their readers, present a narrative that they think we poor, dumb schmucks are capable of understanding. Of all the skydiving accidents I came across during my investigations, I never found a single example of where the facts matched the subsequent findings of the official investigation. (Spoiler alert: It is hardly ever gear failure).

However, to keep things exciting, lazy journalists produce attention-grabbing, exploitative and sensationalist headlines such as,

"Tragedy as family watch brother's parachute fail to open".

or,

"Disaster in Detroit as Faulty Chute Downs Diver"

Now, my beef with all this is that it leaves potential skydivers with the idea that your safety in this wonderful sport is largely a matter of chance. And who wants to leave the organisation and general placement of their internal organs to chance?

A similar process is in play in the sailing world regarding 'uncharted' reefs. Strangely enough, the incidence of uncharted reef collision seems to have grown with the increasing reliance on electronic charts...

Some true stories

In 2016 I was hired to deliver a million-dollar yacht in the South Pacific. When I met the owner, I asked whether he had paper charts on board. His rather condescending reply was,

"No. I don't have a steam engine either".

The implication of course is that paper charts have been made obsolete by technology and only beardy-weirdy luddites like me still use them (and I don't even have a beard).

Fortunately for him, I always bring my own paper charts on deliveries and was glad I did! The course the owner had entered into his

$12,000 electronic chart plotter would have ended in disaster, shipwrecking us no less than three times![21]

The problem is that there are many obstructions not shown at certain magnifications on the electronic charts and others that are not shown at *any* magnification. Over-reliance on electronic charting is now almost epidemic and all over the world yachts are colliding with 'uncharted' reefs, islets and obstructions. A minority of these incidents are indeed uncharted reefs, but increasingly the fault lies (once more) with premature abandonment of solid seamanship in favour of gadgetry and inappropriate attitudes. Like rabbits blinded by the headlights of twenty-first century marketing, many sailors now assume that hi-tech *always* equals better. This is certainly an erroneous and dangerous assumption when it comes to charts.

The media must also take some of the blame. When a story breaks and the skipper claims there was, 'no reef on the chart' the reporter takes it at face value and prints the headline, 'Yacht Lost on Uncharted Reef.' Later, when it turns out that the skipper was referring to the electronic chart, the story is yesterday's news and the online news consumer has already moved on to an article about a cat that looks like Hitler.

There are seemingly endless cases of this, but recently, an Amel 47 *Morning Dove* hit an 'uncharted' reef just east of where I was

---

[21] One part of the course had us passing across the centre of Palmerston Island which looked (on his electronic chart at least) as if it were a group of islands with water between them. In a way, they are, but the water is only a foot deep. That is why it is called Palmerston Island (singular). The clue is in the title.

anchored in the Tuamotu Archipelago. Here is a taste of how it was reported in the media and the reaction from other sailors on blogs:

From the (excellent) magazine Latitude 38:

"At roughly 8 p.m. Tuesday, what should have been an easy inter-island passage turned tragic, as the Alaska based Amel 46 ketch Morning Dove *— one of 183 boats registered with the Pacific Puddle Jump fleet — struck a submerged reef in the Tuamotus, while en route from Apataki atoll to Rangiroa, a passage of about 80 miles from entrance to entrance.*

Owner Bruce Moroney, 67, explains, "Morning Dove *was motoring in no wind and light seas... It was dark and there was no moon. I was in the cockpit monitoring the chart plotter and radar, which showed no hazards. With no warning we hit something. We could see reef from the cockpit, we were lodged on a reef......"*

The accident report gives the position of the rescue as 15°25'S 146°42.1'W. If you plot that on one of the mid magnifications on an electronic chart plotter, this is what you get:

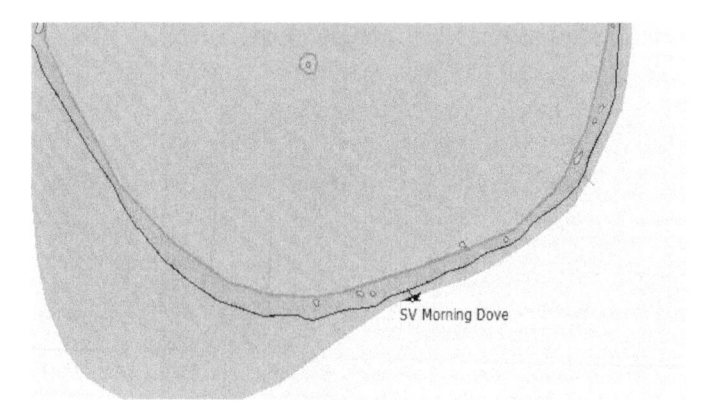

As you can see, what *Morning Dove* has collided with is the thriving atoll of Arutua – 31km x 24km with a healthy population of lobster fishermen and pearl farmers. It even has an airport. It is certainly a long way from being anything like the 'uncharted' or 'submerged' reef that seems so beloved of lazy journalists. Now zoom out just one order of magnification and this is what you see:

SV Morning Dove

Nothing. Nada. *Morning Dove* is surrounded by open water. See the problem? This is how the incident was reported by popular vloggers *SV Delos*:

"SCARY STUFF! It's tough to see an Amel, just like Delos, that's been washed onto a reef. In 2010 we sailed this exact same stretch of ocean between Rangiroa and Apataki in the South Pacific. Although it's rare for things like this to happen, this tragedy really hits home as we prepare mentally for our cruising season that will take us to uncharted areas in the Indian Ocean. Sending love and hugs to the owners of SV Morning Dove!"

A kind sentiment to be sure. I fully understand how awful it must be to lose your boat on a reef, but it is a mistake to let the fear of appearing unsympathetic distract us from acknowledging the ultimate cause of this type of tragedy, namely, the attitude that considers paper charts outdated. This was not so much an accident, but (like so many others) an avoidable incident caused by the over-reliance on electronics[22].

Now would seem a good time to point out that the atoll *Morning Dove* was wrecked upon is clearly marked on every paper chart of the area – including the large scale admiralty chart of the whole South Pacific. I can even make it out on my second generation $1 photocopy.

Nor is it only inexperienced cruising sailors who are falling foul of this. In a recent Volvo 65 Ocean Race, team *Vestas Wind* – all of whom were professional sailors - crashed into the Cargados Carajos Shoals in the Indian Ocean, severely damaging the boat and putting the lives of the crew in serious danger.

The Cargados Carajos Shoals are 35 miles long and clearly shown on paper charts - including the large scale UK chart which encompasses the seas of Indonesia all the way to Africa. They are even visible on my god-daughter's, $2.95 school atlas.

Thankfully, the official report into the incident has drawn the right conclusions as to the cause of this disaster when it clearly states that:

---

[22] In the case of Morning Dove, the skipper was also relying on radar which is mysterious as reefs are too low to be visible on radar.

"The navigator did not use the paper charts carried onboard to check for any dangers that were not apparent on the electronic chart systems"

Yet hardly anyone reads the official reports and everyone reads newspapers and social media, so I still overhear fellow sailors bandying the expression, 'uncharted reef' around as if they were strewn all over the ocean like Perrier bottles.

But don't blame the electronic charts!

The electronic chart manufacturers often get criticized for producing inaccurate charts, but this is not really fair. It may sound like an easy way out, but electronic charts nearly always have the phrase, 'Not Suitable for Navigation' somewhere in the small print. Even Navionics charts (which are highly regarded by many sailors in the South Pacific, including me) have the ambiguous phrase, 'only intended for reference' in their terms and conditions.

Admittedly, they could make that disclosure more obvious, but it seems fair to point out that not even the manufacturers are claiming that their products are intended as *replacements* for paper charts. Using a tool for a purpose for which it is not intended certainly puts the responsibility of any repercussions more squarely on the shoulders of the user than on the (admittedly much narrower) shoulders of the manufacturer – you can't blame Home Depot if you hit your thumb with one of their hammers – and here lies the root of the problem: Electronic charts are so convenient and fun, we sailors *want* them to be something they are not. But wishful thinking is almost the opposite of good seamanship. I would love to be able to cook, but here I am dipping bread into anything less solid than bread. Wishing something were true, does not make it so and is the complete antithesis of staying real.

More wishful thinking

Whenever I do something dumb (which is often – the most recent was fibreglassing my vernier gauge to the inside of the hull. It is still there now, acting as an expensive bit of reinforcement), I always confess. That way, others can learn from my mistakes and have a jolly good laugh too. Learning from the mistakes of others is a cheap and efficient way to become a better sailor and makes a good yarn too. Not everyone feels that way though.

On a routine passage, the catamaran *Tanda Malaika* hit the fringing reef of the Island of Huahine (near Bora Bora) and was lost. She was travelling in the dark at 9 knots under full sail with both engines flat out trying to enter the lagoon. The skipper had such confidence in the electronics, he didn't even slow down. How is that for wishful thinking?

As any experienced sailor knows, the best course of action would have been to heave-to until the morning and enter slowly, preferably with somebody partly up the mast to look for the changes in sea colour which often suggest a sudden change in depth. Over confidence in electronics has encouraged this particular skipper (as it has many others) to abandon this long-established practice of good seamanship as 'quaint' or 'old fashioned'. On this occasion though, this over-confidence cost the skipper his boat and seriously endangered his family.

On her Facebook page, the skipper's wife exonerates him of any responsibility due to his being, 'an experienced pilot and navigator' and goes on to state that they would do nothing differently if they planned the passage again which - is something of a missed opportunity to learn from a mistake if ever I saw one. That does not mean that *we* cannot learn from it though.

But before you go and deep six your chart plotter, I am not saying that electronic chart plotters have no place on a sailboat, just that ocean sailing will never simply be a video game. 'Game Over' is real at sea. You don't get to re-boot.

Used correctly though, electronic chart plotters can be very useful indeed: they can provide information on tides, currents, moon cycles and close-up diagrams of ports and harbours. They are good for gauging leeway and drift too. Just always remember – wishful thinking is the diametric opposite of good seamanship, and however much you would like the electronics you just dropped several thousand on to be accurate, they simply are not.

Not even the manufacturers are claiming they are.

Certainly never abandon the hard-won lessons of the seafarers, upon whose shoulders we all stand, for the false promise of some flashing lights. Forget this and you may end up as the sorry subject of the next lazy journalist's report about a yacht colliding with an 'uncharted' reef.

Now, if the above is enough to deter you from going to sea without paper charts then this book has already paid for itself. If you are still on the edge, this is probably a good time to remind you that to receive even the limited benefits of electronics, they have to actually be working. So let's take quick look at how marketing has changed the word 'waterproof' in such a way as to make that an increasingly optimistic assumption.

Waterproofing v water resistance

If you are on a diet and somebody offers you a huge slice of chocolate fudge cake and you accept it, you have effectively failed your diet. If you reject the cake immediately and all future offers are similarly rejected, you could be said to be 'temptation proof'. Pretty straight forward so far.

If however, somebody offers you a piece of cake and you say, "oh, I shouldn't really…. okay, go on then" then you could be said to be 'temptation resistant' because you did not fail immediately, but offered a bit of initial resistance before succumbing to the yummy stuff. But for how long did you resist? Did you hang on for ten minutes or a whole hour before capitulating to the chocolate fudgy yumminess?

These are the grey areas, where marketing people and lawyers like to make their foetid nests.

In the old days, if a piece of equipment was really waterproof, it would have the same description as your watch, i.e., the word 'proof' would need to be in there somewhere and a depth given to which that description applied.

When my cruddy, ancient $50 Seiko watch was designed and the manufacturer wanted to write the word 'waterproof 50M' proudly on its dial (or as proudly as you can when the font is only 0.025

points) it had some pretty serious obstacles to overcome because the manufacturers would have to replace it if it failed due to water ingress. It meant something. I wore that thing on my wrist in the bath, in the sea, free diving, scuba diving, white water rafting and when the police turned the fire hoses on us in the poll tax demonstrations in London - and not a drop of water ever got into it[23].

Ahhh , the good old days eh? They say that nostalgia isn't what it used to be, but I miss the old, easy to understand distinction between water resistant and waterproof.

Now of course, in true Kafkaesque style corporate double-speak, we have the IPX system of 'waterproof' which is in fact, largely a classification of water resistance, not water proofing. The system is nothing more than a bit of legal chicanery that allows manufacturers to splash the word 'waterproof' on items that are barely water resistant by any real definition of the term[24]

Here is the official description of the IPX waterproofing levels:

---

[23] Unfortunately, despite being stainless, it was not guaranteed rust proof and eventually the clasp gave way and it sunk to the bottom of the ocean where I am confident the mechanism is still as dry as a Amish wedding.

[24] You may be interested to know that the same kind of corporate 'double speak' is now going on in the waterproof descriptions of watches. A watch that has the words "Waterproof 50M" proudly emblazoned on its face is no longer actually waterproof to 50M (or 5 x atmospheric pressure) in water, as any normal person might expect. If you read the small print of most "water proof to 50M' watches, you will find it now means waterproof to 5 x dry atmospheric pressure and you are being advised to remove that watch in the bath.

- **IPX-0** offers absolutely no protection against water, destroying the device
- **IPX-1** offers protection from dripping water from above the device for 10 minutes
- **IPX-2** offers protection from dripping water when the device is rotated 15 degrees any direction from vertical for 10 minutes
- **IPX-3** offers protection from a spray of water in any direction when the device is rotated up to 60 degrees in any direction from vertical for 5 minutes
- **IPX-4** offers protection from a splash of water in any direction for 5 minutes
- **IPX-5** offers protection from a 6.3mm spray of water at 12.5 litres per minute (or about $1/8^{th}$ the flow rate of an average garden hose)[25] in any direction for at least 3 minutes.
- **IPX-6** offers protection from a 12.5mm spray of water at 100 litres per minute(about the same as an ordinary garden hose) in any direction for at least 3 minutes
- **IPX-7** offers protection from complete water submersion up to 1 meter deep for at least 30 minutes
- **IPX-8** offers protection above that required by IPX-7. Exactly how much will be defined by the manufacturer, but anything that is waterproof for 31 minutes at a depth of 1 meter (or indeed 30mins at 1.01 meters will qualify)

---

[25] I achieved about the same flow rate whilst suffering from benign prostrate hyperplasia and kidney stones back in the 90s.

So only IPX-8 (and possibly IPX-7) fit the description that you and I would even begin to call 'waterproof', but the IPX rating system allows manufacturers to splash the claim "waterproof to IPX standards" all over their products – some of which cannot withstand the slightest drip of water if anything other than completely upright. As most of us (except me, it would seem) have better things to do than research manufacturing standards, the IPX system, like so many standards in the marine industry, is used more to obfuscate than illuminate.

While IPX-8 has the potential to be closer to what we would think of as waterproof, I know of no such marine displays. Therefore, pretty much all of them (and if you produce anything different, I will be happy to test it for you and be proved wrong) will be destroyed as soon as a decent wave or two enters the cockpit.

You will undoubtedly meet many sailors in your travels who have never had a problem with their electronic gear and claim that they have never had a wave in the cockpit. These sailors have either been extremely lucky or have not sailed too far offshore.

I confess that I was the similarly naive. My Simrad autopilot worked seamlessly for three years in the protected waters of the Sea of Cortez and I was very happy with it. As soon as I poked my head out into the Pacific though, the first wave in the cockpit drowned it.

Many gizmos don't even wait for a wave – a bit of rain will do it. As long as the first downpour doesn't kill them, you have no comeback because the gizmo has to some extent, 'resisted' the ingress of water by not immediately capitulating.

IPX6 standard only requires a piece of equipment to resist a 12.5mm spray (smaller than an ordinary garden hose) for all of three heroic minutes. So as long as they last a few weeks of (the much more intense) tropical downpour, they have exceeded that requirement and you have no comeback. Much Raymarine equipment is built to IPX6, including some of their most popular chart plotters.

Nor are Raymarine the only manufacturer making marine gear that is only waterproofed to IPX6. Simrad's top of the range Halo 6 radar, which one would assume has to operate in all kinds of ugly conditions and needs to be positioned out in the gnarly elements to get a good line of sight, is only rated at IPX6 despite costing nearly $10,000. Don't you miss the good old days when the meanings of words were defined by dictionaries rather than lawyers?

Researching for this chapter, I noticed that some bits of gear from major manufacturers do not have the IPX rating published anywhere in their descriptions, yet happily bandy the word 'waterproof' around as if the categories had not been nailed down, were somehow optional or only to be published when to the seller's advantage.

One such product is Raymarine's range of tiller pilots which are described as having 'improved waterproofing' but no IPX number given. I made many attempts to contact Raymarine and clear this up, but my question was repeatedly ignored. Eventually I did get a reply, the details of which went some way to explaining their initial reluctance to be immediately forthcoming:

The ST1000 and ST2000 tiller pilots are not rated *at all* on the IPX standard. The top of the range EV1 autopilot control head is rated

IPX6 but the drive unit, which has to sit out in the weather and push the tiller, has no IPX rating either. (Having owned one of these units on *Marutji*, that explains a great deal indeed). Yet these products are often marketed with the word 'waterproof' in the description despite having no claim to such as far as the official ratings are concerned, or indeed, any kinship with the dictionary definition.

Nor am I picking on Raymarine particularly. I have also made several enquiries in writing as to the IPX standards involved with Simrad's tiller pilots and have yet to receive a single answer, so one can only assume that the news is not particularly stellar.[26]

A further bit of obfuscation that seems fairly common with Raymarine and other large manufacturers is the tendency to describe a gizmo's waterproof rating with two figures (i.e., 'Waterproof to IPX 6 *and* IPX 7'). I don't think you need to be a particularly cynical person to suspect that the point of this is to focus the eye on the higher rating, despite the common knowledge that any chain is only as strong as its weakest link. Is it really any consolation that the screen of your autopilot still works if the ram has failed because it is full of water? At least you will know the course it *should* be steering, I suppose.

---

[26] Big shout out to Garmin and CPT here. Most of Garmin's products are at least IPX7 rated and they are transparent in their descriptions. The same is true of CPT Autopilots who share my dislike of the IPX system and merely say that their products are 'designed to work indefinitely submerged'. I bought one (with my own money) and can confirm that they work perfectly in all kinds of gnarly conditions. Furthermore, CPT autopilots do not have those pointless LED screens, thus bypassing another weak link in the cynical chain of built-in obsolescence. Please note that the author does not receive payment from any of the companies mentioned.

To make matters worse, it seems that the skippers with the most complicated electronics are also the most likely to have eschewed the good practice of using paper charts as 'quaint'. These are the very boats most vulnerable to a salt water attack and yet these are the very boats that seem to have cockpits that look like the Kennedy Space Centre – bristling with vulnerable (and expensive to replace) electronic bleepy things. Making expensive stuff with a good mark up that breaks easily, then redefining the meaning of 'waterproof' may be a great business model, but it totally sucks as a human attitude (despite having become so standard that it is hardly news these days).

Another reason that modern production boats particularly, should consider their electronic vulnerability in the cockpit area is that owners of narrow-finned, spade-ruddered boats are often convinced that heaving-to is not possible on their boats and generally prefer running off (running downwind) as a storm tactic (we will get into why this is later). There is absolutely no way that you can avoid water in the cockpit if you are running downwind in bad conditions – with or without some kind of drag device. You are going to get pooped sooner or later and there is no point in not planning for it.

There are several ways of making your electronics less vulnerable. On *Calypso,* all her instruments were mounted on varnished hardwood plaques (the backs sealed against the rain) and hung on hooks in the cockpit when required (and when conditions permitted).

When the conditions were bad or just as a matter of course when 'putting the boat to bed' after sailing, I would take the instruments out of the cockpit and hang them on hooks below. This not only protected them from the elements, but also removed one of the trump cards of the marketer of items such as these (i.e., items that have a high degree of built-in obsolescence) by ensuring that the delicate LED screens that seem to be a fact of life these days, spend the majority of their time away from their biggest enemies - sunlight, moisture and intense heat.

My radar screen was permanently mounted down below and could be easily seen from the cockpit. On *Marutji,* everything was on one screen which lived below and flipped into the companionway on a stainless bracket that I had made for a couple of hundred bucks. In bad weather it was well protected and at anchor, far less likely to be stolen as it was locked away below – rather than visible in the cockpit like most systems are. (Note: If you do this, you need to be able to lock the bracket in place. The first prototype was a bit of a disaster ☺).

I replaced the three original, fixed Simrad cockpit displays (all of which were quickly drowned when first exposed to blue water sea conditions) with pictures of my heroes; Jon Sanders and Tom Cunliffe. The third one is still empty. That space is reserved for whoever persuades Jimmy Buffet to stop using that faux Caribbean accent.

I understand that this may seem a little overkill for many sailors. Again, this is because they leave on some big rally like the Atlantic Rally for Cruisers (ARC) and feel exonerated because all the other boats also have a cockpit like a recording studio. But it does not have to be this way and many of these sailors will soon be tearing their hair out trying to get replacement parts shipped to Nuku Hiva and bemoaning how expensive sailing is to anybody who will listen. Even if you get away with it, the fear of losing all your electronics every time a tropical downpour occurs or a little thunder or wave action is around, will spoil the peace of mind of all but the wealthiest sailors and even they won't enjoy waiting in some remote location for their new gear (and someone to install it) to arrive, or negotiating the often glacial import process of many developing countries. Again, the trick is to control the risks you can identify so that you have time to fix the ones you missed. If you don't do this, you will be constantly overwhelmed by damage control as all your little problems start holding hands to form a daisy chain of precisely the same form of misery and money-worry that you had on land. With a little planning and adherence to simplicity, this type of stress could easily dwindle until it is not much more than a vestigial remnant of a former life.

It is up to you of course, but simplicity really is a kind of bliss.

CHAPTER SEVEN

Staying Simple:
Furling mainsails and other nonsense.

I covered these briefly in the last book, but due to the amount of emails I have received on the subject, I thought it might be useful to expand upon why they are such a rotten idea.

One reader writes,

"I totally get that the thing could jam when you most need to use it, but are there any advantages to in-mast furlers?"

I think the writer answered his own question here. This increased likelihood of malfunction at critical moments is enough to dismiss in-mast furling out of hand, as it could cost you your boat or worse.

"It could kill me but might be easier", is no real argument.

We could end the conversation here as, for a voyaging boat, it is advisable to have a different mindset than that of the coastal sailor. We must always keep in mind that increased complexity nearly always means increased risk of failure, so rather than judge things on how convenient they may or may not be, the nautical nomad must always apply the following logic in respect to essential systems:

Any rise in risk must be 100% necessary, not simply convenient.

Read that again, because it will save you so much thought and internal debate when considering any 'improvement' in your little escape pod. In-mast furling certainly increases risk through complexity and is certainly not 100% necessary. Therefore it really has no place on a voyaging boat.

To support the argument for in-mast furling, one reader suggested there may be some advantages to being able to reef quickly. I absolutely agree – reefing quickly is an essential skill. But conventional reefing is also quick (quicker if you are set up properly). It takes a few seconds to drop the main into the jacks and hook the reef point over the gooseneck. Admittedly, you will now need to spend a minute or two trimming the conventional main, but once the canvas is reduced, the danger has passed and you can usually bimble around all you want, scratch your butt and generally take your time tying in the bunt or tidying up the trim.

Furthermore, in-mast furling sails cannot be battened and must be made of thinner material to fit inside the mast, thereby reducing both their effectiveness and durability. There is only one reason they are popular and that is because the market is driven by weekend yachtsmen who rarely go offshore and therefore do not really mind the extra risk of being caught in bad weather as they generally head back to harbour when the forecast looks bad and never have to face the possibility of being laid down flat by a 50 knot squall whilst swearing at their ****ing in-mast furler.

Even in situations where the extra complexity does *not* lead to serious issues, the in-mast furler can still be problematic. Non life-threatening malfunctions might be easy to deal with when you have several chandleries nearby and spares are easy to get, but soon start drifting into the arena of the dangerous in the Cook Islands when everybody else is skedaddling because a cyclone is on its way and you are still waiting for the UPS guy to look up Avarua in his A-Z of New York.

If you are determined to have one of these ghastly things then in-boom furling is a much better option as, should the furler jam, the mainsail can be dropped easily in the conventional way. In-boom furling also allows for the mainsail to be fully battened which makes them more efficient.[27]

Even better, get yourself a junk-rigged boat if reefing is worrying you as they are marvellous to reef - way faster and easier than any other system, furling or otherwise. You can spend the money you save on a stack of t-shirts so you don't wear your skin out patting yourself on the back every time you feel the confidence of knowing that you can reef your mainsail with one hand whilst holding hold your curly pipe in the other.

One reader suggested that the rise in popularity of the in-mast furler is because yacht owners are getting lazier and trying to replace good seamanship with button-pushing. This feels a bit harsh to me but probably has a grain of truth in it as the only obvious benefit of the in-mast mainsail is labour saving. Some are even electrically operated which makes reefing totally effortless (while of course introducing even more complexity). Furthermore, a furling main does not need to be flaked or a cover put on it when you have got the anchor down,

---

[27] I always find it bewildering that so many people seem happy to risk their lives in flimsy boats with spade rudders simply because they are a knot faster and then immediately surrender that advantage by installing inefficient in-mast furling mainsails. I just can't parse that one.

thereby getting you into the, 'feet up with Mai Tai' position a few minutes earlier.

This all sounds great, but one of the advantages of this lifestyle is staying fit, so labour-saving by adding complexity raises both the risk of gear failure and the spectre of the health risks that come with indolence. Add to that the significantly increased expense and there are few things that are as counter-productive to the simple, healthy life at sea as in-mast furling.

Having said all that, if you find yourself strolling so far from the leafy glade of youth that you can no longer perform normal sailing duties, then the in-mast electric furler might be exactly what you need to get out on the water. That is great news for older sailors (although I still think a junk rig would be a better option), but if you lack the fitness to flake a mainsail or turn a winch then it is probably best if you don't venture too far offshore. Everyone else with a little muscle tone left should always try and stick to the KISS principle. (Keep it Simple, Stupid).

CHAPTER EIGHT

Getting Smarter: More on buying

While I accept that real estate agents are not the devil incarnate, I do not accept that they are totally unrelated to the Dark Lord either. However you feel about them, we all know that they speak another language. Words like 'cosy', 'bijou' or 'rustic' can easily mean, 'poky', 'old' and 'ruined' in the mouth of a realtor. And so it is with yacht brokers.

I often receive emails from readers with a link to a boat and a request for advice. I am more than happy to give my opinion from afar, but enough people are having their time wasted by brokers who give incomplete information that I thought it might be useful to briefly go into the more commonly used techniques of yacht brokers so that the prospective buyer at least knows the right questions to ask in order to avoid a wasted journey.

As we know, there are thousands of boats for sale online and we cannot see them all without blowing our entire wee budget on travel and surveys. One of the few disadvantages of buying a budget boat is that the search will always represent a greater proportion of the overall cost than those buying a more expensive vessel. Hopefully these tips and tricks will help you minimise your wasted time and limit the 'non productive' drain of travel and inspection on your escape fund.

How to speak fluent 'Broker'

While most brokers are fairly honest and genuine people, it is in the nature of the job to be a little less than totally forthcoming. All boats have their strengths and weaknesses and the broker's job will always be to underplay the weaknesses and overstate the strengths. That is to be expected from anyone selling anything.

What is perhaps less acceptable are the following techniques which are far from rare. Chief amongst those is:

Using old pictures

Some brokers visit every vessel (the *Boatshed* group is a good example here) and take their own pictures and that is to be applauded. However, the majority of brokers rely on pictures supplied by the seller and do not check how old they are. While this is more a failure of due diligence than outright scurrilous lying, it has the same misleading effect on us buyers, so the distinction is immaterial in practical terms.

Either way, there is nothing more annoying than having gone to the trouble of getting a baby-sitter, putting some kerosene in the old jalopy and trekking across three counties to inspect that wonderful little Westsail you saw online, only to find out the piccies were taken in 1972 and since then the boat has been squatted by several homeless *Grateful Dead* fans and now smells like the inside of an enormous aquatic bong.

Do that a few times and you will be spitting blood and finding yourself more than a little disillusioned with the sea gypsy life before you even get your beak wet. So, it is very important to ask the broker exactly when the photographs were taken and whether they truly represent the condition of the boat.

An example

In 2018 I sold my beloved *Calypso* in order to buy *Calypso II*. When I sold her she looked lovely – always the best looking boat in any anchorage and I was very proud of her. Unfortunately, the new owner of *Calypso* was less than fastidious with her upkeep and now, three years later, she sits abandoned and forlorn in the corner of a boatyard in Fiji. Her bowsprit is broken, her rigging rusty, the exterior wood rotten and the sails and canvas are black with mould – an ignominious end for a noble boat.[28]

So imagine my surprise when I saw her for sale recently with a broker in New Zealand, looking magnificent in the full colour glossy pictures. And well she might! This is because I took those pictures almost a decade ago after an extensive re-fit. The listing goes on to show other photos from nearly a decade ago – enough to get the most fastidious buyer into a Hawaiian shirt, buckled into a Fiji Airways 747 and dreaming of palm trees and vahines, only to find the object of their desire looking sad, forgotten and as close to being a total write-off as you can get without actually being any of my attempts at lemon drizzle cake.

---

[28] I know selling a boat is a financial transaction and you shouldn't care, but you can't help it. That boat has so much of my blood in her, she may actually be my closest living relative.

> Code: A817 CL/DJ
> Year approx:1984
> Design:
> **Hans Christian 36**
> Price:
> **US$ 64,300**
> Plus taxes
>
> *Gulf Group* MARINE BROKERS   nzmarine

How the broker portrays her – a great beauty indeed and nothing like her current condition at all. Eagle-eyed readers will recognize that this picture has been lifted straight out of my last book.

As you can imagine, you only have to do this a few times and the search for a boat starts becoming a significant proportion of the cost of your great adventure. So again, always find out how old the photographs are and get something in writing so you will have some comeback with the broker if the discrepancy is as stark as the example of poor old *Calypso*.

What is not said.

Whenever a broker starts waxing lyrical about storage space, beautiful lines and glorious sunsets, you should pay special attention to what is not being said.[29] All cruising boats have good storage and most have nice lines. All will show you some beautiful sunsets. What you are interested in is the things that will cost money to fix, not some Jimmy Buffet sailing fantasy about how great the margaritas

---

[29] Or as my Scottish mother would say, "when somebody says 'trust me', it is time to count the silver".

will taste. Most often I find the things that get conveniently left out of the description are:

- **Engine hours.** Brokers always tend to give the engine hours when they are low and attempt to draw your attention away from them when they are high. Although some people (and I include myself in this description) can keep old engines chugging away almost indefinitely, a modern marine diesel is pretty much past its *reliable* lifespan at 5000 hours. So if an engine is approaching (or has passed) this limit, the broker will either not mention the hours at all or he will write something like: "reliable engine that has served the owner well" (I am sure it has, but how does that help you?), or "diesel engine just serviced!" (as if that will roll back the clock). You absolutely need to know the engine hours and if they are high, then you will need to re-power - and sooner rather than later as reliability is a much more important commodity at sea than it is driving to the office.
- **Engine servicing.** I am amazed at how many people write 'engine fully serviced in 2018'. Given that it is now 2021, this is something to be ashamed of, not a selling point. Yet those that do not understand the service needs of marine diesels can easily be persuaded that service intervals of two or three years are a good thing.
- **Standing rigging.**[30] Insurance companies will not insure a boat whose standing rigging is more than 10 years old.[31]

---

[30] Standing rigging is the stainless steel wire that holds the mast(s) up.

Most sailors know it and every broker knows it too. If you have a quick trawl through *Yachtworld* or any other brokerage website, you will see that in the space allotted to describe the standing rigging, there will be one of two answers. If the rigging is under 10 years old, you will see something like, "standing rigging renewed 2018". If it is older than ten years, you will see something like, "all stainless standing rigging", which is plain obfuscation as pretty much all boats have 'all stainless standing rigging' and that statement is simply there as a substitute for any good news about its age. Or my favourite, "rigging recently inspected". It is nice to inspect your rig (as it is all your systems) but as stainless often gives no visible signs before failing catastrophically, a visual inspection is not a guarantee that all is good. Nor is it a substitute for a young rig. But if the broker can introduce the idea of 'recent' into your mind with regards to the rig, you may overlook that. Misdirection is everything, so stay real and stay focused.

- **Just circumnavigated and ready to go again!**
  Very much a favourite expression of brokers used to glorify a boat that has had a hard life. If a boat has just circumnavigated, in the majority of cases it most certainly will *not* be ready to go again without a serious out-of-water

---

[31] Or, more accurately they will, but with the caveat that any damage or loss caused by the loss of the mast will not be covered. As it is not uncommon that the loss of the mast can mean serious damage to the hull and sometimes total loss, this is a fairly serious caveat.

inspection and re-fit. Unless the seller has already done this, you will be doing it.

- **Osmosis treated as a 'preventative measure'**
  Another favourite bit of 'broker-speak'. I have never met anyone who has dropped 20-30k on their boat *in case* it develops osmosis. This statement usually means that this particular boat has suffered from osmosis in the past and has been repaired. Not a deal-breaker, but osmosis often returns after about ten years, so it is important to see the receipt for the treatment and pay attention to the date.

Brokers generally have as many sales techniques as real estate agents, but also the added advantage of a less informed clientele. Most people are familiar with the problems of buying a house, but even so, will still choose to engage a lawyer to make sure they have not missed anything. Furthermore, most people may move house several times, gaining experience each time, whereas the experienced boat buyer is far less common, and this provides a much more fertile soil for the seeds of indiscretion and general spreading of bullshit. So (at the risk of sounding like a stuck record) always use a marine surveyor and not the one recommended by the broker.

Of course, surveys are expensive, so hopefully the tips above will help you reduce the amount of them you will need in order to find your awesome little ship.

Speaking of which, many readers seem to be a little confused as to how the buying/selling process actually works once you have identified your wee pocket of air. So, here is a brief synopsis of the process.

1. Trawl internet and traditional media for possibilities.

2. Narrow them down with questions – including those suggested above.

3 Go and see the boats that still interest you.

4. Make an offer 'subject to survey and test sail' for the one you like and if the offer is accepted, leave a 10% (refundable) deposit.

5. Find a surveyor and instruct a survey.

6. On the basis of that survey, you can now do one of three things:

- If the survey was unacceptable, you can decide to walk away and get your deposit back. You will still need to pay the surveyor and the costs of lifting the boat.
- If the survey was acceptable but found a few problems, you can either grin and bear it (if the problems are trivial), ask the owner to put them right, or re-negotiate the price to allow you to do so. If you cannot reach an agreement with the owner over the repairs, then the owner must return your deposit.
- If the survey was good, sign off on it and move on to the sea trial.

7. Sea trial. If you are not experienced you should ask a friend to come with you who is more accustomed to what to expect from the particular sailboat you are interested in. Be careful not to pick someone who has only sailed fin and spade boats as they tend not to like the boats we are interested in and often erroneously assume that directional stability means that there is something wrong with the steering.

Even better, ask the surveyor to come with you.

8. Assuming the sea trial is good (and most are - very few deals fall flat at this point) pay the balance and do the transfer of ownership paperwork.

This is a pretty good system which protects both parties and I would advise you stick with it (rather than buying sight unseen on EBay which is becoming increasingly more common). If you go through a broker, this will most certainly be the way they do things. The broker will hold deposits and monies in escrow until all the paperwork and conditions of sale are met.

If you are buying (or selling) privately, then it still pays to use this system. There is a very good generic contract that I have used a couple of times. You can download it here:

https://mariner.co.nz/forms-documents

(scroll down to 'other forms' and click 'Sale and Purchase Agreement') but please read the caveats.

Right, having cleared that up, I want to answer what is overwhelmingly the most common subject I am asked about.

CHAPTER NINE

Staying Solvent: More about the money

A wise person should have money in their head, but not in their heart.
                                                            -Jonathan Swift

Wealth consists not in having great possessions, but in having few wants.
                                                            –Epictetus

Next time somebody says, "time is money", ask them to print you some time or stop wasting yours.
                                                            -Me

Money, money money, must be funny, in a rich man's world.
                                                            –ABBA

In *Get Real, Get Gone* I covered some of the many diverse ways my briny brothers and salty sisters keep their cruising kitty topped up whilst bimbling around on the wobbly blue stuff. And this, not surprisingly, generated the largest amount of queries.

I get that completely. I will never understand why money is a subject that so many sailing writers are vague and reticent about. After all, there is no point in planning a new life you can't afford any more than there is in chasing Angelina Jolie – both are unattainable and their subsequent pursuit will turn you into some kind of spiritual (or actual) stalker. So if we want to pluck this great adventure out of the dreamscape and give it corporeal form, it is quite sensible to give finances a serious amount of consideration, assuming you would rather surf the wonderful wave of reality than whack the uncharted reef of unattainable fantasy.

Interestingly, the most popular question about money I receive is not about the various occupations undertaken by us budget buccaneers - I suppose most people don't have too much difficulty with the concept of moving their trade or occupation offshore, particularly after the Covid experience where remote working is almost becoming the order of the day.

No, what most people wanted to know was how I was getting 6.6% interest on the little nest-egg I had in the bank. In a way, this is a question I helped create because many of the readers who were planning to buy a huge, flashy coastal boat have found themselves spending half the money on something smaller and more robust, leaving a wee pot of cash to put towards their income generation.

This is something that always cheers me up as, having a little less boat and a little more income, is always a winning combination. Even if your nest-egg is tiny and only generates a little income, having a small stipend really takes the pressure off your other income-generating activities and always leads to a happier wee sea gypsy.

In this chapter then, I will explain how I get my little nest-egg to yield a big omelette. But remember, the secret to an economically and environmentally sustainable lifestyle at sea without a care in the world (a point endlessly and clumsily bulldozed home in *Get Real, Get Gone* and yet put so succinctly in the Epictus quote above) lies in keeping your overheads low by buying a small, sea-kindly boat that was designed with 'sail' and not 'sale' in mind, identifying the important things to spend money on and kitting her out accordingly with the simplest, best quality gear you can afford. If you cannot bring yourself to abandon the ego-driven nonsense of having the largest boat with all the latest novelties, then you are going to struggle with this and almost certainly become one of those people that fill every marina in the world with the depressingly common refrain, that cruising is:

"Fixing your boat in exotic locations" or that,

" B.O.A.T stands for Bring Out Another Thousand."

Don't join them! It does not have to be that way! Yes, those people exist (and you are most likely to meet them when you don't own a boat because they normally either live on land or in marinas) and you will feel obliged to accept their advice because they are 'experienced'. Politely thank them, smile and walk away as it is entirely possible to be experienced, genuinely nice and spectacularly wrong all at the same time (look at Tom Cruise).

Your 'reality' is defined by your decisions and your decisions by your attitude. If we buy a high maintenance boat and keep it in a marina, our wallets will be the major player in our lives, just as if you married Rhianna and bought her a penthouse. This does not mean that 'sailing costs a fortune' any more than it means 'all women are high maintenance'. We just need to make the right decisions, informed by the right attitude as to what is actually desirable and what is all botox and gel coat.

By the time this book goes to press, I will have updated the 2015 edition of *Get Real, Get Gone* to reflect the costs of cruising today. But just to save you looking it up (or buying another copy), here are my activity/expenses as laid out in 2015, adjusted to 2021 prices. I have included the activities of that year too because any fool can vegetate in their boat in one spot, living off charity and the barnacles that grow on the hull, so it is good to know what the money represents in a fun per dollar sense.

Number of Nights

At anchor: 283 (77%)

On passage: 50 (14%)

In the boatyard: 17 (5%)

On a mooring: 15 (4%)

In a marina: 0 (0%)

On land: 0 (0%)

Total sea miles: 4696

Longest passage: 32 days (Mexico – Marquesas)

Total days passage-making (not including day sailing): 86

Motoring hours: 167

Litres of fuel: 270 (twice normal consumption. This was an unrepresentative year for engine use)

Money in Euros (USD in brackets)

April: 800 ($937)
May: 331 ($388)

June: 290 ($340)
July: 592 ($694)

August: 205 ($240)

September: 1018 ($1193)

October: 1000 ($1172)

November: 293 ($343)

December: 1034 ($1212) incl. new autopilot control head.

January: 411 ($482)

February: 654 ($766)

March: 666 ($781)

Average Euro 607 ($711) per month for two people. [32],

I would like to re-iterate that it is quite possible to live, and live well, on this budget, but only if you follow the rest of the advice in the book. I have had several letters from owners of 48 foot marina-

---

[32] Note to single-handers. All of my crew (including long-term crew like Steph, Jasna or Fee) contribute only towards food. Although a great help in the day to day running of the boat, my crew do not contribute financially towards purchase, maintenance, fuel, docking, insurance etc., of my boats. So, these figures will also be about right for a single-hander if you halve the food expenses (which are about 30% of the total budget). However, a single hander can further reduce her budget by buying a smaller boat. My previous 34 footer Marutji was 50% cheaper to maintain than Calypso and more than adequate for a single hander or cosy couple.

dwelling 'flashy flimsies' claiming that my budget is unreasonable and misleading. I agree with them. If your boat is as thin as a hermit's address book and loaded up to the gunnels with high-maintenance 'convenience' contraptions, you will have to live with the mess you have made. But instead of peeing in our own shoes and then complaining how wet our socks are, we can choose a path to happiness that is a lot less strewn with diversionary cow pats by shelving the ego and becoming happy, smiling sea gypsies with warm welcomes, small boats, big hearts and a sense of the amazing privilege it is to see the whole of creation from the deck of your own cosy, wee home. Let others concern themselves with their Instagram image or whether their boat is sufficiently bling to keep up with the Kardashians.

Cherry picking just the bits of getting real that that suit (normally those bits that don't require any real personal change) will yield an unrecognizable experience (see the introduction to part one). So, in case you have not read *Get Real, Get Gone,* here in a nutshell is the ABC of safe, budget, sustainable voyaging on the wobbly place where fish live.

- A. Remove all debt. Declare bankruptcy if you have to, but remove all debt.
- B. Remember SSSSS: Get a Small, Simple, Solid, Seaworthy Sailboat and do NOT fill it with every gadget the salesman recommends at the boat show. (Best not to go to boat shows at all actually – even if I am speaking there ☺). Identify what gear is important at sea, and buy the best quality you can afford.

C. Develop a small income.
D. Don't skip a step
E. Enjoy your new life.[33] (Then come find me, tell me your story, get a signed copy of my latest book and claim your free glass of Chardonnay).[34]

There is no jumping straight to E without passing through A to D.

It has now been my pleasure and privilege to have helped hundreds of couples and single-handers on their own transition from turf to surf and I have never had a letter from anyone who has done ABCD and not got to E. If you are that rare person, then check you have done all the things recommended and then write to me. I will be happy to help identify a way forward.

Sorry for the diversion. I am aware that this chapter is meant to be about money, but I wanted to reiterate that very important point that if you have few expenses, your income only needs to be small and your path to sustainability becomes that much easier. (Yes, that does appear rather obvious doesn't it? But you would be surprised how many people find it hard to absorb).

---

[33] I am aware how simplistic this sounds, but I go into great detail as to how to achieve each step in *Get Real, Get Gone*. At the risk of sounding like a salesman, I recommend you read that first, or if you read it some time ago, pick it up again and have a skim through. It can be read for free on Kindle Unlimited or downloaded to your phone, tablet or reader on Amazon for about the price of a latte.

[34] Not subject to any terms or conditions whatsoever (unless you play chess or tennis).

So, now that is out of the way and the trolls have either thrown the book away or are angrily logging into cruising forums to protect the world from such clearly subversive communist ideas, let's look at how I make my little nest-egg sweat like a mugger in church.

How a doofus got smart about money.
(This section is a bit rambly, but I will get to the point, I promise).

Every dark cloud really does have a silver lining, although sometimes it is not obvious at the time. How could it be? If the silver lining was obvious, it would not appear like an ominous, dark cloud at all, but simply as good omen.

For example, one of my best friends met his paramedic wife in the ambulance when he accidentally amputated one of his toes whilst cutting the lawn with an industrial weed-whacker. St Paul discovered God when he had an epileptic fit on the road to Tarsus bought on by lack of good drinking water. Such misfortunes must have been wholly distressing at the time, but both went on to do very well for themselves through these unpleasant, formative experiences.

Some of the best experiences are born from situations that seem less than ideal at the time. You never can tell. The trick to being happy on a daily basis is, naturally, to try and be aware of it at the time rather than just in hindsight.

This is of course, easier said than done. It is far more difficult to think, "I bet I will meet the love of my life because of this" whilst holding your pinkie toe in the spring edition of *Gardeners' World,* than it is to paint the sky blue with words containing unusually high concentrations of the letter 'F', and ranting on about how life is singling you out for a particularly thick shit-sandwich.

What has all this ersatz eastern wisdom got to do with financial sustainability?

Well, one particular instance (one of many) of this ever-present, but difficult to see silver-lining has had more impact on my financial sustainability than any other single factor (I confess that I did not see it at the time either, but that is rather the point I am making).

I never imagined that losing a heap of cash, then having a financially dependent partner living on my boat with me and eroding my small savings like a beaver locked in an IKEA warehouse, would be the best thing that ever happened to my understanding of finances. I would have enjoyed the whole process a lot more if I could have seen the silver lining in that particular cloud.

Let me back-track a bit. To go a-watery wandering, I had sold my small farm in rural Spain, paid off the mortgage and thought I had a tidy little sum left over to qualify (RYA Yachtmaster fast-track), get some experience, buy a boat, drop out of the madness of life on land and have a sustainable lifestyle in peace at sea. Unfortunately, I put my money from the farm into one of those banks that did not survive the global financial crisis and although it was bailed out by the government, I took a big hit because my deposit was above the limit guaranteed by the state. Undeterred, but now with only about a third of the money I had envisioned, I still managed to buy a small, simple, seaworthy boat and get trained and qualified. Soon I found myself living the dream, making small forays up the east coast of Australia (which is absolutely festooned with great anchorages and helpful sailors who are mercifully free from any hint of snobbery towards doofus newbies like myself) whist I learnt my sea-craft.

When I met Jasna and it became obvious that we might sail together for a while, the situation was further exacerbated as two do not live as cheaply as one on a boat[35].

My already unsustainable lifestyle had just become even more untenable and I decided that I had to make my little nest-egg work a lot harder if I was to support both myself and a charming, but penniless, backpacker whom I had fallen for.

Knowing absolutely nothing about money (and being a little nervous due to having recently lost a fair amount of it), I had my little nest-egg in a long-term savings fund which was paying a little under 7% interest a year (this was back in 2008 – good luck getting this from a bank today!) which gave me an income of about AU$12,000 a year (which, at the time was about US$12,000).

Spending all of it would have meant that inflation would erode my wee nest-egg pretty quickly, so I needed to live on less and return some of that income to the bank if I wanted to be truly sustainable. My practical *sustainable* income was therefore about AU$10,000 a year (US$10,000). This was just about do-able on my nearly new, low-maintenance 34-foot steel Van de Stadt in Australia (which is

---

[35] As explained in Get Real, Get Gone, if food and drink are your largest expenses, then you are probably doing it right. Add another person to your crew and your food expenses (and therefore your overall expenses) should increase substantially.

quite an expensive place) but impossible now I had a dependent partner. Just to add insult to injury, worldwide quantitative easing (money printing) meant that interest rates for depositors were plunging like amnesic skydivers as governments all over the world were trying to kick-start the economy by encouraging people to borrow with fantastically tempting interest rates.

This was good news for mortgage holders and those living on debt, but for savers it was a catastrophe. Every month, my little nest-egg produced less and less as the world's governments, in their wisdom, chose (and continue to choose) polices that reward the financially less responsible whose ability to buy more crap is constrained only by their access to credit, at the expense of frugal savers like me. Something had to be done!

Firstly, I managed to raise some money by selling *Marutji*. I was sorry to see her go, but I was offered an insane price for her at the same time that the AU$ had spiked and was buying an unprecedented US$1.15, so I took advantage of that rather unusual glitch in the exchange rate, sold my Van de Stadt in Australian dollars and headed for nearby Malaysia (where boats are sold tax-free in US dollars) and after more travelling adventures and stories which I shan't bore you with, eventually bought *Calypso* for half the money I had raised by selling *Marutji* and put the other half in the bank.

That helped increase my income for a while, but interest rates were still dropping so I signed up for an online course on investing in equities and bonds and have never looked back.

Now, before you throw your hands in the air and cry "too risky!" I would like to dispel a few myths. While there are cases of enormous successes and failures, overnight millionaires and precipitous market crashes that could scare any fund manager half out of his BMW, the majority of investors are quietly investing in relatively safe stocks and receiving relatively modest, reliable returns week in, week out, year in, year out. Like professional musicians, we only hear of the most extreme stories of rock stars choking on their own vomit or hanging off the back of bathroom doors auto-asphyxiating in random hotel rooms. Whilst in reality, 99% of professional musicians are fairly anonymous and live quiet lives earning a living to support their families. Ahh, such is the media and our almost limitless appetite for prurient gossip!

I do not care about the extremes and, like most people reading this book, I am not trying to get rich and conquer the world, but would like to have a small, steady, low-risk income that I can use to explore the world without worry and create a permanent break in the connection between time and money. Time should only be money in the sense that each month you get a bit more for doing what you love. In other words, time should be a resource that increases the distance between you and the poor house, not one that pushes you towards it.

⚓

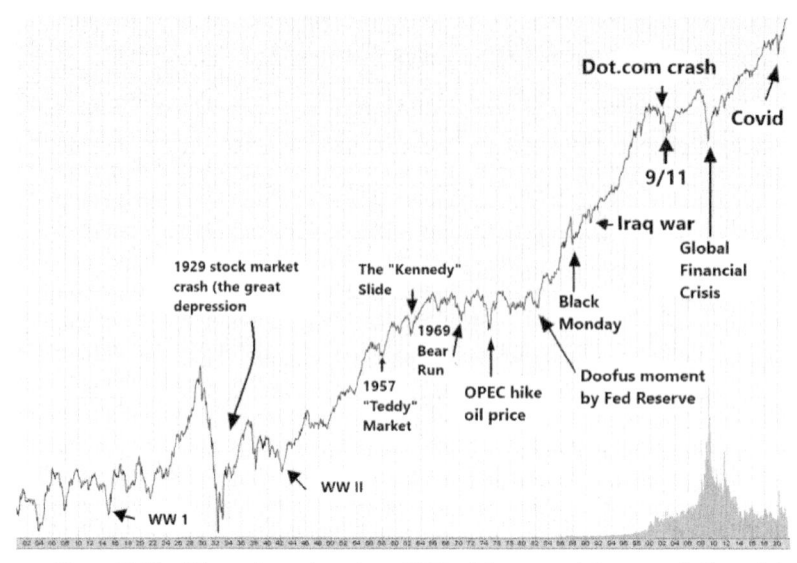

Figure T: The US stock market since 1900 with some of the more influential points in history that caused sudden dips.

To get a better grip on the real risks of investment and how us sea-sliders can mitigate them, have a look at Figure T. The above chart shows the US stock market since the beginning of the last century. I could have just as easily picked the stock market chart of any developed country as they all tell a similar story. While they have all had their ups and downs there is one overriding, unquestionable truth about all of them: They usually tend to go up in the long term. If a hundred years ago you had put $100 in the stock market and your friends had put their money in the bank, they would have $46,000 now and you would have a staggering $2 million.

To put it another way, you would be 43 times richer than your cash-loving friends who, rather ironically, probably stayed away from the stock market because they considered themselves 'risk averse'. Interestingly, the majority of short term investors or 'day traders' actually make a loss (as many as 85% of them according to some sources).

So, the trick to mitigating risk is clearly to think in the long-term, rather than join the massive casino of speculators trying to get rich by predicting short-term volatility. Fortunately, this works out rather well for nomads who have taken to the sea, or to many other forms of off-grid living, as the stats clearly show that nearly all successful investors (including the great Warren Buffet) owe their success to taking the long, 'hands off' view.

The attempt to make massive, short-term gains is the origin of nearly all the disaster stories (and of course, like any casino, just enough success stories, to inspire the terminally gullible) and this is largely what gives the stock market such a bad reputation - just as most sailing disasters occur when sailors (or designers) try to push the outer limits of their boats to win races or join up meaningless, man-made lines on the planet.

There are a lot of parallels here. Just like picking a good boat, identifying where the real risks are in investing (compared to the media noise) can go a long way to seriously reducing the actual risks involved. More on that later, but for now, back to the story....

So, there I was, having a wonderful time with a new squeeze and a new boat, but a little concerned that my small savings were getting even smaller on a monthly basis. By now though, I was optimistic and fully committed to my online course in investing. I spent many an evening reading every single thing I could get my hands on about long-term, 'value investing' and the whole Warren Buffet ethos in general.

When I thought I was getting a handle on things, I started 'paper trading' my decisions. There are many different websites where you can set up practice accounts and 'paper trade' stocks. These accounts track stock movements and allow you to see what would have happened if you had invested at certain times, without actually risking any money. A kind of 'dummy run' as it were.

This is actually quite fun. I had several paper accounts on the go, based on different criteria or sources of advice, until I got a reasonable idea of who/what could be trusted. I then started buying stocks with real money, but only at a fraction of a real stock portfolio. For example, I allocated $10,000 of my wee nest-egg and imagined each dollar was ten dollars.

This is where you really start learning.

Let's face it folks, finance, as a subject, is as dull as Jimmy Buffet's record collection and it is nearly impossible to read about 'dividend re-investment plans', if you are remotely sauced or can hear reggae music playing in a bar ashore. Actually, even if you are in prison and have to choose between showering with rapists or reading Benjamin Graham's classic book, *The Intelligent Investor*, it's a coin-toss as to whether you will find yourself immersed in its dusty pages or reaching for the soap while a guy called 'Bubba' is whispering in your ear about how much you remind him of his wife.

If you are the type of person who is reading this book, then you will probably be as bored by financial information as I am. However, all that changes when you put a bit of skin in the game by investing your own money (however small the amount) in the hope of creating an income with which to buy your freedom. Using a small stake is a complete game changer and provides the motivation to do your research into the night when the breeze is in the palm trees and the mango daiquiris are calling your name.

As alluded to earlier, it turns out that the skills we identified in *Get Real, Get Gone* as being important to develop in order to get afloat safely on a budget are completely transferrable to the world of investing. It is all a question of noticing your own psychology and biases and looking through the flashy hype at the bones of what lies beneath. Is it all marketing, shiny gel coat, flashing lights and marble table-tops or is there a decent keel and fully supported rudder underneath?

It is beyond the scope of this book (and its author!) to delve into the process of analyzing businesses, but I thoroughly recommend that you make this journey if you have a little nest-egg that you need to make work for you – particularly in this money-printing environment that is penalising savers so much. What I *will* tell you though, is that as a small, domestic investor, you have one major game-changing advantage over the large fund manager and it is exactly the same advantage you have as a boat buyer in a buyers' market.

You can do nothing.

You can simply walk away in the total confidence that there will be a better deal around the corner.

Yup, the sea gypsy's favourite pastime (doing nothing, goofing off or generally lollygagging) is as much your key to good investing as it is to getting a good deal on your new floating home. The world's most successful investor, Warren Buffet, claims that the key to his success is:

"Lethargy, bordering on sloth".

Most professional fund managers are under enormous pressure to provide a good return on the money you (or your pension/insurance fund) hand over to them as well as pay their staff, rent, bills, etc. Doing nothing is not an option for most professional fund managers, as doing nothing will lead to bankruptcy. Imagine how many bad deals you would make if you simply *had* to buy a boat every month – even when the only boats for sale were utter dogs?

When the markets are looking sketchy we salty sea-sliders, mercifully free from the ravages of the time payments that afflict our land-dwelling counterparts, can follow Warren Buffet's advice to the letter - by doing absolutely nothing.

In extremis, we can even turn all our stocks into cash and put the lot into a government guaranteed deposit (or term deposit, or government bond) at 2% and wait for the crash (at which point we can buy our favourite stocks back at a fraction of the price).

Of course, that is easier said than done. Many investors (including the majority of professional fund managers) were entirely blind-sided by the 2008 Global Financial Crisis (GFC) and so would you have been too. But the important thing to bear in mind here is that even those who held on at the bottom of the crash and did nothing were soon much better off than before the GFC and waaaaay better off than those who sold low in a panic.

"So Rick, you annoying, myopic, British hobbit", I hear you justifiably ask, "if it is that simple why doesn't everybody hold on in bad times and wait for the recovery?"

The answer to this is a toxic combination of bad attitude and something called 'margin loans'.

Avoiding margin loans

Every stock you buy will have 'Loan Valuation Rate' (LVR) number attached to it. This number represents how much the bank will lend you if you buy this stock, expressed as a percentage of its value. For example let's imagine a company and call it Acme Industries.

If it is a large, fairly well established company with a good track record (sometimes called a 'blue chip') it will have a fairly high LVR. For the sake of argument, let us say that Acme Industries' LVR is 80%.

Now, your research has led you to believe that this would be a good company to put a portion of your little nest-egg in. Good. If you have done your research well, you will receive your fairly low-risk, modest returns (more on that later). That is not the whole story though. Many investors are not satisfied with this type of modest gain and use the LVR facility to borrow from the bank to try and supercharge their returns. This is called 'leverage'.

For example: Thinking that the stock of Acme Industries is sure to go up in value, a brave investor may take the full LVR loan offered by the bank to buy $100,000 worth of stock by using $20,000 of her own money, plus the full extent of the LVR to buy another $80,000 of the stock with the bank's money. The bank has now leant you 80% of your total $100,000 investment. No problems so far.

Now, if the stock goes up 20%, she sells the lot for $120,000, pays the bank back their $80,000, pockets a nice $20,000 profit and has effectively doubled her money. Yaay! Take the rest of the year off! All well and good.

Until it isn't.

If the stock should fall 20% in value, then the investor has a big problem as she cannot simply do nothing and allow the effects of time to work for her. Why not?

Well, remember, the maximum the bank will allow you to borrow is 80% of the total value of your investment. When the stock you bought was worth $100,000 ($20k of your money and $80k of the bank's), the bank's $80,000 contribution represented 80% of the total value of the investment, as agreed. Now that the stock has fallen in value 20% and is now only worth $80,000 in total, the bank's exposure of $80,000 now represents 100% of the value of the investment - which is not something the bank has agreed to at all and some prawny-faced, yeasty landlubber in red spectacles with bad breath, a worse tie and a thoroughly undeserved confidence in his own superiority, is already picking up the phone to make the dreaded 'margin call'.

Margin calls

Once your LVR has exceeded the allowable maximum, the bank will ask you to re-balance the investment by buying $20,000 more of the stock (thus returning the percentage the bank owns to 80%) or to pay them $20,000 in cash transfer. The banks are absolutely adamant about this and are as likely to enter into negotiation as a Taliban at a gay bar. You are in the big leagues now and there is no debt relief, no safety net and you won't get let-off if you blub.

Now, remember that a falling market is like a falling tide and tends to effect a whole raft of stocks simultaneously. So, if you have several margin loans out, you may have several other margin calls coming in all at once.

You can easily see what a compromising position that puts you in. Most small investors will not have the cash available to absorb this kind of impact and will be forced to sell perfectly good stocks at exactly the wrong time in order to meet their margin obligations and will be forced suck up huge losses. It is no good throwing up your hands and saying, "I just don't get it, the market is so irrational" because in the short term, the market *is* irrational and more importantly, it can stay that way longer than you can remain solvent.

In short, when you use money from the bank via the LVR mechanism, you surrender your only real advantage as a small, domestic investor – the ability to do nothing, sit tight and sell at the most financially advantageous time, which is usually when the market has stopped being negatively irrational and has become positively irrational.

Using the bank's money like this to super-charge returns also requires near-permanent vigilance and I am guessing that being stuck to your laptop screen like a porn-addicted millennial YouTube influencer is not the manner in which you were hoping to change your life.

This type of leveraged investing is risky and is the source of many of the horror stories that have kept us all in enough fear to continue lending our money to the bank for free so that *they* can make it sweat and pocket the difference.

But, as always, we have to look through the hype to focus on the mundane and try and remember that, while the motto of the glamorous, high-risk investor may well be, "buy low, sell high", the central tenet of low-risk investing will always be, "protect your investment".

And that cannot be achieved with margin loans. [36]

---

[36] The reason I have spent a lot of time on this is that there is a fairly popular book available, written by a sailor who claims it is possible to fund your sailing life this way. He claims that 'all' you have to do is increase your little nest-egg 5% every month by using this (and other) risky strategies. Sounds quite reasonable until you realize that 5% a month is 60% a year and that would make you the best money manager the world has ever seen by several factors. If something seems too good to be true....

Dividends, Australians and alcohol.
"Okay", I hear you say, "I will only use my own money, but what am I expected to live on when the stock market isn't growing"?

The answer to that is the sweetest and most misunderstood aspect of stock ownership namely, dividends.

Dividends (yay!)
Many people believe that the stock market is one giant roulette wheel. While there is more risk than sticking your money under the mattress, this is an unfair representation. The key to using the stock market for sea gypsies is dividends and time. To explain, I have taken as an example a stock I own called Ale Properties (stock code LEP). Nobody has ever heard of them, but they are a great little property company that own pubs in Australia which, as you will have correctly surmised, is as steady an investment as owning a brothel near a French navy base.

I hold shares in Ale Properties and will probably never sell them. I have chosen them as an example, not because they are a stellar performer in my micro-portfolio, but because they are a plodder – boringly reliable, relatively risk-free, steady and dependable. So let's look at them and what this type of 'hands off' investment can brings to the passive, sustainable income of a nautical nomad who would rather not screen-gaze the rest of her life away. Have squint at the chart on the next page.

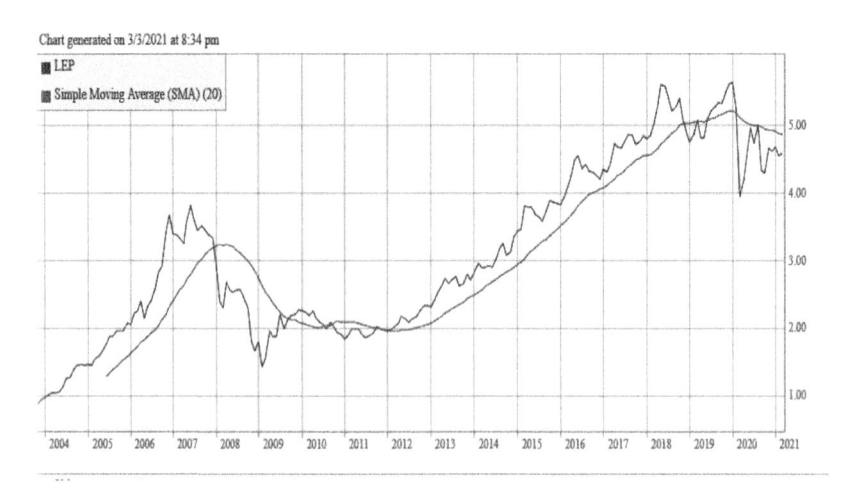

Performance of ALE Properties (LEP) since 2004. Chart courtesy of Commsec

I have held these shares since 2012. In that time, they have more than doubled in value. But that does not really affect me as I have no intention of selling them. This company is interesting to me because its assets are bricks and mortar. It owns real estate, which it turns into bars, rents out to people who like filling Australians with beer and kindly shares the rents with me via a dividend while I am asleep or sailing in exotic locations and generally goofing off (hard to believe we live in such a wonderful world, but we do).

A dividend is a payment usually paid out twice a year to shareholders. For every share you hold, regardless of what you paid for that share (and this is a very important point to keep in mind, so store it away for later) you will be paid a dividend. In the case of Ale

Properties, this dividend is currently (in late 2020) 23 cents per share, per year[37]

So a quick sum...

(0.23 dollars / 5.00 dollars) x 100

... gives us a percentage yield of 4.6% a year. (For those who have forgotten their arithmetic, remember to do the sum in the brackets first and then multiply the answer by 100 to get the percentage).

Now, that is a fairly decent return on its own in 2020, but there are not one, but *four* magical things going on here. The most obvious is:

1. **The stock price has risen.**
   This is the most obvious, but in a way, the least interesting as (strangely enough) this makes little difference to my income as I don't intend to sell these shares unless there is a material change in the company. This is not to say that the rise in price has no effect on my income, just that the real effect is far less obvious. The real impact this has on my income is that, due the rise in stock price...

2. **... the dividends have increased while staying the same.**
   Confused? So was I, but it is worth taking a little time to understand this process as it is the secret to a long-term,

---

[37] There are companies that pay higher dividends (BHP Billiton, Sydney Airport, Unibail, etc) and other companies that pay less or none at all. Those that pay a decent dividend are often called, "income stocks".

sustainable income (and also why the rich always seem to get richer). So let's look a little more closely.

The directors of Ale Properties have decided that paying a yearly dividend of 4.6% will be tempting enough to keep attracting investors so that the company has the cash it needs to continue to grow, buy more pubs and fill more Australians with beer.

To achieve this at a share price of 5.00, the dividend payout will have be about 23 cents per share (as demonstrated on the previous page). If you own a thousand shares, the payout will be $230. If you own ten thousand shares, the payout will be $2300. If you own a hundred thousand shares, the payout will be $23,000, etc. So far, so good.

Now, assuming you have done your research and chosen wisely, your stock (like most stocks) will hopefully rise in value over time. Let us say that Ale Property shares rise to $7 a share (as I expect they will in a few years). Now, to maintain a 4.6% dividend payout (the level the directors consider to be the sweet spot for attracting new investors) 23 cents per share is no longer cutting the mustard. To maintain a 4.6% dividend, the dividend per share must rise to 32 cents. In other words, those who buy shares in Ale Property (in a few years time and assuming it has risen to $7 a share), will need to get 32c a share if Ale Property wants to maintain the 4.6% dividend rate.

But hang on though, what happens to us who bought Ale Properties at $2 dollars a share back in 2012 and lethargically held on to them through the ups and downs? Well (and pay attention now as here comes the money shot) *we also get 32c per share, because dividends are paid per share regardless of what you historically paid for that share.*

So, now, after 8 years of doing absolutely nothing, we are getting a payout of 32 cents per share for a stock we bought for $2, which is a dividend of 16%. (Even at today's dividend of 23 cents, I am getting a return of 11.5% without including any profits from the rise in the share price).

And this is far from fanciful. One of the most 'boring plodder' stocks of all time is mining giant BHP Billiton.[38] BHP is an enormous conglomerate that is currently paying a dividend of about $2.00 per share. A share in BHP at time of writing costs about $50, so a $2 dividend represents a healthy return of about 4%. Now, take a look at the chart overleaf which shows the BHP price for the last 30 years.

---

[38] I don't hold any BHP shares personally because I have reservations about their environmental policies and this, like any other stock mentioned here, should not be considered as a recommendation.

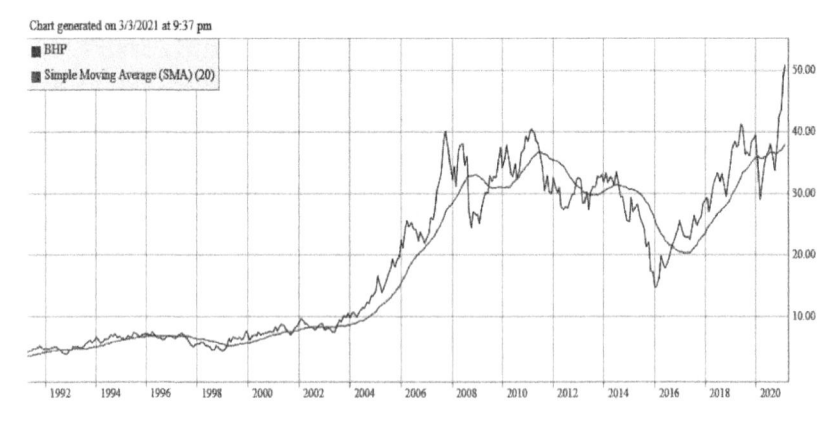

BHP Performance since 1991

BHP as a company go back to 1851, but this chart only goes back to January 1991. However, if you had bought your shares in BHP back in 1999 (and that was not SO long ago!) at $4.90 per share, you would still be entitled to the same $2 per share dividend as those investors who are buying BHP today at $50 a share. While their dividend may be the same *per share* as yours, when expressed as a percentage of the investment, recent investors are receiving a payout of 4% whilst yours is a whopping 41%! That is a really good return by anybody's standards and again, without even considering the gains you have made in the value of the stock. You see how 'old money' just seems to make the rich richer?

Nor do you have to pop into your time machine and go back to 1999 to get a good return (but if you do, don't forget to party like you were an artist formerly known as alive). There have been several opportunities to get into BHP (and stocks in general) in more recent history. Have another look at the chart above.

An opportunity was created in 2006 by a drop in resource prices (oil, Iron ore and minerals which BHP produces) and by the subsequent rush by investors to sell their shares to service those pesky margin loans. The stock price fell to $22.56. Buying at that price would mean that your investment would now be paying you just shy of 9% every year.

The stock quickly recovered but then fell again to $20 during the global financial crisis of 2008. Buying then would mean that your investment would now be paying you 10% a year.

In 2016 there was another global slump in iron ore prices and a dam failure in Brazil which caused the share price to bottom out at $15 a share. Getting in here would mean that your investment would now be paying over 13.5% a year.

Very recently of course, we have had the pandemic which, tragedy notwithstanding, provided another opportunity to top-up on BHP at $27 giving a return today of around 7.5% per year .

All the above is in addition to the gains made by the rising stock price (which only really affects your income because rising stock prices tend to mean an increase in dividends), but you will be glad of that increase in share price should you need to raise money suddenly because your spade rudder has dropped off and you are bobbing around on the ocean feeling sorry for yourself (just don't expect too much sympathy from me).

3. **Dividends are trying to go up.**
   Like most companies, BHP and Ale Properties will try to increase or maintain their dividends as a way to attract new investors. Obviously, the bigger the dividend, the more attractive that company is to investors looking for income. This is not to suggest that Ale Properties, BHP (or any other company) are obliged to pay a dividend (they are not), just that it is in their best interests to do so. This means that you have a second force working for you to increase your income. (It is very easy to check the track record of any company to see how reliable its dividend payments have been historically).

4. **Generally there are tax advantages to receiving income via dividends**

On top of all this, there are also some tax advantages to receiving income via dividends. These are called, 'franking credits' or 'imputation credits'. To encourage investment, many countries offer tax breaks for those receiving their income via dividends that super-charge those earnings further. For example, my Ale Properties dividends are around 11% a year now but with the tax rebate, that gets boosted to 12.1%. It is of course impossible to dive into the murky depths of any specific country's tax laws in a book about budget sailing (and much depends on your own personal circumstances anyway), but at time of writing, the USA, Canada, UK, Germany, Switzerland, Finland, New Zealand, Hong Kong, Singapore, Ireland, Australia, South Korea, Mexico and many other countries have tax laws that favour those receiving their income in the form of dividends. Check out what the laws are in your country by googling 'imputation credits' or 'franking credits' in your country's tax office website.

Money in the bank

So let's have a quick look at a 10-year comparison between a term deposit (sometimes called a 'time' or 'cash' deposit) and shares in Ale Properties over the last ten years. The best deposit rates over the last decade have been in the USA, so let's take those.[39] Just to make this a very conservative comparison, I have chosen the 3 year cash deposit rates as they are always higher than the annual ones.

If we assume that in both cases we are not reinvesting the interest/dividends, but withdrawing the cash to buy sails and mango daiquiris, then the comparison looks like this:

---

[39] Some developing countries offer extremely attractive rates, but they are too high risk to be included in a conservative strategy that has, 'protect your investment' as its mantra.

Term/Cash/Time Deposit

	Capital	Interest rate%	Yearly income
Year 1	$50,000	1.09	$545
Year 2	$50,000	0.74	$370
Year 3	$50,000	0.52	$260
Year 4	$50,000	0.45	$225
Year 5	$50,000	0.47	$235
Year 6	$50,000	0.48	$240
Year 7	$50,000	0.49	$245
Year 8	$50,000	0.49	$245
Year 9	$50,000	0.96	$480
Year 10	$50,000	0.94	$470
Total Gain	$0	Total Interest	$3315

Figures courtesy of FDIC and based on average returns for 3 year cash deposits under $100,000.

So, your nest-egg has produced a total of $3315 or 0.66% a year (6.6% in total for the decade). However, if the historical inflation for that period is factored in at 1.75%, then your $50,000 capital actually only buys today what $41,250 did ten years ago. [40] In other words, your capital has generated $3315 but is worth $8750 less than it was 10 years ago and you don't have to be Warren Buffet (or even Jimmy Buffet) to see that this only ends one way – with the wealth from your money being magically transferred to the shareholders of the bank in

---

[40] The predicted inflation rate for the US in 2021 is 2.24% according to Statista. So if interest rates do not rise significantly, cash deposits will be even less good value.

one of the most common, legal and breathtakingly audacious pick-pocketing operations ever invented.

Also bear in mind that money received as interest is treated as income and taxed accordingly in (as far as I can see) every single tax system in the word except some Arab countries and French Polynesia, so you may have to pay tax on it as well, depending on your personal circumstances.

Now, let's have a look at what your income would have been had you spent that cash on 27,173 shares(@ $1.84/share) of a fairly low risk bricks and mortar stock like Ale Properties ten years ago.

	Capital	Div/share	Yearly income
Year 1	$50,000	0.21	$5706
Year 2	$55,161	0.16	$4,347
Year 3	$68,204	0.16	$4,347
Year 4	$79,073	0.16	$4,347
Year 5	$103,800	0.17	$4,619
Year 6	$113,855	0.20	$5,435
Year 7	$121,735	0.20	$5,435
Year 8	$139,397	0.21	$5,706
Year 9	$107,886	0,21	$5,706
Year 10	$123,909	0.21	$5,706
CapitalGain	$73,909	Total Divs	$51,354

Figures courtesy of Commsec

As you can see, even if we exclude the tax advantages of receiving your income as dividends, the returns of a cash deposit do not even get close to those offered by even the most unspectacular company like Ale Property. Had I used any of the FAANG stocks (Facebook, Amazon, Apple, Netflix, Google) as my comparison, the results would have been even more stratospherically one-sided.

But couldn't I lose everything?

While it is true that there is no guarantee that any particular stock will rise in value, there are ways to reduce the risk to acceptable levels – even for a penny-pinching Brit with Scottish heritage like me who thinks Ebeneezer Scrooge was a profligate wastrel. I picked Ale Properties as my example because they are a real estate company with tangible assets. The value of this company is in bricks and mortar and that will always have value which you, as an investor, become a part owner of (without having to find tenants or fix the roof). It may have less value some years than others but it is a well managed company and it is extremely unlikely that it will ever be worth less than the bricks and mortar in its portfolio. So, assuming you can buy the stock at fairly close to that value, (which is what I did and why I did it) then the risk is minimal.

Some people lost money on Ale Property though. As you can see in the chart, the pandemic in year nine had quite an effect on the share price and those who bought in year 6, 7 or 8 and were forced by margin loans or other financial considerations to sell in year 9, lost money. For wily investors like us, who do not have the dark shadow of the margin loan hovering over us, the downturn in year nine was an opportunity to top up on some more. As highly leveraged greedy people were forced to dump good stocks to re-balance their relationship with the bank, we were laughing all the way there.

Yet margin loans are not the only way to lose your shirt. Investing in 'pie in the sky' start-ups that promise 1000% returns based on an untested product is a great way to ensure you are playing for the 'skins' team. As is Bitcoin. There is no doubt that people have made amazing returns on both, but they have no substance, could disappear overnight and as such, mark the dividing line between investment and gambling. I don't gamble, so I won't cover them here.

But, like you, I am not interested in risking my little pile of cash in the hope of striking it lucky and getting rich, but trying to create a small, reliable income stream so that I can live a more authentic life. To that end, I buy only reputable stocks with good track records that my research has lead me to believe are either undervalued by the market or have steady future prospects, or both. As a result, I sleep soundly and don't care if I am offline for weeks. My (non-writing) income these days now comes mainly from dividends and actually results in a negative tax bill (rebate) rather than the kind of figure that looks like an iPhone serial number and pre-empts some mild tachycardia. However, even if my very cautious approach still fills you with the cold sweats, there is a way to mitigate the risks even further.

Investing for the terminally risk-averse scaredy-pants.
Ha. Sorry about that. I don't really think being risk-adverse about your wee pile of freedom tickets is anything to be ashamed of. Quite frankly I would rather eat a whole dolphin on toast than have to go back into the job market, and having a reasonably safe little nest-egg certainly keeps the likelihood of ever having to endure a

'performance review' from some nineteen year old yeasty codpiece at acceptably low levels.

Yet there is no escaping the fact that with the current levels of interest and inflation, something has to be done to generate a better return, no matter how risk-averse you may be, if you want to get your wee pile of cash to start cranking out some spendables rather than watch its value wither on the vine in the bank.

I am pleased to say that there is a fairly simple answer to this and that is diversity.

Diversity.

Now as a lover of all races, genders and sexual orientations (with the possible exception of real estate agents and people from Coventry) I already like the word diversity. If you are a risk-adverse sea gypsy with a bit of cash you want to make sweat, you are going to love it.

Let me explain:

The stock market is a zero sum game. If you buy something and it goes up, the person who sold it misses out. If you buy something and it goes down in value, you lose out. The trick of course is being on the right side of any trade. If you put all your cash into one or two stocks and they do very well, you are laughing all the way to the chandlery, but there is also a chance that you could be on the wrong side of those deals and booking a spot for the next swap-meet to sell all your spare parts. However, as the stock market always rises over time *as a whole*, you have a much higher chance of being on the right side of those deals if you invest a little bit in many stocks in the market. Having a multitude of stocks in your portfolio is known as 'diversifying' and is the best way to reduce risk. Individual companies may come and go, but the market as a whole, marches on. Therefore, if your nest-egg is invested in the whole of the market (or a large, diverse section of it) then your wee pile is fairly secure over time.

Now, there are over 2000 stocks on the New York Stock Exchange. Same for the UK, Canadian and Australian Stock Exchanges, with stocks drifting in and out all the time as companies get formed and go public or go bankrupt, and this creates two problems for our wee nest-egg. Firstly, when you buy a stock, there is a brokerage fee (usually about $15).[41] So, if we divide our small pile between 2000 shares that would attract a whopping bill of $30,000 just in brokerage fees and the BMW dealer would be very busy that week. The other problem would be time – how the hell do we analyse which companies are sound investments and then keep track of them all when we are sunning ourselves on some atoll and already having enough trouble trying to remember where we left the dinghy?

Well fortunately, this is made easy and fairly doofus-proof for us by a little device called the Electronically Traded Fund (ETF)

ETFs

ETFs are traded just like stocks but allow the investor to gain exposure to a broad range of shares, for one brokerage fee. For

---

[41] There are several 'no commission' brokers but I don't really trust them to hold my stake as they are not part of any government deposit protection scheme. I am particularly nervous about 'Etoro'. Obviously a professional company, but they are based in Cyprus where the government recently froze all bank accounts over a certain amount and simply kept the money. If you use any company based in Cyprus, keep your stake somewhere else and transfer only what you need to make any particular trade.

example, you can buy an ETF today that splits your money over all the tech stocks in the USA. Obviously this has performed very well recently and delivered consistent healthy returns. As your money is not entirely in one company, should there be a bankruptcy or two, you are not as adversely affected as if your entire investment was exclusively in one of those unfortunates. An ETF can be based on virtually any commodity or basket of stocks – tech stocks, mining stocks, consumer staples, oil companies, the gold price – practically anything at all. But the safest of them all are those that derive their value from the biggest 50 or so stocks of an entire exchange because they are the most established and reliable. These stocks of course do not promise the huge up-side of more risky assets, but the more risk-adverse investor could do a lot worse than take a look at these. There are risks involved of course, but significantly lower due to the inherent quality and diversification. I could prattle on about them for another hour, but I want to get back to prattling on about boats. However, there is a good synopsis of the risks of ETFs for those that are interested, here:

www.investopedia.com/articles/mutualfund/07/etf_downside.asp

Generally though, over time and with much less risk than you might imagine, it is fairly easy to get your little income to go into bat for you if you pick diverse ETFs or low risk companies that have a good moat (barrier to competition), a history of maintaining or increasing their dividend and management with a good track record. Now all you have to do is avoid the greed and temptation offered by margin loans - and then don't panic every time there are gloomy headlines.

My dividend income this year was about US$12,000 which generated a US$900 tax rebate, so let's say about 13k all up, and while that hardly makes me the Sultan of Brunei, it is a good feeling to know that it is always there and usually (in the long term at least) increasing.

As always, *amounts* are irrelevant to calculating sustainability. If you need 100k a year to service your 80ft carbon fibre yacht *Speed Demon*, then my weedy little income represents less than 13% of what you need to live without financial worry. For me (and hopefully for you), 13k is practically all I need and sets me free - and freedom has always seemed a better purchase to me than the latest touch-screen chart plotter.

A quick word about government guarantees.

After the Global Financial Crisis, many people (including me) discovered the hard way that the expression, 'money in the bank' may be as good a metaphor for financial security as, 'too big to fail' turned out to be for Lehman Brothers. Even if you were not affected directly, you probably knew somebody who was.[42] All around the world, people rushed to withdraw their little nest-eggs, threatening to further deepen what was already a financial nightmare by emptying the banks completely. Governments around the world (under pressure from their friends in the banking sector) moved to assure domestic savers by using tax-payers money to guarantee deposits up to a certain amount (depending on country, but around

---

[42] Even if you didn't, you do now.

the US$200,000 level). In return for this guarantee, savers around the world were suitably reassured and left their money in the bank. The crisis was averted, but now this meant (and still means) that savers are now effectively lending the banks money at interest rates as low as 0.1%. The banks could then invest this virtually free money more wisely and keep the profits. The government guarantee made us all confident enough to trust the banks again so they could put our money to work for themselves and their shareholders.

But there is another guarantee I want to talk about.

Putting your money in the bank at low interest rates is pretty much the same as sticking it under the mattress. As inflation rises more quickly than the interest you earn in the bank or under your mattress, your money will eventually be worthless – the value of it sucked out by more financially astute landlubbers who care more about this kind of thing than you do. And that my fellow watery wastrels is 100% guaranteed.

But before anyone accuses me of being a communist (again), all we are really doing when we educate ourselves about money, is becoming better capitalists by trying to find out why the bank wants our money, where the bank puts it and why, then using that information to put that value into our pockets instead of letting them put it into theirs. Nothing communist about that at all.

Learning about money has been a real eye-opener for me and I am still enjoying the journey. Strangely I have found the that learning to be financially astute is not much different from learning to sort the wheat from the overwhelming chaff that constitutes the yachting industry - it is all a case of telling the smoke from the substance and if you have already come this far with me on this journey, then the skills you have acquired (or already possessed) are entirely transferrable to the task of becoming financially literate. In the end, every step you can make towards self-reliance, whatever the subject area, is a step towards realising the dream of getting gone and staying gone, and as money is one of the larger issues, learning how it works is one of the major steps towards oceanic independence.

I must point out though, that although I am 100% happy to help in any way I can, I am no money expert and nothing I have said anywhere in this book should be construed as financial advice, as much will depend on your own circumstances, risk tolerance and stage of life. Certainly do NOT buy BHP or Ale Property shares as they are now quite expensive and not particularly good value for money.

It is a damning indictment of the lawyer-driven society in which we live (and yet another good reason to flip it the bird and sail away) that I am bound by law to make the following statement:

Stocks may go down as well as up and past performance is no guarantee of future performance.

Like you didn't know.

CHAPTER TEN

Staying Real About Steel

In my last book we spoke of the virtues of steel and how much has changed with the development of modern epoxy coatings. Briefly, I was keen to point out that the lingering fear caused by pre-epoxy rust-buckets meant that there were some very good, modern, steel boats going for a song and those who could learn to tell the difference between 'good' steel and 'bad' steel could do well – often (as I did) ending up with a newish steel boat for the same price as a 30 year old GRP boat.

Admittedly, one needs to keep a weather eye on the rust, but the gist of the chapter was that by owning a newer, stronger steel boat the nautical nomad was being well rewarded for that risk and might even end up doing less maintenance. That was certainly true for me and I have met several sailors who would confirm this.

This turned out to be the most misinterpreted chapter in the book. I have received so many requests from readers for advice on old steel boats they were considering buying that it is obvious that the point of the chapter was lost somewhere along the line. So, just to be clear, the point I was making was this:

As it is often possible to buy a newer steel boat for the price of a 30 year old GRP boat, the advantages of having everything else on the boat (rudder, bearings, engine, gearbox, mast, boom, rigging, chain, winches, windlasses, anchors, electrics etc) in near-new condition, can seriously outweigh any lower maintenance advantages that fibreglass hulls may generally have to offer.[43]

If one then opts to buy an *old* steel boat, those advantages are lost.

Yet many readers were using the relatively cheap price of steel boats, not to get a better condition boat than they could afford in fibreglass, but a bigger or cheaper one of the same age. I most certainly would not (and certainly did not intend to) advocate the purchase of old steel boats as a path to happiness.

If you are buying an older boat that needs work, then do not look at steel unless you are an expert in the material and the price is rewarding you for the risk. There are old steel boat out there that would cost you money just to dispose of. As a first time buyer on a restricted budget, it is far better to go with a solid fibreglass hull with minimal signs of osmosis. I hope that is clearer now.

Holy hulls!

While it is important to have a strong hull, the holes in the hull can often be more of a safety issue than what it is made of. I am of course referring to the holes that are put there by designers for various reasons, and if you do not manage them well, the material your hull is made of could be, well, immaterial. There may be up to twenty hull penetrations or 'through hulls' in the design of your new boat and it is worth taking a quick look at them before we finally leave the subject of hulls and sail into more interesting waters.

---

[43] With the possible exception of northern Europe, where steel boats seem to be more expensive than elsewhere.

CHAPTER ELEVEN

Hull Integrity

An old salty fisherman from Port Douglas with only slightly more teeth than decades once told me that there are only two really essential things you need to make sure of on a boat.

"Oil and Water!" he would spit through a half-closed mouth that seemed more intent on clamping a cigar in place than effecting clear communication.

"The oil should be on the *inside* of the engine and the water should be on the *outside* of the boat".

Obviously, this is what passes as a joke up in the further reaches of rural Australia, but there is no smoke without fire and keeping the water on the outside of the boat is in fact the single most important role of our little pocket of air on the ocean (after all, a well-corked bottle of rum will come through most storms intact and with its message still readable). Yet achieving this is much more complicated than it sounds as most boats have numerous holes built into the design to suck in seawater for the engine, the head, the galley, watermaker, etc., and to let out the washing-up water and the less mentionables. So, once you have bought your boat, you need to take a good hard look at those 'designer' holes.

As you will probably be aware, I tend to avoid overly technical subjects (all that can be found in Nigel Calder's excellent books) in favour of the broader issues of design and the psychology of sailing happiness, but I hope you will forgive me if I dip a toe into the technical side of this subject as it is so important and very likely to need attention on the type of older sailboat we liquidy layabouts are likely to be buying.

Know your enemy

Hull penetrations are definitely something all sailors need to worry about far more than we do. According to a survey by the insurance company BOATUS, hull penetrations account for a whopping 43% of sinkings at the dock alone. I imagine this figure is replicated for boats at sea, but it is impossible to know for sure as it is difficult to discern the cause of a sinking at sea without spending millions trying to raise the boat off the seabed. Even when people live to tell the tale, their reports must be taken with a pinch of salt as the insurance boffins are not likely to pay out if the recently rescued sailor confesses to a dodgy through-hull. It is much safer to claim that the boat 'struck a submerged object' because the insurance company is not going to raise the wreck in deep water to prove you wrong. Either way, this means that designed holes in the hull are your real enemy and far more likely to ruin your day (particularly if you are uninsured) than the odd osmotic blister that seems to freak everybody out to a much greater degree.[44]

Another report by US Surveyors found only 30% of through-hull penetrations operative on pre-purchase surveys, so it is fairly likely that you will have some duds too. If you cannot shut off a through hull in strong conditions, then the entire integrity of your boat is reliant on a length of hose and a couple of hose clips. Not good.

Through hulls generally come in two parts (Fig 23).

---

[44] On the bright side, this also suggests that there could possibly be less floating obstructions than reported. I have no data for this, but the anecdotal evidence is suggestive.

Figure23: The two parts of a Groco 'bronze' through-hull.

Part A is the bit that actually goes through the hull (the 'skin fitting') and part B contains the shut-off valve. Now, if you only need to change part B, this can actually be done in the water by sending your squeeze over the side with a bung to stop the water rushing in (I do not recommend doing this alone. If anything goes wrong, you need somebody in the water. If your squeeze is not prepared to help you with this, you might wish to consider exchanging him/her for a more amenable one).

I have used this method in the past and it is satisfactory as a temporary repair, but before passing your new boat as seaworthy, I cannot emphasize how important it is to get the boat out of the water for a really good look.

The main reason for this is to check the colour of the skin fittings and the condition of the fibreglass around them.

Colour

If you have bought a fibreglass boat, the chances are that you will have bronze skin fittings. Bronze is generally an excellent material for nautical purposes but much of what is often called bronze is actually a bronze alloy more accurately described as, 'red brass'. The most commonly found through-hull fittings are made by a company called Groco who, in the great spirit of obfuscation that is a constant frustration in today's marketing-driven world, label their products 'C83600 Bronze'.

What's wrong with that? Well, you can't really have C83600 Bronze any more than you can be a fat, thin person – you are either one or the other. It is a contradiction in terms like 'genuine fake', 'jumbo shrimp' or 'posh spice'. Bronze is a material made from 88% copper and 12% tin. Its chemical description is $CuSn$ because it contains only copper (Cu) and tin (Sn). What Groco (and most other manufacturers) make their through-hull and skin fittings from is actually an alloy called 'red brass'.[45]

This is important because red brass contains zinc and goes through a little drama all of its own (which does not affect real bronze) called 'dezincification'. This is where a stray electrical current (electrolysis) or the current caused by having two different metals in a salty

---

[45] I have absolutely no idea what legal chicanery allows manufacturers to call this material 'bronze'. I have written to Groco for clarification and while they have confirmed that their products are indeed red brass and not bronze as advertised, they have declined to comment on why they describe them as bronze. I suspect the answer is probably related to the same reason manufacturers can state "waterproof to IPX 1" on their products which, to any rational person, means "not waterproof".

solution (galvanic corrosion) has caused the zinc to leach from the red brass, leaving behind a dangerously weakened material.

On the bright side, red brass lets you know when it is dezincifying by turning pink. This can be very confusing though as you and I (like everybody else) thought we were buying bronze skin fittings (as advertised) and are now scratching our heads wondering how they have defied the laws of chemistry.

Anyway, back to the inspection of your wee escape pod. Once you remove the gazillion layers of bottom paint from the skin fitting, if there are any pinkish spots to it, then it has to go. There is a tendency for those new to the enormous task of becoming marine engineers in a shockingly short space of time, to look at the nice thick walls of a well made skin fitting and think, "what harm can a little colour change do to such a sturdy-walled piece of metal"?

Well, actually not much. But the *threads* are thin and vulnerable and if they are weakened, then the retaining nut will start to lose its grip and only bad stuff follows. So a stitch in time really does save nine here. Don't scrimp on this - it is an essential part of safety and much easier to do when the boat is already out of the water! Only this time, be a little more sceptical regarding the manufacturer's descriptions and try to get real bronze (or at least the red brass that has the lowest zinc content).[46]

---

[46] There are also some new materials on the market that are made from plastics. The most promising of these is Marelon which would totally eliminate the chance of any sort of corrosion. Apparently they exceed the strength of metal skin fittings and could very well be the answer to this problem. Certainly worth keeping an eye on. You never know, one day 'though-hull' could join 'explosive' to become the only two expressions not fatally diminished by the prefix 'plastic'.

Keep up to date with your sacrificial anodes too. Forewarned is forearmed and now that you know that your 'bronze' hull penetrations are actually red brass and much further down the nobility table than you thought, you have to add them to your 'at risk' substances that will start to suffer once the zinc in your anodes have sacrificed themselves. If, however, your inspection reveals that the penetrations are all nice and bronzy without a hint of pink and as healthy as trawlerman's cat, then we can have a margarita and move on to the next step.

Surrounding fibreglass

If your hull penetrations have not been properly seated or the bedding compound has broken down over time, seawater could have found its way into the exposed part of the hull and the fibreglass may eventually become unstable. You need to get a sharp tool (I use a dental pick) and dig around as this can often be hidden by years of bottom paint. I found two such offenders on my 1984 Hans Christian *Calypso* and it is not unlikely that you will find a similar problem on an older boat. If you do, under no circumstances patch it up and forget about it! I know it hurts, and I feel your pain, but you must remove the skin fitting and dig out ALL the suspect fibreglass and grind it back until you reach the good stuff before laying new fibreglass and then re-drilling the hole.[47] Sorry brothers and sisters, but there is no other way. On the positive side, you will feel great when it is done and when the wind pipes up you won't have the

---

[47] I don't have the space to get into fibreglass repair, but there is an excellent free resource from West System that can be downloaded from
https://www.westsystem.com/wp-content/uploads/0121-Fiberglass-Boat-Repair-and-Maintenance-Manual-lr.pdf

worry of a dodgy section of fibreglass gnawing away at your already over-stimulated worry glands. Anyway, assuming that your fibreglass is as solid as my recipe for lemon drizzle cake, let's move on.

Nigel Calder in his essential book *The Boat Owner's Mechanical and Electrical Manual* (don't leave home without it!) rightly suggests that all through-hull penetrations should have hardwood backing plates in order to spread the load more evenly across the inside of the hull (fig 24). From an engineering point of view, this is a great idea and I would be the last person to contradict the great Nigel, but I don't know a single boat that has them. I certainly have never had them on any of my boats.

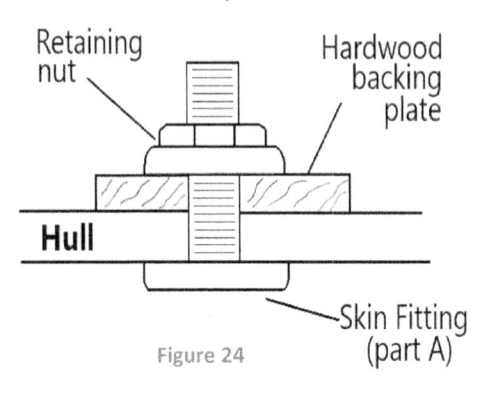

When I was anchored in Puerto Vallarta, I visited the fleet that was preparing for the 2015 Pacific crossing and they graciously allowed me a wee nosey around their boats in general and at their through-hulls in particular. None of them had hardwood backing plates either, so I am uncertain what to recommend here as I bow to nobody in my respect for Nigel Calder. But certainly don't fly into a panic if your recently acquired boat doesn't have hardwood backing plates. Obviously, you will need a flat surface to screw the retaining nut (of part A) on to, but as we are only discussing the inspection of existing through-hulls (rather than relocating or adding new ones) I think it is fair to assume that they will already have been positioned with that in mind.[48] If however you decide to use (or replace existing) hardwood backing plates, epoxy covered hardwood will provide a more reliable, long-term platform than bare hardwood.

One last problem to cover is the length of part A of the skin fitting. The example in fig 23 has already been cut to size, but the most common makes are long and will need to be cut down so that the shut-off valve (part B) does not protrude so far into the hull that it becomes dangerous (by becoming a lever when you step on it) or bloody annoying (when you bark your shin on it).

With bronze through hulls, I have found that as soon as you cut Part A down to size, the threads can become tight so some time and WD40 needs to be spent just to make them run freely again. So, once you have cut them to size and before you cover the whole lot in bedding compound, just work the threads and make sure they are running freely or you will be doing a great deal of swearing later on when covered in white sealant and looking like the statue of Lord Nelson when the pigeons are flocking.

Final assembly

Traditionally, people tend to install part A first and screw on part B once the bedding compound is dry. If you do this, it is essential to get someone on the outside of the boat to hold Part A in place. There are usually a couple of tangs in the throat of the penetration that you can lodge a flat bar of some sort in. I use the handle of an adjustable wrench (which I have ground down slightly to be a perfect fit) and then open the jaws of the wrench to take a long bar so the holder has

---

[48] Bear in mind that a lot of boats have strengthening around the hull where a penetration is placed and you will need to think long and hard before moving it or adding a new one.

some leverage). If you don't do this, as soon as you tighten part B on to Part A, you will spin part A in the hull and weaken or break the seal of the bedding compound which leads us back to the problems of water ingress into the laminate, or even the boat, as described earlier.

A good way to avoid the above problem is to do everything at the same time. Prepare your bedding compound and Teflon tape (for the threads when fitting part B. Teflon tape is not necessary for the retaining nut) then position your assistant outside with a suitable device to stop Part A turning. Splooge the bedding compound on all surfaces (making sure you have the right type, i.e., one that says 'suitable for below the waterline'. Sikaflex and 3M 5200 are both excellent products) and don't worry about using too much of it. Have your assistant poke part A through the hole from outside. From inside, put some more bedding compound around the hole where the locking nut will land and screw down fairly hard while your assistant stops the movement. Before letting your assistant wander off, immediately put your Teflon tape on the thread of part A and screw Part B into place. Wipe off the excess bedding compound on part A with a rag, but do not use alcohol or acetone as that will stop the bedding compound curing properly.

Doing it all at once takes a little organisation, but means that if your assistant lets part A slip a little, it doesn't matter too much as the bedding compound has not yet cured and will still adhere in its new position.

Attaching the hoses

Surveyors used to advise that every hose should 'always' be attached to through-hulls with TWO stainless steel hose clips , whether there was sufficient space for a second hose clip or not. This has since been revised down from 'always' status to 'where possible'. This is a very positive step because if you stand any chance of insuring your boat, the advice of the surveyor must be acted upon, even if inappropriate.

A second hose clip that is not tightened onto the underlying metal will pinch the hose and do more harm than good, and it is a great move forward that this recommendation is no longer treated as such a hard and fast rule (Fig 25).

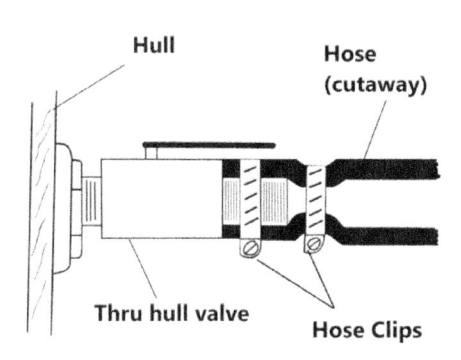

Figure 25: The hose clip on the right is tightened only on the hose itself and is doing more harm than good.

However, two is always better where possible. If you have enough space for three, then use three as they are a relatively cheap way to decrease your chances of sinking. Always use 316 grade stainless hose clips or better. Take a little fridge magnet with you when you buy hose clips as not all stainless (or bronze, it would seem) is what it claims to be, even when stamped on the metal! A 316 grade stainless steel hose clip will not be attracted to the magnet at all.

Stayin' alive

All of the above excellent prep is totally useless if you now ignore your through-hulls lurking down there in the bilge like the forgotten cousin in the cellar that nobody likes to talk about. Pick a day (I do Sunday because it gives it the religious status it deserves) and open and close them all a few times as if your life depends on it. And if you are tempted to miss a week because the footy is on, remember that it actually does.

The forgotten step of hull integrity

I am unashamedly the nosiest parker alive when it comes to other people's boats. One of the things I like about changing boats (something I am doing right now as it happens) is that boat shopping gives me a legitimate excuse to have what the Aussies call a 'sticky beak' into other people's lives. I don't think I have ever been aboard a boat where the owner has not made some cunning little adjustment that I can learn from. I find the whole process of how people manage their little escape pods of air on the sea quite fascinating.

Having said that, I am also quite shocked by the amount of boats that cannot keep the water out if they are inverted.

The main safety advantage that mono-hulls have over multi-hulls is that if they are inverted, they will normally right themselves.

Unfortunately for their owners, catamarans are fantastically stable upside down whereas monohulls are totally unstable upside down and are unlikely to remain that way for too long. Unfortunately for monohull owners, most monohulls are not nearly as watertight when inverted as they should be, thus surrendering this great advantage for the want of a little preparation. If an inverted monohull is not properly watertight, she is going to ship a lot of water in a short time. That water will now either sink her or sit on the roof of the upturned boat and make it a little less likely she will right herself. The water on the upturned roof acts like ballast and fights against the efforts of the keel which is now in the air, trying its best to drop towards the centre of the earth and pop you upright again, save your bacon, give you a few bruises and a fantastic story to tell.

The longer this goes on the worse your chances get. Even if you don't actually sink and still manage to pop up nicely, having large amounts of water in the boat never ends well and can mark your cushions as well as seriously dilute your rum. Self-righting is the monohull's 'get out of jail free' card. So let's have a look at how most monohulls give up this great self-righting super-power without a fight.

Companionway.

It does not matter how much you have just spent on your latest Bavjenben Oceanator. If the companionway hatches are not lockable from the inside and outside, it is not as safe as a little Westsail 32 that has this modification. There are endless stories of boats being knocked down and water pouring through the companionway, yet somehow it seems to go largely unmentioned as long as the life raft worked okay. If you can also find a way to keep the companionway washboards permanently attached to the boat with some kind of lanyard, that will go a long way to making sure you are properly stoppered and more seaworthy than most of the boats currently sailing.

Calypso, like so many other boats had pretty, louvered doors at the companionway. These are great to keep fresh air circulating when the boat is closed up, but about as watertight as Julian Assange. I had some lockable washboards made and would replace my pretty louvered doors before I went to sea. I made the lower one with toughened safety glass so that I could keep an eye on things below while in the cockpit and (much more importantly) see what was going on in the cockpit when I was down below, as well as make sure the correct amount of people were still there.

TIP: To check you have the correct amount of people aboard, count their legs and divide by two. Divide that answer by the amount of people you started with and the answer should be 1. If your answer is any less (and particularly if is a fraction) you have issues.

Dorades

Lots of boats have these and they are virtually indispensible in the tropics where humid temperatures and torrential rain can act in opposition. The humid temperatures make you want to open the hatches and the rain forces you to close them. When this happens, dorade vents provide just enough cooling and circulation to stop you actually murdering somebody. But you must be able to remove them and seal them up when on passage because when you are upside down (or even when a big wave crashes over them) they will squirt water into your boat like four fire hoses.

Make sure you have the offshore plates for them and if you don't, it is money well spent acquiring some as they are not expensive.

Cockpit lockers

Some cockpit lockers are completely sealed, but most lead into other parts of the boat. Water than finds its way into the cockpit locker normally then finds its way into the rest of the boat. So put some weather seal around it and keep it dogged down.

Spurling pipes

These are the openings where the anchor chain enters the deck. Make sure you can close these off in some way. You may have to disconnect the chain from the anchor to do so, but why not do that for a long passage? You can even stow the anchors down below while you are at it - you won't be needing them for a while and it always improves the motion to get the weight off the bow. If that is not practical, make a bung with just the width of the chain cut out, bang it into place and seal the gap with plasticine. It won't stop everything, but a drip is better than a deluge.

Cockpit speakers

I bet that surprised you! Lots of people fit cockpit speakers by cutting a hole in the fibreglass and setting the speakers nice and flush. If the boat you buy has these, then you have a little problem to sort out as this means the only thing stopping water fire-hosing into your boat through two giant 8" holes, is the cardboard cone of the speaker. If you are fitting cockpit speakers (I love mine) there are plenty of stand-alone models that can be affixed to the stainless frame of the spray hood, or elsewhere, without cutting holes. They don't look as nice as the flush ones, but they won't cave in and flood your boat either.

A last word about being upside down.

Most sailors, including me, never suffer an inversion (obviously I am assuming you don't have the type of boat that the keel drops off). Hopefully you will remain forever upright and magnificently erect, but it certainly improves your confidence and helps you manage fear in bad weather offshore to know that you are prepared – you may actually start to enjoy 'bad' weather. I certainly find that my enjoyment or otherwise of heavy weather is entirely based on how prepared I am. When I have cut corners or I am delivering a badly prepared boat, the enjoyment of sailing can disappear as quickly as

Bill Cosby's fan club. And in the end, we are doing this for the enjoyment are we not?

The above tips are about keeping the water out long enough for the next wave to knock you the few degrees one way or the other that will set the ballast in the keel heading for the centre of the earth again and flipping you into the correct, upright position. But once you are confident that the water is going to stay, as the old salt at the beginning of this chapter said, "on the outside of the boat" long enough for this to happen, give a little thought as to what will start flying around on the inside.

Are your batteries secure? What about your lockers with all your heavy spare parts? It is one thing being playfully boffed on the noggin by a stray cockpit cushion and quite another to be kerranged by your spare starter motor.

What is under the floorboards and can they be dogged down? In short, where will everything be when you find yourself momentarily sitting on the ceiling of your boat with a rather bemused expression on your face?[49]

All the floorboards on *Calypso* had wonderful little dogs on them that I picked up in a swap meet. All the lockers were made lockable and these are easy, cheap and rewarding jobs that can increase your safety in a very real way.

Most of the things that are going to start flying about on your boat will be pretty obvious to anyone with eyes and a smattering of

---

[49] This is where not having excessive headroom can work for you. I always think a lot of headroom is undesirable. I don't want to fall too far if the boat goes over.

imagination, so I would just like to point out two things that get overlooked.

Anchor lockers

If you have a boat with an external anchor locker, it needs to be lockable. If it is not dogged down, all that chain is going to spill out if you are inverted and work against the efforts of the keel to right the boat (as well as put some nasty scratches in your pride and joy). The dogs I have seen on boats with external chain lockers (including my own on *Marutji*) are not nearly strong enough to resist the weight of a quarter of a ton of chain pressing against them and will probably need beefing up. Don't forget the hinges on the other side as well, because the world's strongest locks are no good if the hinges are as weak as a resort cocktail.

Gimballed cookers

As you probably know by now, a boat's cooker sits on a little arrangement called a gimbal, allowing it to swing with the motion of the boat, which helps keep the porridge off your pants. All well and good, but all the gimbals I have ever seen are shaped like the letter 'U' and the bars from the side of the cooker sit inside them held there only by gravity (fig 26).

This means that should you be unfortunate enough to go turtle, this heavy, spiky, sharp thingy will start spinning around your boat like an epileptic robot. It will also probably disconnect or damage its

Figure 26: A slightly exaggerated gimbal on a marine stove

flexible gas pipe at the same time (another good reason to always turn the gas off at the bottle). I looked for a better gimbal for a while for *Calypso* and did not find one. So what I do now as part of my offshore prep is wrap several layers of stainless steel locking wire around it, effectively turning the 'U' into an 'O'.

This still allows the gimbal to perform its pants-protection duties, but hopefully (and this is purely theoretical as it has never been tested) this will keep it in place if my world gets turned upside down. I am sure you could come up with something better. Drop me a line if you do and I will pop it on the website.

As I said, the chances of turning turtle are very low, but enough people do it and don't live to tell the tale that it is important not to rely on only what you hear. It is worth making some little alterations to your boat so that not only can you come back and tell the tale, but the telling of it will give the listeners such satisfaction that we will sit open-mouthed an enthralled while you happily hold forth whilst surreptitiously scarfing all the rum.

The real value of this type of preparation though lies in the way it helps you stay focused and calm when other, less well prepared, captains might tend to be consumed by their nerves. Anything that helps you keep a cool head is always worth the effort. A calm disposition will lead to better decision making which is the skill at the heart of any good leader who works in a high pressure environment.

So do not be put off by those who say inversion is unlikely, as that is to miss the point. I ride my motorbike like a granny and probably will never have an accident, but I always check my tyre pressures and wear my leathers – not because I think I will fall off, but because it gives me a feeling of safety and confidence which improves the riding experience and makes me a better rider. But please don't think this lifestyle is one endless disaster after another – all I am saying is that you will enjoy it much more if you have confidence in your preparations.

So having prepped you not to get too depressed by talking about disaster preparation, let's undo all that good work by talking about the other big question that is so often asked...

CHAPTER TWELVE

Staying Real About Risk: Storms

If you were unfortunate enough to see my less than photogenic face on the Ben Fogle TV series *New Lives in the Wild* or *Where the Wild Men Are* or *New Lives in the Wild Revisited*, you may already think that to live as a sea gypsy is to be at the constant mercy of the weather.

I enjoyed making those programs and, on the whole, they are a good portrayal of the sea gypsy life, but always remember that TV is about making a drama out of everything – it is not malicious or fraudulent, it is just better telly when stuff happens.

So, forgetting entertainment value for a moment, how *do* we deal with storms? Here are some pointers in order of importance.

Avoidance

This is by far the most important point. In the TV show, Mr Fogle has a moment to camera where he says that he admires the freedom of the sea gypsy life, but would not enjoy being at the mercy of the one thing we cannot control – the weather.

There is of course, an element of truth in this, but much of the ravages of so-called 'chance' can be avoided with the right attitude. Remember what I said about buying a boat and setting off around the world in *Get Real, Get Gone?*

Don't do it! It is just the ego talking you into feeding its insatiable hunger to always be 'achieving' something. If you wish to avoid bad weather as much as possible, please abandon that idea, as this type of ego-driven list-ticking is probably the most dangerous thing aboard any boat.

Having set yourself this goal of joining up imaginary lines on the planet, it will colour your judgement of everything – including what you consider to be an acceptable weather forecast. Even when you are aware of the universal human tendency towards self-justification, you can still get caught out. I have been caught out by my own self-justifications in the past and you would think I would be the last person to get self-conned, considering how much I bang on about it.

What we plant in our minds as our goals will create a lens through which we will judge everything – including the chances of bad weather in any given forecast. Someone without agenda can see a forecast for what it is. Those who are on a deadline begin to develop selective blindness and start negotiating with themselves.

That is why our attitude is such an integral part of our arsenal (and why I harp on about how having no other agenda than enjoying your time on the sea, is such an essential safety feature).

You control when you are ready. If in doubt, miss it out! There will be another weather window along soon enough and as you are a happy, relaxed sea gypsy just bimbling along in our beautiful blue world with no need to feed the ego, who cares? Learn the ukulele, practice your French, squeeze your partner and wait for a better opportunity.

This is another reason I eschewed the racing mentality so much in my last book. Races are set to start at a given date – often decided a year in advance. Obviously, it is impossible predict the weather a year in advance, so you could get anything on the day. But having made the preparations, acquired your crew and your sponsors, you are likely to have a seriously thick lens to look through when deciding whether the conditions on the day are acceptable or constitute too much risk. Hardly surprising then that so many sailing disasters happen in race situations.

There is nothing heroic or daring about what I do, despite the tendency of adrenalin-fuelled racers and TV producers to make it sound otherwise. When you see me on the telly crossing the Pacific on *Calypso*, you don't see the years I spent sailing locally, coastal hopping, learning my craft, altering my boat (three full haul-outs!) and waiting for the right weather conditions. And quite frankly, if I hadn't felt that the conditions, boat and crew were capable, I would still be happily day-sailing from one great anchorage to the next in the Caribbean, the Sea of Cortez, the Great Barrier Reef, the Greek Islands or a thousand other magical places worldwide where you are never too far away from safe harbour. Absolutely no shame in that and don't let the 'miles under the keel' braggarts tell you otherwise. We don't pull out into traffic just because some impatient prick behind us with 'goals to achieve' toots his horn. We hold our position and pull out when we are ready, based on nothing other than traffic conditions.

Enjoy your sailing, learn slowly, at your own pace and don't be pressured by other sailors to depart in weather windows that you are not happy with or do not consider settled enough. Always bear in mind the most dangerous thing onboard is our own egos which tend towards conformational bias and wishful thinking if left unchecked.

Hopping off the old soap box for a minute, if you decide to go ocean bashing, then knowing that you and your boat are not simply 'at the mercy of the weather' will help you get real about the risks and manage your fears of the unknown.

We have already covered how preparing your boat for the unlikely event of inversion can help you feel calm, make better decisions and give you the confidence to get the most out of your sailing experience, so keep that head on while we hit the subject of what to do on the rare occasions that you do hit bad weather.

More on heaving-to: How to stop the train when you wanna get off.

I briefly covered heaving-to in the last book, but would like to expand upon it here and particularly its use in severe weather. Just to remind you, heaving-to is basically arranging your deeply reefed mainsail and helm so that the bow of your boat sits quietly about 45-55° off the wind and waves. In most well-keeled boats, the arrangement would look something like fig 27.

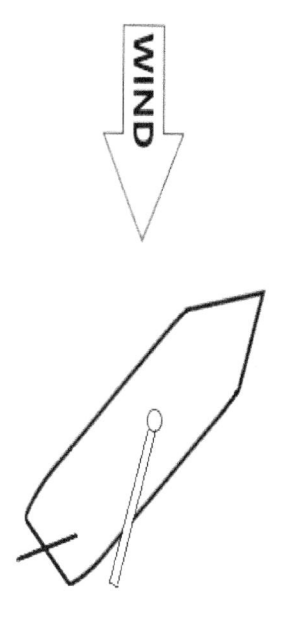

Figure 27: Hove-to

Forget all that stuff on the internet about backing the headsail – it works well for a quick sandwich break in an Adriatic regatta, but it will just flap and chafe itself to death in the kind of conditions we are currently discussing.

A well keeled boat should be able to heave-to with

just a third reef in the mainsail or a dedicated trysail.[50]

Get rid of your headsail and if you find you are still nosing up to the wind, simply adjust the helm and ease mainsail to bear off a bit. If you have bought a ketch and have been putting up with a bit of a ribbing from sloop owners, now is your chance to feel uber-smug, as ketch rigged boats generally heave-to very well indeed using the mizzen only or a combination of mizzen and deeply reefed main or trysail.

Pouring oil on troubled waters

We have all heard this expression, but few know its origin. Back in the grand old days of sail when wind was the only source of power and real men would rather die than wear skinny jeans, ships in extreme weather would heave-to and, as an extra measure, attach bags of whale oil to the windward side of the boat (that would be the port side in Fig 27). As the boat drifted sideways downwind, the sailors would put tiny needle holes in the bags of oil to create a slick upwind of them. A tiny drop of oil can cover a surprisingly large area of sea as it spreads out in a layer only a few microns thick. Next time you are in your galley, drop a little olive oil in the sea and see how the tiniest drop will create a disproportionately large slick (although don't do this anywhere you can be seen or somebody may think you are dumping engine oil and, quite rightly, report you to the coppers).

---

[50] A trysail fits behind the mast and is not to be confused with a storm jib which is a rugged headsail. Some boats have three reefs in the mainsail while others (including mine) have reefing points at position 1.5 and 2.5 with a dedicated trysail (rather than a third reef) on a separate track for when the excrement hits the extractor.

Now for reasons that are far too technical for a book that is supposedly about attitudes and the broader issues of the sea-gypsy lifestyle, this slick would prevent waves breaking in that particular spot. We won't go into the physics. The old salts didn't know the physics either, just the results and that is all we need to know too.

This is important because wave size itself is not really a danger. Whatever the height of a wave, a good boat will rise to meet it. Even tsunamis go largely unnoticed at sea. It is when the waves start breaking and the crests begin tumbling down their faces that they become dangerous.

So, there the old salty seadogs would sit in their own little slick of whale oil, watching waves break everywhere else except on them.

"But hang on you nauseatingly nostalgic endomorph", I hear you cry, "I don't have any whale oil and I am not about to be dumping Castrol GTX into the sea".

Fair point! However, we can create the same effect using our keel. All boats with a keel can do this, but only a nice *long or long-ish* keel is really effective (do I need to say it? Hold me back, hold me back).

As you drift downwind, the water to the leeward side of the boat (that's the starboard side in Fig 27 and Fig 28) is forced under your nice long keel and when it emerges on the windward side it has the same, disturbed look that the old salts produced with the whale oil, back in the days when nobody had heard the word 'metro-sexual' and a crèche was something that stagecoaches occasionally had. I am pleased to say that it works the same way too. The waves will not usually break in that artificial 'slick'.

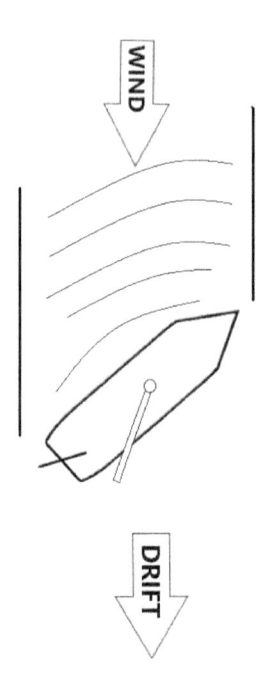

Figure 28: As your boat drifts downwind the water from the starboard side is forced under your nice long keel and re-emerges on the port side all messed up.

I know, I know, it sounds farcical and too good to be true and I confess that I shared your scepticism when I first read about it, but since then I have spent several days sitting on my cabin top in foul weather with my imaginary curly pipe, quite mesmerized by this and it is truly uncanny.

Having said all that, whether you manage to get this effect working for you or not is perhaps immaterial, because even without the slick effect, heaving-to is still such a fundamentally important tactic that I would not buy a boat that was anything other than stellar at it (not for ocean crossing anyway) because none of us are the supermen/women we really think we are sitting on our couches reading about sailing.

We like to think that we will be calm, tough and crap actual bullets, but so few people are naturally this way, there is a fair chance that after a few hours of trying to hand steer downwind, what you will actually do is try to run in several directions at once before collapsing in a gibbering heap on the cabin sole.

We must try and notice this about ourselves if we don't want to be so terrified out of our minds at the first sign of bad weather that we give up sailing at the next port.

As with all things safety, trying to wing it in the hope that 'it will be all right on the night' is inadvisable. Prep is everything and that goes for managing the central control unit of safety at sea – the brain of the captain. This is such an important factor that I would like to take a little break from the physics of heaving-to (we will get back to it shortly) to talk about the psychological aspect of heaving-to, which is every bit as important.

A small diversion

"Twenty years from now you will be more disappointed by the things you didn't do than by the ones you did do. So throw off the docklines. Sail away from the safe harbor. Catch the trade winds in your sails. Explore. Dream. Discover.

Mark Twain

Despite this quote appearing with increasing regularity on the less imaginative sailing blogs, this is nonsense on stilts. The idea that whatever you do is less likely to produce regrets than the things you don't do is just reckless and plain untrue. Now might be a good time to reflect upon the fact that the hundreds of corpses being revealed by the newly melting snows on the lower slopes of Mt Everest were all highly motivated people following their dreams and simply, 'casting off the docklines'.

This type of bumper-sticker mentality does us a great disservice. Yes, you have to be tenacious and push your dream through the muddy swamps of reality, but many sensible people with a bit of imagination are understandably turned off by this type of meaningless glib bravado.

I have known some sailors (mainly from South Africa, but I don't know why this is) that are truly fearless. Do not confuse this with competence. That is just the absence of fear. It takes no competence at all to overcome an absence of fear. Furthermore, all the truly fearless people I have ever met owe that fearlessness not to hard-won experience, but to a chronic lack of imagination. Now, that tiny percentage of people may be happy with the above platitude from the venerable old gentleman of southern wisdom, but for most people, it will take more than this type of Athena-poster mentality to persuade them that simply casting off the docklines is a virtual guarantee of twenty years of regret-free life.

And that is a good thing!

Many people I have spoken to find this 'just do it' attitude that seems so fashionable today amongst 14 year old snowboarders and energy drink manufacturers, both intimidating and irritating. It seems that those who value preparation and caution are being made to feel somehow 'stuffy' by those who either know no fear or do not value their lives sufficiently to elevate preparation above bravado. Do not be put off by them (most of them are full of it anyway). Happy and successful sea gypsies use their fear to motivate them to prepare properly.

So, let the 'just do it' brigade steam in with all guns blazing if they like, but most of us need to know where the emergency exits are.

Having a boat that heaves-to well is so much more than just an academic exercise of balancing forces or a last-ditch survival tactic. It is all those things, but most importantly, it provides the safety valve that ordinary, rational adults like you and me require to satisfy themselves that leaving sight of the coast is not a semi-suicidal, 'at the mercy of nature' roll-of-the-dice that can only be accessed by a unique realm of fearless supermen with biceps like Baltimore and no imagination.

Your fears are a super-power and a gift from Neptune! Be proud of them and let them guide you towards good choices, great preparation and solid seamanship.

Okay, back to heaving-to. Sorry about the diversion.

Meanwhile, back on the boat...

I have been hove-to in bad weather often enough now that I actually quite enjoy it in a strange way. I know what to expect, what to do, and I feel relatively safe. I have just enough fear and imagination to predict the likely results of my actions and enough confidence in my simple, rugged little boat not to be consumed by nerves. I have several seasons of whatever crummy TV series I am binge-watching at the time ready to go and I know how to make my boat lie so quietly in the hove-to position that I am usually quite surprised by the sea state when I look up long enough from an episode of *Desperate Housewives* to pop my head out on deck and scan the horizon.[51]

So, heaving-to is great for anyone who is not a fearless superman and the type of boats I recommend will normally do it well.

---

[51] Always pick something brain-numbingly dull to watch as it quietens the mind. Don't pick anything challenging as you will already have quite enough of that kind of thing occupying your brain. When Jasna felt insecure she would watch Sandra Bullock films. Personally, I can't imagine ever being that scared.

However, due to any number of factors of boat design, weather or sea state, your hove-to boat may not lie quietly, but instead make a little forward progress. This is where heaving-to officially becomes 'fore-reaching' and in most circumstances is no problem at all. It does mean though that you could be fore-reaching out of this little protective artificial 'oil slick' you are creating and no longer be getting the benefit of it.

I would like to point out here that this is usually not the end of the world. Not even close. It's not even the end of Coventry (more is the pity). Of all the times I have been hove-to, I have only been in conditions foul enough to need the protection of the slick once. In most cases, a little fore-reaching is fine.

However, when the faeces hit the windmill and the waves are breaking regularly, you will have to stop all forward movement so that you can remain in the protected area. Fortunately for us, there is a quite simple way of doing this using a drag device called a parachute anchor (Fig 29).

Figure 29: Using a parachute anchor to hold your boat at 50 degrees off the wind /waves and stop her fore-reaching out of her protective 'oil' slick. There is not enough space in the diagram to represent the length of the line which could be several hundred feet.

A parachute anchor is literally a parachute on a long and strong line that you set to hold yourself about

45-50 degrees off the wind/waves and arrest forward movement (as well as backward drift). I have a Fiorentino parachute anchor and have used it in anger only once, but I am very happy with it and the build quality is light years ahead of anything else on the market.[52]

Because I do not lie to myself about weather conditions in order to satisfy my ego, win races or justify my itchy feet, I have limited experience with setting the parachute, but can confirm everything Larry Pardey says in his excellent book *Storm Tactics*. Larry (who died this year, unfortunately) was a hive of information on traditional seamanship and the world's leading expert on heaving-to, both with and without a parachute anchor. I strongly recommend you read his book (see appendix) and completely ignore the few critics with their thin fin and spade boats (oh no, he is off again!) who contradict him. Larry had a boat like the ones I have been recommending and his advice is specifically aimed at sailors like us who do not feel sufficiently pacified by Mark Twain's platitudes, but need to know we have some real control over our own safety and survival before we 'cast off the docklines' and start not regretting things.

Read Larry's book (twice!) and practice setting your parachute in easy conditions until you can do it automatically. You may never need to use those skills, but knowing you have them and knowing your boat can roll without sinking or tossing an oven at your head, will change the entire complexion of your sailing life. For those still to make the decision to get gone and who are perhaps struggling with fear of the

---

[52] I think their sizing chart is a bit generous though as my parachute anchor is a bit snatchy sometimes, so if you are on the cusp of their sizings, ask them whether you should pick the larger or smaller one, but I would err on the side of smaller next time. In my dealings with them, they have been refreshingly straight talking. Note: The author does not receive any consideration from Fiorentino.

unknown, I hope that this approach will resonate with you more successfully than the 'no fear' mantra of the 0.1% of the truly fearless and catastrophically unimaginative.

Stay Real. Leave the fantasy behind, and prepare well for your beautiful adventure my watery comrades. You are too unique to give in to a bumper-sticker and your life far too precious. There is *way* too much fun to be had out here on the blue stuff to give it all away so cheaply.

CHAPTER THIRTEEN

Getting Off

"What about the storms?" is the second most commonly asked question from readers thinking about becoming nautical nomads and while it is essential to have an understanding of how to deal with challenging conditions, there is another skill that you will be far more likely to be using when you start sailing which, strangely, nobody ever asks about.

When you first start out on your new life, you are much more likely to be sailing in coastal waters and inland waterways than crossing oceans. This is good and necessary. While some people seem to feel that their wealth means that they can bypass the gaining of experience, purchase a 'top of the range' (according to the salesman at least) boat at the boat show and set off around the world, it is not something I ever advise. In many ways, this is why sailing is not really about money as only knowledge gained by direct experience will place our brains on the fast-track to getting real.

Full of contradictions, conformational biases, endowment effects and general 21st century demands for immediate gratification, our brains will not give up without a fight though. Experience can at least moderate our less appropriate tendencies to the point where our biases and attitudes are more suited to life afloat. But to get to that point you have to put the hours in. It cannot be bought, can only be acquired slowly and the best way to do that safely and enjoyably means staying coastal for a while. Therefore, storms, cyclones and the ability to heave-to or set a parachute anchor will not really be part of the day-to-day reality of your early experiences.

A set of skills you are far more likely to need is the ability to get yourself afloat when you have run aground in shallow water or on shifting sandbanks.

Running aground happens to coastal sailors and estuary explorers all the time and can occur even to the most diligent planner because sands can shift quicker than charts can get updated. Plus, of course, there is the usual, 'doofus factor' that is inherent in any new venture you are brave enough to try. Don't beat yourself up – it happens to everyone. Embrace your inner doofus, learn from your mistake and move on. Most importantly, don't forget to have a good laugh at yourself.

Having said that, prevention is always better than cure and while you may not be able to avoid running aground entirely, there are a couple of measures you can take that will not turn a drama into a crisis.

Slow down.
The amount of people you see charging around at full speed in marginal areas beggars belief. The result of this is that when they do go aground, they don't just nudge a meter or so of their boat onto a sandbar but, carried by the momentum of several tons travelling at several knots, they launch themselves upon it like a beached whale. This makes getting off that bit more complicated. A low-speed nudge of a sandbar can often be overcome with a hard burst of engine in reverse, but with your boat half beached, some more active measures will called for (more on those later).

Pick your moment

It is always advisable to pick the right moment of the tide to explore or sail through shallow waters. If you choose a falling tide and are unfortunate enough to get stuck, every moment you remain stranded reduces the likelihood of escape as the water gets lower and lower leaving you increasingly sticking out like a redneck at an Enya concert. If you run aground at the top of a king tide (which only occur twice a year) you had better hope you stocked up with food and water before you left and have lots of good books and Sudoku.

If possible choose a rising tide to explore marginal areas as, when you run aground, you only have to employ the favourite tactics of the sea gypsy – doing nothing – to get off again. The rise in water level alone will probably be enough to free you, but even if it is not, it will make your subsequent tactics much more likely to be effective.

Tactics

Oops, so your doofus moment has arrived and you have sailed the wrong side of lateral marker and come up against a sandbank. You were going fairly fast because you thought you were in the channel so you have travelled quite a way into it. So what do you do? Assuming that we are near the top of the tide (or on a falling tide) and there is no advantage in waiting, there are still a few tricks that will get you off, but first we need to see what exactly happens when you run aground in the type of boat that I have now been advocating for 500 pages or so.

The Problem

When you go aground, it is actually your keel that has touched, rather than the boat's topsides and you will likely be in this position (Fig 30).

So the solution, in pretty much every case, is simply to lift the keel off the bottom, at least partially, which in turn means less force is required to get off and there is less chance of any damage to the rudder.

Fortunately, most sailboats come supplied with a 50ft lever attached to enable you to do this. Otherwise known as 'the mast' it also conveniently has a line attached to the top of it. So, if a passing boat has come to help you (or you can launch a dinghy) pass one of your halyards out to her and ask her to slowly motor away from you until you tip far enough to lift the keel off the sand[53]. At this point you can use your engine to

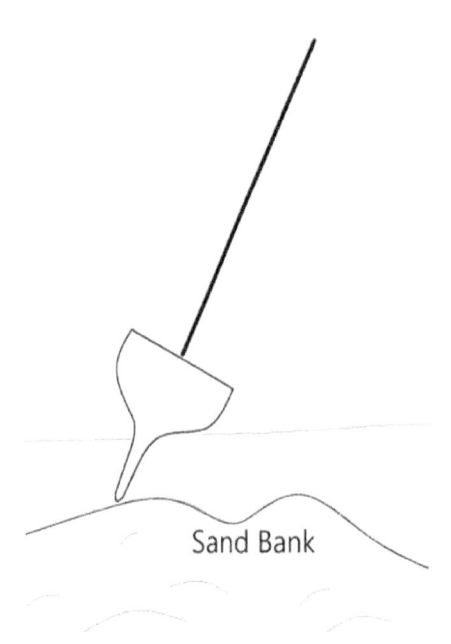

Figure 30: Aground

---

[53] For those yet to start sailing, a halyard is any line that lifts a sail. They usually exit at (or near to) the top of the mast.

gently reverse out of your doofus predicament – and move on to the next one. (Fig 31)

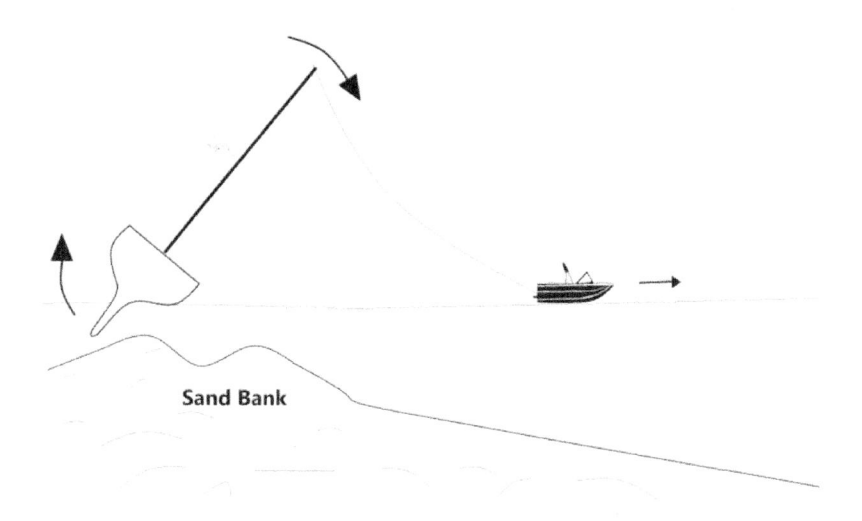

Figure 31: Using the mast as a giant lever to raise the keel is a great way to recover from your doofus moment in style.

There are a couple of risks with this. You have to trust the skipper of the other boat not to be too ham-fisted and speed off at 10 knots, tilting you so far that water is now running over the gunnels and down the companionway. This can be mitigated by putting your washboards in and battening down the hatches before attempting this manoeuvre as well as controlling the main halyard. For example, if you find the skipper of the other boat is pulling you over too much, you can easily release a little of the halyard (or dump it altogether in an emergency) to bring you back to a more reasonable angle while signalling the helpful captain, in the strongest acceptable terms, to ease up a bit. This is why you should never tie the halyard or use locking turns on a cleat, as they will be irremovable under load. Wrap it around a winch instead.

Most fellow sailors you meet will be experienced and competent enough that this should not be a problem – it just makes sense to prepare for it and know you can control the situation yourself should the worst happen.

The other danger you have to be aware of and prepared for, is the release. Once you are clear of the sandbank, the boat can pop upright fairly quickly, so be ready for that. Hopefully the skipper of the other boat will keep a little tension in the halyard and you will become gracefully upright again as the falling keel tries to overcome the weight of the pulling boat, but if she simply dumps the halyard (or you are using a dinghy with no weight), your return to upright status can be 'corky' to say the least. So it pays to hang on, just in case.

If there is nobody around and you don't own a powerful dinghy fear not, there are other ways to lift the keel.

Sails

As you no doubt know, when a boat is sailing with the wind forward of the beam (beam being the side of the boat) she will lean over or 'heel'. This can work in your favour if there is a wind blowing. If the wind is blowing from a favourable direction, raising the sails might heel the boat sufficiently to sail you off the bank or allow the engine to slide you off it.

No wind, no help, no dinghy, no problem.

This is precisely the situation I found myself in with *Marutji* whilst sailing up the mighty Clarence River in Australia. There is a gorgeous, virtually empty anchorage about halfway up this beautiful river. Out of the main current and about the size of 10 football fields, it is a very beautiful anchorage, full of pelicans and black swans (by coincidence, *Marutji* means 'black swan' in the local Aboriginal dialect) and a great place to stop for a while. However, there are no charts that show depth so you have to use your eyes, depth sounder and spider-senses to fathom a good place to drop the hook. I found what I thought was such a place only to discover that, as I swung on the change of tide, I was not nearly as clever as I thought and *Marutji* was aground. With no dinghy (well, no outboard) and nobody about, I was in a bit of a spot. In addition, the anchorage is fabulously well-protected from the wind which, while comfortable, did not leave me the option of raising the sails in order to try and heel the boat over. If you find yourself in this position all is not lost as there are still a couple of things you can do individually or in combination.

Kedging

This is where you row out an anchor in your dinghy as far as is practical (the further the better) and drop it. You then use a winch to slowly drag the boat off the sand bank. This can be a forward anchor or a stern anchor depending on which way you have identified as being the shortest route to deeper water. All situations are different, but in my case, *Marutji* had gone aground when swinging at anchor with the tide, so she was already facing the deeper water with her anchor down and pretty much in the kedge position. Had I gone aground whilst moving forward, I would have had to row out a stern anchor and pull her off backwards. If you act quickly before the tide drops further (obviously if you are on a rising tide, wait until you have reached high tide) this can be enough on its own to drag you out. The rudder can easily get damaged coming out backwards, particularly a spade rudder (don't start me off again) so keep it centred by lashing the helm amidships and winch the anchor in slowly. This might be enough on its own to get you off, but can (and really ought to) be used in conjunction with:

Self-induced heel

This technique may also be used on its own and, for me, is the first place I go as it is quick to set up. Even if it is not sufficient to get you off, it will certainly make the kedging easier and reduce the likelihood of rudder damage. The theory is simple:

Tie everything heavy you have to the end of the boom and swing it out as far as you can. Obviously if you have a grand piano (or a particularly fat husband) you may overwhelm the rigging and add a dismasting to your increasingly doofus scorecard, but generally the rigging can hold more than you would think. However, as a safety precaution, I always take the main halyard (the line that lifts the mainsail) and attach it to the back of the boom to give a bit of extra support to the topping lift (this is the line that holds the boom up) as the topping lift is probably the weakest link in this procedure (assuming your rig is in good shape).

As you can see in the Fig 32, I am using a spare anchor and some jerry cans filled with water. There is only about 70kg (155 lbs) in absolute weight here, but the boom is 4.5meters (15 feet) long. So bearing in mind the cantilever effect we discussed in chapter one, when we swing the boom out 90 degrees, the weight is magnified by the length of the boom which gives us a massive 315kg (nearly 700 lbs) of force to heel us over and lift our keel off the bottom. In this instance, this was enough to lift the keel sufficiently to enable me to power forward with no kedging required, but feel free to use both techniques at the same time. If nothing is moving you, it is time to use your patience, get your tide almanac out and try again at the next high tide. If you have bought a boat with a longish keel and protected rudder, then waiting for the next tide, whilst a little uncomfortable, should not cause any real damage.

Figure 32: Using weights tied to the boom to induce heel.

Attitude

Again, this can be a fun experience or a real humiliation and financial strain. Once you have the right boat, then that should keep the worry of damaging your keel and rudder (and the expense of hauling out and inspecting after each grounding) to a minimum, but if you need to always look like a 'winner' or are in a rush to be somewhere or show everyone how fast your boat is, you will feel frustrated and embarrassed. Which is a shame because being aground can be fun - I maintain to this day that you always meet the nicest people when you are aground. I think it is because only empathetic people are motivated to help and the dicks sail right on by. Anyway, with the right attitude it is just another fun day on the water with interesting problem solving, learning opportunities, belly laughs and the possibility of great people.

Being aground doesn't bother me because, not only am I never in a hurry, I am happy to admit that I am a colossal doofus and do not claim to be an expert or own a flashy white cap, blazer and slacks.

I am quite often saddened by how many couples I see screaming at each other and trying to deflect the embarrassment they feel as they criticize themselves and others for an error. Whether it is docking, running aground, anchoring or any other activity, the wrong attitude will cause you to forget that the feelings of others are way more important than making a great job of docking or spending half an hour getting off a mud bank – particularly if they are the feelings of someone who is important to you. If you accept your own inner doofus (and I really hope you do) it becomes that much easier to accept the inner doofus of others. Remember, we all came here for a different, more rewarding life and I would hate to see you fail to access it by setting impossible standards for yourself and those you care for. Even as an experienced sailor you will make mistakes. As a new sea gypsy, you will make hundreds. You need to be prepared for that and not engage in a harsh inner (or outer) dialogue with yourself, your crew or your squeeze. Embrace your inner idiot, learn, laugh and move on. In sailing, whatever doesn't kill you may not make you strong, but it will certainly make an awesome story for the beach camp fire.

PART TWO

Staying Gone.

Sailing does not have to be stressful.

Introduction to Part Two

It is often said (though not nearly often enough in my opinion) that money can't buy happiness. This is well illustrated by the (admittedly small) amount of hate mail I receive which almost invariably issues forth from the latest iphones of the more well–heeled yachtsmen who (though for reasons I cannot begin to fathom) seem outraged that a book such as this exists at all. Some have even expressed genuine anger that those who have to concern themselves with the vulgar subject of money are daring to take to the ocean or even have opinions regarding safe yacht construction. They seem to feel that their wealth and endless consumer choices somehow trump hard-won experience and engineering reality.

One critic was almost spitting blood that I had dared point out that the spade-ruddered, flimsy-keeled, production boat he had just dropped $500k on, was less seaworthy than a $30k Westsail 32 (which has an excellent keel/rudder and is laid up thicker than a bowl of whale custard). He then went on to conclude that the point of the book was to, "encourage the dregs of society to set sail on any piece of floating jetsam."

Given how much I tend to bang on about the constituents and importance of seaworthiness, I find it hard to imagine how he drew that conclusion, but even if that *was* the message, it would still come down to who you think the dregs of society are and what constitutes floating jetsam. A merchant banker wearing a blazer and slacks on a flashy yoghurt pot with a poorly attached keel and an unprotected spade rudder certainly gets my 'dregs and jetsam' vote.

What is enlightening about all this anger and vitriol is that it illustrates, far more clearly than I ever could, that once you have enough money to get by on a modest boat, pots more of the stuff is the least important component to happiness at sea. If anything, it seems to get in the way.

So, if money is not the engine of long-term voyaging happiness, then what is?

Welcome then Salty Sirs and Marine Madams to the second, and much less technical, part of the book. I hope you find something here to help you maintain your equilibrium and contentment in the face of the depressingly common and wildly erroneous belief that sailing nirvana can only be accessed by the profoundly deep of pocket.

CHAPTER FOURTEEN

Staying Happy on a Budget
Establishing new 'normals'

"All happy families are alike; each unhappy family is unhappy in its own way."

— Leo Tolstoy in Anna Karenina

There is a tendency for some to assume that because we don't have washing machines, freezers or air conditioning, that we budget buccaneers are being deliberately Spartan or purist in some way.

One reviewer on Amazon (going by the screen name Fantomfears) typically grabs the wrong end of the stick when he writes that,

"The writer believes that he is not as extreme as some purist sailors, but to my taste he is still off. I believe that creature comfort adds to the sailing experience and so would recommend including it in your boat, especially if it pleases your partner."

What Mr Fantomfears and others do not realise is that our rejection of things like air conditioning and washing machines is not because they are luxuries but because, for the nautical nomad, they are quite the opposite. If, for one moment, I believed they added to my comfort (or that of my partner), then I would add them immediately and without question.

As explained in *Get Real, Get Gone*, all additions to the power demand have a knock-on effect. The addition of say, a washing machine, means a generator, more batteries to store the charge, a watermaker and expensive spare parts shipped around the world. This, in turn, leads to standing in customs offices, hiring clearance agents, paying bribes (hard to do in a foreign language without ending up in jail). Once you have negotiated all that, you still have all your work ahead of you, fitting, maintaining and eventually replacing whatever supposedly 'labour saving' device you have imported.

Not too much hassle for the weekend sailor who plugs into the dock every night, lives near great services and goes back to work the next day to earn some more beer tokens, but for the sea gypsy on a limited budget, it is an absolute nightmare and as far from luxury as lying on a bed of nails and being body-slammed by the Fijian rugby team.

Two very good friends of mine have just spent the best part of six months trying to fix their generator in Tahiti. It has been out of the boat twice to the workshop where, after several attempted repairs, it was concluded that a total rebuild was required. The parts were ordered, sent all the way around the world to several wrong destinations, before arriving in Tahiti. These were then blocked by customs, resulting in the hiring of a clearance agent. The duty was finally agreed and the parts sent to the workshop which made such a bodge of it (quite common in developing countries) that it only worked for a week. The whole process had to be repeated until it was finally installed. It then stopped working and a further inspection determined that a new cylinder head was also required. Off we go to the races again - parts ordered, shipments chased, customs clearance agent engaged, work done to a questionable standard and generator re-installed in boat. Finally it seems okay-ish. And for what? So they can operate their washing machine. Now they are stuck waiting for parts for their roller furling because six months of inactivity has frozen the bearings... and on it goes.

I have covered all this before, but let us make a quick calculation. Assuming they get a year of trouble-free running out of the generator/washing machine/watermaker combo (quite an assumption with marine stuff) and do one wash per week, then each load will have cost them $62 and 3 days not sailing before we even factor in the operating, servicing and replacement costs.

Whereas using a tub with a sturdy lid and a few big rocks in it costs me 0 minutes not sailing (the wave motion whilst sailing provides the energy) and about 3 cents in cash, freeing me up to spend my days exploring, meeting awesome peoples, spear fishing and chasing the best margarita in town instead of chasing spare parts, cursing bruised knuckles and whining about how expensive sailing is.

And *that* my fellow watery wastrels, is as good a definition of 'luxury' as I know.

Yet my friends with the washing machine (who are experienced sailors by the way) still believe that nautical nirvana (when everything works fine, forever) is just around the next corner, 'as soon as we get this part' or, 'the moment that this gadget is fixed' and nothing seems to be able to convince them otherwise.

Psychologists call this the 'endowment effect' which is the tendency to ascribe more value to things (and habits) simply because they are yours, and is one of the many psychological traits that contribute to discontent and bad decision making at sea. But it doesn't have to be that way.

Examining and recalibrating the instrument of judgement (our own brains), is one of the best ways to enhance our life at sea as well as giving us more, 'happiness bang for our buck' than all the gadgets combined. Which leads us neatly to the greatest weapon in the attitude arsenal of the seeker of sailing happiness on a budget.

Establishing new normals

It seems to me that the secret to happiness is fairly universal. It often *appears* to have many different forms as it wears many different masks. This is partly because we confuse the pursuit of novelty with happiness itself.

For example: Bob might think he will be happy when he gets a promotion, whereas Debbie may be convinced that her happiness will arrive with the booking of a holiday. Sue might think a new car will do the trick and Mark may be convinced that happiness is the result of getting hold of Sue for a weekend. They all appear to have different paths to their happiness, but those differences hide what they all have in common. Regardless of what they are individually chasing, they are all convinced that the acquisition of some new status or object will be the key to their future happiness, and in that respect, they are all doing exactly the same thing – substituting the fleeting pleasure of novelty for genuine contentment.

And maybe they will be happy when they get what they want.

For a while.

Then it will be on to the next thing and then the next. And so on, in constant pursuit of the temporary buzz of novelty, then back to feeling that things are not quite right until the next novel thing or situation is identified and pursued.

If you have unlimited resources, this can go unchecked almost endlessly. Film director Steven Spielberg sold his 282ft motor launch to buy a 300 footer on the grounds that the previous one was 'too small'. Read that again, because we have become so numb to the madness of this type of charade that it just seems to glance off us now. But Spielberg's discontent only illuminates what we all do to some extent (only his example is more obvious because it seems to be on steroids and walking on stilts).

We humans are an adaptive species. We enjoy the thrill of the new thing or change in status for a moment or two and then we quickly adapt to it and incorporate it into our new 'normal' and go out looking for the next thing.

This can be a very useful trait, and you will need it if you are ever to overcome the bowel-loosening moments that will occur when you step outside your nautical comfort zone. It is this very process that will allow you to take challenging experiences, incorporate them into your new lifestyle and increase the width of your comfort zone accordingly. This process is the key to becoming confident and happy at sea – whatever the conditions.

However, every human trait (noble or otherwise) can be understood and manipulated by marketing people to sell a product - and this one is no different. So it is important to take control of it so we can know the difference between the moments when our natural adaptive inclinations are helping us learn and become better sailors, and when they are being manipulated in order to sell us another piece of needless nonsense that some marketing exec is trying to convince us will make us "happy".

Know your enemy

Imagine you have now bought your small, tough little ship with its decent hull, keel/rudder and rig (perhaps you already have). You are looking forward to safely immersing yourself into the sea gypsy lifestyle and embracing your inner pirate. Lots to learn, lots to do! It is hard to see how you are ever going to establish this as the new normal. But as the months pass by and you slowly start making little forays out to various destinations and learning how to live your new life, you will gradually become accustomed to certain things. Great! This is how you build your skills and expand your comfort zones. But this can work against you too, if you let it.

For example. Also imagine you have a nice, little, hard, rowing tender with an environmentally sensible and economically prudent little 2hp outboard on the back, and you have been happily putt-putting ashore in the sunshine every day feeling like Captain Cook in your new vessel. Hurrah! 'Aint life grand?

As time goes by, the adaptive process of your mind establishes this as the 'new normal' and the three minute journey ashore stops seeming like the lovely trip on the sea it once was and starts to feel a little boring. After a while, three minutes to get ashore begins to seem a bit excessive and you start looking around at all the huge, planing RIBs with 50hp, turtle-mashing outboards on the back who can bounce ashore in half the time it takes you and, before you know it, the downhill process begins with this thought; "I will be happy when I get a faster tender and don't have to waste so much time getting ashore".

The problem is of course, that you won't. You may buy a RIB and an 8hp outboard and be happy for a while until you adapt to that, but once it has come to be the new 'normal', you will be looking for something better (or at the very least you will become so blasé about your new acquisition that it no longer makes you happy and only gets noticed when it breaks down and you start swearing at it).

And on it goes to absorb all your time (and a large portion of your budget) in the process of 'novelty yearning' for the next thing that will make you 'happy' - and you will find no shortage of marketing execs willing to support you in this illusion for their own gains. If you are fantastically rich, this process can continue indefinitely until you are in the rather ridiculous position in which Mr Spielberg found himself, of being unsatisfied with his luxury 282ft yacht because it was, 'too small'.

Fortunately for us, we sea gypsies don't have unlimited resources to indulge this kind of spiritually lazy and environmentally disastrous thinking.

And when I say 'fortunately' I really mean it. In the last book I covered some of the benefits and rewards available to the less well-off sailor in some depth and this is yet another example.

If you have a mountain of cash, you can keep upgrading everything and confusing the temporary cheap thrill of novelty with genuine happiness until you run out of spending power - and if the sales of Spielberg films are anything to go by, that is unlikely to be any time soon. So the richer sailor may never be forced to confront his addiction to novelty, which is shame, as novelty addiction is a real barrier to genuine fulfilment.

We poorer sailors are more fortunate. Having seriously limited resources, we are forced to confront this addiction much earlier.[54]

So if you find yourself envying the super-fast, centre console, 50hp dolphin-liquidizing rib as it crashes through the waves sending spray, noise, pollution and the unmistakeable scent of mid-life crisis throughout the anchorage, simply so the skipper can spend less time doing what he came to do (be on the water) and are wasting your precious time and sea-gypsy soul in the act of yearning for novelty, then here is the answer:

Row.

Row until you have established this as the 'new normal'. You might even like it (I do). Even if you don't enjoy rowing (perhaps especially if you don't enjoy rowing), a week of pulling the sticks will reset your mind and when you put your little, affordable and eco-friendly 2hp outboard back on, you will once again realise what a miracle it is to be able to release the energy of fossilized dinosaurs to get you ashore while you sit motionless like some Arab sheik on a magic carpet. More importantly, you have embarked on the first step towards taking back control of your own satisfaction from those that seek to profit from manipulating human nature.

Do you need a freezer? No, you need to live without your fridge for a while. When you turn it back on after a month of warm beer you

---

[54] This, incidentally, is also why rich, rock-star drug addicts can often get into such a bad way. Poorer people hooked on heroin often lose their jobs or turn to theft to support their habit and tend to come to the attention of the authorities where they are forced to confront their addiction by the courts. A rich heroin user can fly under the radar almost indefinitely.

will experience exactly the same rush of satisfaction without adding weight (and complication) to your boat, blowing your budget or increasing your carbon footprint.

I received a fair bit of criticism (and some hate mail -though I have no idea why) for the anti-marketing tone of the last book, but none of it enlightening, challenging or even coherently argued, so I won't bother addressing it here. Trolls notwithstanding, it is very important to keep in mind that, despite our tendency to think we are all totally unique, many functions of our brains are universal and certainly not a secret known only to us. They have been understood by psychologists and neuroscientists for decades. Much of this knowledge is employed by marketing companies to target our tendency to believe that the next 'new normal' will make us happy. There are entire departments in most large companies whose purpose is to understand the mechanics of the universal human search for happiness and use it to loosen our purse strings (which is why psychology graduates are so highly sought by marketing departments). But the benefits of recognizing this are more important than simply saving a bit of cash or being a 'purist'.

I am a sybarite, a hedonist and enjoy pleasure above all things – a million miles away from the image of the Spartan Calvinist that seems stuck in the minds of the less charitable commentators. But unless we start to see the difference between genuine happiness and our universal addiction to novelty-seeking, we remain terminally vulnerable to the marketing people and the fleeting happiness of consumerism they offer. We will remain locked in an endless, doomed treasure hunt because we have not noticed we are holding the wrong map.

So, my watery cousins, take heart. There really is no long-term advantage to wealth or supposed 'luxuries' or 'upgrades'. Not if your aim is to have more time for really living or to find some inner peace - and I don't imagine that you have chosen the sea gypsy life because you like the smell of bilge water.

CHAPTER FIFTEEN

Staying Healthy:
Do I need health insurance?

"Until you make the unconscious conscious, it will direct your life and you will call it fate."

Carl Jung

This is a very common question and a difficult one to answer. Like everybody else, I would rather not die and would like to have access to world-class health care 24/7. I would also like to have a heap of cash in the bank, but to achieve that, I would have to join the rat race, get a 'proper' job and that would suck the joy out of my life – much too high a price to pay.

The price one has to pay for 24/7 access to world-class health care (never going anywhere too far off the beaten track, never taking any physical risk, never having an adventure, etc.,) is similarly too high for me. Every adventure must carry some risk, or it is not an adventure.

Being in the middle of the Pacific and totally reliant on yourself and your body is either fantastic or foolish, depending on your outlook. Personally, I find that level of self-sufficiency the very stuff of life. You may feel differently and in which case, you should keep your sailing limited to coastal hopping and one or two night passages in fairly developed places.

This may sound restrictive, but that gives you the UK, the majority of the Med, the French Canals, much of the Caribbean and Mexico, large parts of the USA, the Aussie east coast, the Florida Keys, south east Asia and hundreds of other places to explore without ever being too far away from weapons-grade hospitals.

I do not have a scrap of health insurance and that sounds crazy to many of my American comrades and quite normal to my European brothers and sisters. While it is true that not everybody is as blessed with the rude good health that it has been my good fortune to enjoy, it is also true that the health insurance industry is built on lies and fear-mongering. I wrote a wee article a while ago which expresses my views on the subject and have reproduced it below:

Do I need health insurance? By Rick Page

This is a question that often seems strange to us Europeans (or Canadians, Australians and Kiwis) who have grown up in societies with advanced social health programmes, but is a very real cause for concern for our American cousins who are thinking of sailing off into the horizon — and that is partly due to the astronomically expensive nature of health care in the US and partly because of a failure to understand that medicine is an entirely affordable commodity virtually everywhere else in the world.

To get a better understanding of the physical and cultural barriers that our American brothers and sisters have to face, try imagining you have grown up in a country where vegetables are 1000% more expensive — where a carrot costs $10 and a veggie stir-fry could easily run to $100. On top of that imagine that your government and media had also managed to convince you that vegetables elsewhere in the world were sub-standard and even dangerous to consume.

What do you imagine would be the first question you would ask anyone who was daft enough to leave your country and travel abroad to live on a boat? Probably something like,

"How do you eat?" or,

"Where do you get safe vegetables?"

"How could you afford to live?" or something like that.

I mention this because we (along with many European sailors) are often perplexed by, and sometimes a little unfairly dismissive of, the attention our American cousins seem to focus on the subject of health insurance. For those that don't understand why this is, under no circumstances should you get sick in the US.

US citizens have been so grossly overcharged for health care, for so long that they have come to accept it as normal. Furthermore, the American medical machine tries to justify this over-charging by claiming (contrary to all evidence) to be far superior to anywhere else in the world. Years of this propaganda have had their effect as many American sailors I meet have policies that involve immediate repatriation to the US should they become ill, which suggests that at least some have bought the idea that health care outside the US is sub-standard or even dangerous[55].

---

[55] The widely respected Health Care Index actually places the US in 30th position, below countries like Australia, Turkey, Spain, Thailand, Sri Lanka and Mexico. (I picked those examples because they also have great sailing). For those who need some serious medical attention, it can pay to buy a boat in Thailand (ranked 8th best healthcare in the world) because the exchange rate makes normally prohibitively expensive operations and treatments, very affordable indeed. You are also more likely to survive your surgery in Thailand.

Self treatment can cure most minor things and is very economical. My entire drug cabinet pictured here cost less than US$50 and was available on prescription once I paid for a doctor's consultation to help define our on-board needs. The consultation and prescription cost just US$4. (Mexico).

The good news is that health care around the world is a lot better than many have been lead to believe, often better than the US and much better than many of our parents had anywhere.

In my 30+ years of being on the move, I have been treated in Kenya (malaria), Tanzania (dengue fever), Malawi (wisdom teeth), Zimbabwe (facial and rib trauma), UK (head trauma and dengue), Spain (chipped bone), Mexico (kidney infection), and now Fiji (wisdom teeth). Some of these treatments required a day or so in a hospital bed – others over a week.

All the treatments I have received have been exemplary. I paid cash for all of them and added up together they come to less than $1500. In the same period, the average American would have spent at least $69,000 in premiums (or just shy of $175,000 for a family policy) *and* had to make up the difference for the many things not covered in the plan.

On a skydiving trip to Florida, my girlfriend Davina fell down the stairs that lead to Flagler Beach and chipped a bone. She spent three days in hospital, the bill came to $16,000 and the service was no better than anywhere else in the world. When I did more or less the same thing in Spain after being thrown from a horse onto a village fountain, the bill was just over 200 Euros (US$238) and the service fantastic with no waiting. Most sea gypsies you meet will relate similar experiences.

I love American sailors. With the exception of the occasional evangelical bore, I always hit it off with the Yanks and it seems a shame that the unnecessary fear of getting sick or injured whilst uninsured and abroad seems to be holding so many of them back from joining us out here on the big blue wobbly stuff.

Sailing is a healthy lifestyle and your health (and chances of survival) will improve immeasurably just by eating well, living with less stress and not driving every day. So, if the fear of not being insured is stopping you realising your dream, worry not. If you can shut out the voices of the 'what if something happens' brigade and stop wondering why nobody else is paying $10 for a carrot, you will be a lot closer to reality, health and happiness than the fantastically over-insured, over-fed and over- stressed.

⚓

Since writing this, I have had a major accident in a storm off the coast of Futuna (my own stupid fault for not following my own advice. I mean, *really*!). I suffered a deflated lung, a damaged diaphragm and double inguinal hernia. I had to sit hove-to for 2 days then sail back to Fiji with little breath and with my lower intestine clearly visible under the skin of my upper leg and groin (which, I will happily admit, was a wee bit spooky). I got into Fiji and was dealt with very well by the Fijian surgeons. I had two mesh implants in the abdomen, my diaphragm patched up and my left lung re-inflated. I was asked to pay $65 for my treatment, so I still have no reason to change the opinions expressed in the article.

Now, I know how the medical marketing machine would react to that. They will (and do) claim that Fijian or Spanish or Mexican (add name of country that is not America here) medicine is not 'state of the art'. That may be true (although quite often it is not). Fiji may be 10 or 20 years behind the US in terms of technology, but I was alive 20 years ago and I assume you were too. Did you feel in danger? Did you worry that your surgeons were 20 years behind the game compared to surgeons of the future? Of course not. This is just fear-mongering.

Almost everywhere you go in the world, the medical system will be better than your parents had and unrecognizably futuristic in comparison to the health system your grandparents were perfectly happy with in the US or Europe when they were growing up. No wonder the old folks think we are all going a bit soft!

Of course there is a little risk when you start crossing oceans and living miles away from medical infrastructures, but I maintain that it is not an elevated risk, merely a different one. As different risk carries that anal-twitching, sugar-frosting of our dear old adversary, 'fear of the unknown', it can often feel more intense and scary until you incorporate it into you 'new normal'. It is this that often makes the idea of getting sick abroad seem so scary, not the reality.

Ironically, the only place I will not go without health insurance is America because, like Monica Lewinsky, I don't want to be surprised by an enormously undesirable Bill.

Okay, joking aside for a moment. When you take on the life of a watery wastrel, you may no longer live twenty two minutes away from medical help and that is indeed an elevated level of risk. However, you have to see the *total* amount of risk in your lifestyle as a whole, because risk is cumulative.

When you set off, you will no longer be:

- Driving on the highway.
- Riding motorcycles or cycling in the city.
- Crossing busy roads.
- Eating junk food.
- Stressing out (big one this for men over 40 and post-menopausal women as it contributes to high blood pressure and heart disease which is still the biggest killer even post-covid).
- Eating processed food (same heart issues + bowel cancer risk)
- Breathing auto fumes
- Sitting on your butt in an office
- Living in a country where there is easy access to firearms. (However you feel politically about gun ownership, there is no doubt that you are much more likely to die from gunshot wound if you live in a country where guns are easily accessible)[56]
- Living in a crowded environment where disease is easily transmitted (I can't remember the last time I had a cold or the flu).
- Vulnerable to pandemics.
- Suffering the negative mental health effects of urban life.

And all those carry a risk that far outweighs the fact that medical care might be a few years behind 'state of the art'.

---

[56] Actually, you are statistically far more likely to die from a self-inflicted gunshot wound (accidental or otherwise) than you are to have it save your life.

Of course there is always *some* risk – it would be impossible to have and adventure without it – but the reality is that if you leave your office job and become a nautical nomad, you will simply be exchanging one set of risks for another (possibly even slightly lower) set of risks which only *seem* scary because they are different.

If you are determined to have a risk-free life then not only are you probably reading the wrong book, but I have some bad news for you: Being a man over 60 for 20 minutes carries a one in ten thousand chance of dying (about ten times the risk of making a skydive). Whatever your gender or age, there is significant risk in just being alive.

Heart disease is still the biggest killer out there and that is a cumulative condition caused by a sedentary lifestyle, stress and a bad diet. You can whistle goodbye to those things when you choose a better lifestyle and that alone should tilt the odds back towards your favour.

Non-specific health worries.

One of the more common questions I get asked is, "what if 'something' happens?" This rather nebulous, non-specific fear is quite revealing as the asker has not been able to negotiate the general maze of health fears to focus on anything specifically.

Unless you are a member of the 0.1% of unimaginative people who are truly fearless, you will probably identify with that question strongly. Like nearly everybody else, you will need to manage your fears because you are an integral part of the ship and your systems have to be examined and checked as thoroughly as if they were part of the rig. So, as the great Carl Jung says at the beginning of this chapter, we really do need to make the unconscious conscious and unpack this non-specific fear of 'something' happening if we are to be happy nautical nomads.

As you will have guessed by now, I am quite interested in the mechanics of happiness and I certainly don't mean to be morose, but it seems that even when you are in your late seventies the fear of 'something' happening still haunts. If you are approaching eighty years old then 'something' is definitely going to happen, and probably quite soon. If you are younger it is going to happen too, not quite as quickly but still relatively soon. Sorry to sound negative, but nobody gets out of this life alive and wishing this were untrue is often at the cause of our non-specific unease.

Oh god, not another skydiving metaphor!

I am afraid so, because in many ways we are all sky-diving accidents in process. Skydiving accidents are rare, but they do happen. Even rarer, but by no means unheard of, are those that actually survive. Curiously, they all report a similar feeling. Peace.

Well obviously, there is a lot of panic at first which gives way to flapping like a demented bird, but once the skydiver realises that there is absolutely nothing they can do, they stop flapping and report an overwhelming sense of peace.

Well folks, as you know, we are all going to get old, get sick and die sometime relatively soon. Nobody likes to be reminded of it and I suspect this is why so many people seem unable to verbalise it specifically or give their fears any sort of corporeal form.

Some people avoid this reality by stuffing their heads full of drugs, alcohol, the false promises of immortality or other diversions to avoid thinking about it. Even those who consider themselves too smart for such diversions often attempt to cope with their inevitable demise by paralyzing themselves with boredom, ennui and existential malaise; making one's life depressingly tragic certainly helps us deal with the reality that it won't be bothering us much longer.

Psychologically and spiritually, these avoidance strategies are the equivalent of the demented flapping that skydivers do when they first realise that they will be meat bombs in a few minutes.

If this sounds like you, I have a suggestion for dealing with it. It is not a complicated suggestion. It does not require difficult yoga poses, blind faith, believing in the impossible or understanding mysterious-looking Sanskrit runes. It is simply this:

Stop flapping.

Embrace the idea that the 'something' you are worried about is definitely going to happen and relatively soon too. Anyone who says otherwise is peddling something that is not only untrue, but is a genuine impediment to the equanimity and satisfaction we all seek by giving us false hope in the efficacy of our flapping. Politely show them the door, accept the truth and stop flapping.

Ahhh, there it is. Peace, understanding, and the impossibility of ever wanting to waste a moment of this short free-fall flapping like a frightened chicken or finding excuses not to enjoy every precious second of it just because it has a definite end.

Fear can be useful. Imagination can be useful. Combined, they help us look into the future and get a taste of how wholly unpleasant it would be to drown in the cold waters of the grey Atlantic and this can provide us with the requisite motivation to do all the physical and psychological preparation necessary to avoid such an outcome whilst steering us towards becoming better, happier sailors.

However, this same combination can cause us to over-think and elevate the risks in our minds to such a level that they scare us into paralysis (or the desire for ridiculously inflated and unaffordable levels of insurance, which amounts to the same thing). Getting real is not just about turning the physical odds in your favour with the right boat and gear, but about finding that sweet spot where one has just enough fear and imagination to inspire good preparation but not so much that the terror of the unknown 'something' happening forces us into stagnation.

So grab what you have and do what makes your heart sing. This is a book about the sea gypsy life, but it does not really matter. The sea gypsy life is just one way I have found to enjoy my own terminal free-fall without ruining it by flapping, and if it works for you then I am glad I wrote this book. Personally, I intend to live forever or die trying, but the accent has to be on *living,* rather than merely existing in an over-insured, under-stimulated, cosseted bubble of boredom.

Now, I could go on all day about how 'the things we have failed to make conscious' are our biggest obstacles to happiness, but this chapter is supposed to be about physical, rather than mental, health and no discourse on this subject is complete without addressing the big, stinking, mud-caked elephant in the room. Covid 19.

CHAPTER SIXTEEN

Staying Covid Free

At the time of going to press, there are several vaccines being rolled out and the international mood is growing more positive. However, many experts agree that pandemics will be with us, in some form or another, for a very long time, possibly becoming a fact of life like the flu. Many epidemiologists consider the risk of rapid-spreading viruses to be nothing new, but simply a product of general population growth and mobility (which is pretty obvious when you think about it) and have warned that Covid may be the first of many inevitable pandemics as both mobility and population growth continue unabated.

With this rather gloomy thought as low level background noise (and the fact that many people have learned that being cooped up indoors with their relatives is about as much fun as chewing aluminium foil) I have received quite a few emails asking how the sea gypsy community has been coping and whether this lifestyle is healthy, or even still possible, in the post-Covid environment.

I am pleased to say that it most certainly is. Generally, we nautical nomads have suffered much less from the Covid outbreak than our land-based counterparts and there are some very good reasons for this.

Good sea boats are almost perfectly designed for self-isolation. Not only are most yachtsmen mentally equipped for, and accustomed to, long periods of self-sufficiency in small spaces, all the features of a well-found sea-gypsy boat are also perfectly suited for self-isolation from infectious diseases.

Unlike the many gin palaces you see permanently plugged into the mains electricity at the marina, a good sea gypsy boat should be self-sufficient in electricity (from wind and sun without the need to return to the dock or rely on generators or starting the engine) and have some way of collecting rainfall to keep the tanks topped up. An over-reliance on complicated systems will also scupper any attempts to self-isolate as you will need to continually return to shore to chase down parts for your washing machine or air conditioner and fuel for your generator to run it all.

Calypso II's directionally stable long keel and windvane steering enables her to virtually sail herself, allowing me to maintain a good social distance from my imaginary friends who tend to appear on long passages.

Once properly set up, a good sea gypsy boat can travel extensively and have a new view every day without actually coming into contact with anybody at all. You will be surprised how much a new view can lift the soul and compensate for restricted social contact.

Attitude wins again

Again, those who set themselves the goal of sailing around the world will be feeling frustration that travel restrictions may mean that their man-made milestones are not being 'achieved', which is another good reason (as if another were needed) to not set yourself this largely arbitrary goal. Your frustration at being stuck in a yacht in paradise will make you seem quite a comical figure. Those of us who have taken the time to get real will enjoy this period to take stock, explore local bays, learn the lingo or do something creative, as well as enjoying the comedic spectacle of watching frustrated A-type personalities shouting at bemused government officials and storming around the dock getting their Mustos in a wad.

Even in a crowded anchorage, *Calypso* (in foreground) always has a moat around her.

Living in a castle

Unless you are lucky enough to have been born into the royal family or are planning world domination from your own secret island, the chances are that you do not have the perfect feature for self isolation. I am, of course, referring to a moat (preferably full of unpleasant beasties).

Anywhere you anchor your yacht is an automatic moat several

times larger than most castles and anyone visiting must announce their presence from a long way off. They then have to get past the marine etiquette of not coming aboard without asking permission or being invited. In nearly 15 years of living aboard I have only seen one person breech this convention (a rather evangelical missionary who came aboard without being asked as he considered the word of his god to be more important than marine etiquette. He soon learned that is not necessarily the case). So, for sailors, it is beyond easy to maintain correct social distancing without really changing one's lifestyle or invoking new or unfamiliar habits. (Plus most boats already have a stock of masks on board for dealing with antifouling paint and epoxy resin).

Self entertaining

In *Get Real, Get Gone*, I quote the Hollywood actor and sailor, Sterling Hayden who claims that, apart from a few pounds of food and six feet to lie down in, a person really only needs some rewarding work for a happy life. I get the point, but only partially agree as I do not think most of us can go too long without some creative pursuits. I like to write and play music and if I do this every day, I find it much easier to forgo the second essential missed by Mr Hayden – the need for human contact. The sea gypsy life can also help us safely negotiate that need.

Trolling for fish from my little sailing tender is a great solo activity...

For example, I have been anchored in the same three or four places for several months now and have come to know those who have also been here for that period, largely isolated in their boats. So when I hear a rap on the hull and an "Ahoy *Calypso*", I already know who I can safely invite aboard immediately and who to keep chatting from the dinghy.

....as is exploring remote areas by kayak (but much less likely to result in lunch).

As the borders open up and yachts start to arrive from New Zealand and other parts of the world, this lifestyle will continue to offer a protective shield as those sailors who drop the anchor in Fiji will have already been self-isolating for a couple of weeks on passage. Furthermore, they would have had to pass the quarantine checks that have been routine for those arriving by sea for decades before this most recent pandemic made 'quarantine' a new word in the landlubbers' lexicon. So, as I have always suspected, largely restricting your contact to fellow sailors really is good for your health (assuming, of course, that you can maintain proper control of your beverages).

Business as usual
Generally then, life has not really changed that much for me – but it is good to know that, should the situation deteriorate, we have been unconsciously practicing how to cope with it for years.

Covid spike

This lockdown seems to have led a great many people to re-evaluate their lifestyle choices – or so it would seem if my book sales are anything to go by. Maybe it has been a close encounter with mortality, a reminder of how little time we have before that 'something' happens or just a little shock therapy, but my inbox has taken quite a pounding since the pandemic took hold. Some people have already made the jump and are asking for practical advice, but the majority are first-timers who have been spurred on by recent events to make the leap and are simply waiting for the restrictions to ease in order to make the change to nautical nomad status. Many seem to believe that the restrictions are going to be a permanent fixture of the 'new normal' and are therefore keen to take this opportunity to leave the land before the next spike in infections causes another lock down. (I cannot see this happening personally, but I am, by design, increasingly out of touch with the supposed, 'real' world and only really capable of answering nautical questions, so what do I know?)

It is easy to self-isolate when your swimming pool covers 75% of the earth's surface.

Silver lining

Even before this pandemic, there were an overwhelming amount of good reasons to embark on the life of a peripatetic puddle plodder. If it takes this virus to kick you into action and join us out here on the big blue wobbly thing, then at least *some* good will have come of Covid 19.

CHAPTER SEVENTEEN

Staying Sane: Taking a Break

However great your lifestyle, however much you enjoy what you do, it is always good to take a break – even if only to remind yourself that life ashore sucks.

Getting off your little escape pod for a while also presents another opportunity for you to pat yourself on the back for buying a small, solid sea boat, because leaving a 45 foot, million-dollar catamaran while you go hiking in a rain forest or fly home to see your mum is a whole different level of expense and risk.

So let's look how much it costs to store various sizes of boat while you goof off on a motorbike adventure for 3 months. There are several ways to store your boat, but let's look at the obvious one first.

In the marina
The marina is a good place for security, but not good for marine growth on the bottom. Furthermore, your boat may be bashed by someone who has not taken the time to develop their docking superpowers as you have (or may not have their own curly pipe). Of course, your boat could still sink at the dock if you have not properly installed and maintained your through-hulls as described in chapter eleven, but generally, the marina is a solid (if somewhat expensive) choice for peace of mind.

The prices below are based on Coffs Harbour Marina in Australia and are in US Dollars. I chose this marina simply because this is the nearest one to me at time of writing. Obviously, other marinas will have different prices, but generally the *percentage* differences are fairly similar across a broad range of marinas. (Boy, you really going to love having a small boat now).

A 32 foot boat is going to cost you $952 to leave for three months.

A 40ft boat is going to cost $1425 – more than 50% more.

Usually a catamaran of the same length is subject to a 50% surcharge, so in the above case, a cat of 40 feet is going to dent your adventure budget to the tune of $2,178 for the three months – well over twice as much as the 32 foot monohull.

I don't want to discuss boats above 40 feet as it makes my sporran twitch.

At the boatyard

Storage fees at the boatyard are similar in both cost and proportion to the marina. Again, catamaran owners can expect to pay significantly more for both storage costs and haul-out charges, but this can be a great way to store your boat if you time your break to coincide with your scheduled haul-out (so as not to incur an added haul-out charge)[57].

---

[57] Haul-out charges vary but to give you an idea, both *Calypsos* weigh a little under 10 tons, and I have paid between $300 and $500 to haul them out. This includes being returned to the water.

When you feel like a break coming on, identify a good haul-out yard, lift your boat, pack her away, have a break, come back, do your antifoul (and anything else) and re-launch – job done! (Of course, really organised people will do all their work *before* they leave, but who really does that? It could be argued that if you are such a picture of organizational mental health, you probably don't need a break anyway).[58]

Not only is there no chance of your boat sinking while you are away, but hauling out for long periods can actually be good for fibreglass boats as they tend to absorb water over time. A good few months on the hard stand will help them dry out nicely and return them to the correct weight (water is quite heavy to lug around!).

Getting by with a little help from your friends.

Obviously, for those with limited budgets, the expense of securing a larger boat in a marina or a boatyard can seriously curtail any land-based forays you had planned. For some sailors on particularly skinny budgets, even the more modest charges incurred by the smaller yacht may still prove too onerous. If this is the case for you, do not despair. You have two options open to you, but both require you to have been nice enough to have developed a good reputation in our little community and be good at making sailing friends (you will be surprised how quickly your boat name will circulate if you never help anyone else or are generally behaving like a dick).

---

[58] If you chose this approach, make sure you check your hull for any osmotic blisters before you leave and grind them out, as they need several weeks to drain fully and you will be kicking yourself if you only discover them after a 3 month holiday.

So let's go make some! Firstly we need to have a look at the type of anchorages where you will find friendly liveaboard communities.

Anchorages

For our purposes, it pays to divide anchorages into two types:

- Open roadstead
- Closed roadstead

Open roadstead anchorages are, as you might imagine, open to the sea. Their attraction as a place to park your little floating home comes from the protection the land provides against prevailing winds (Fig 33). As the prevailing winds increase, the land continues to offer protection, but more importantly, the 'fetch' remains the same regardless of wind strength. Fetch is the distance the wind has available to whip up the waves - the longer the fetch, the bigger the waves. As long as the prevailing winds continue to prevail, the fetch remains the same, regardless of wind strength.

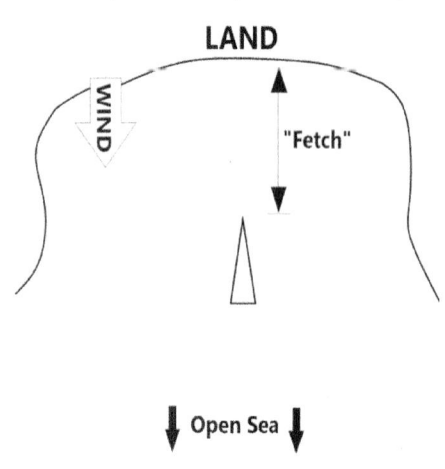

Figure 33: An open roadstead anchorage

Unfortunately, 'prevailing' does not mean 'constant' and, sooner or later, the winds are going to change. They will now have several hundred (or thousand) miles of fetch available to them which will turn your previously calm little anchorage into a hellish cauldron. These anchorages are fine while you are onboard and can keep an eye on the weather, but are terrible places to leave your boat unattended. Although you may see dozens of boats in such an anchorage, this does not constitute a long-term community as, when the wind changes, this anchorage will empty quicker than Hervey Weinstein's social diary, leaving your poor unattended vessel all alone and at the mercy of the sea.

Closed roadstead anchorages are either partially closed to the open sea (such as in lagoons, up rivers or estuaries) or are in inlets so deep that the waves are forced to travel such great distances to reach the anchored boats that most of their power is dissipated in the process. These are the types of anchorage where you tend to find longer-term communities of fellow liveaboard sailors at anchor.

The downside of these more secure anchorages (compared to open roadstead anchorages) is that because they tend to be in deep bays, rivers or estuaries, they are usually subject to a fair bit of tide action.

Now, if you have found a closed roadstead anchorage that has good, inexpensive moorings that you can easily inspect, your journey ends here. Rent one and ask somebody to pop onto your boat once a day to check your lines and your bilge. Moorings are usually pretty good value, so pack your bag and off you go to mix with the mud people. (Don't forget to write, and remember to spend some time laughing at the quaint things that they worry about).

However, if there are no trustable or affordable moorings (or if your budget is so thin that even the modest cost of a mooring gets you clutching your sporran) then we will have to make our own.

Why can't I just anchor normally?
It is true that in many ways, you are safer lying to your own ground tackle than taking a mooring. When moorings fail, they tend to fail catastrophically, whereas anchors tend to fail slowly by dragging which, while unpleasant, normally gives you time to roll out of bed and re-anchor.

Of course, this doesn't help if you are visiting your folks in prison or climbing Mount Kilimanjaro at the time, so a little look at why anchors drag and what we can do about it will help us understand why we need to make a mooring before we get our walking boots on.

If a correctly scoped anchor is properly dug in to a good-holding seabed of mud or deep sand, (see *Get Real, Get Gone*) then it will take quite a bit to dislodge it - assuming the winds/currents don't change direction.

However, when the wind or tide change, the boat swings to face the new direction, and the anchor is rotated. This is the most vulnerable moment in the anchoring cycle because the anchor can now temporarily find itself parting company with the sea bed. Normally the anchor will re-bury itself, but occasionally it only *partially* re-buries itself. Your boat will now start moving slowly through the anchorage, towards the shore or out to sea. Perfectly okay and solvable if you are onboard, but a danger to your boat and others if you are drinking absinthe in Paris. So, if you want to leave your boat at anchor without worry, we are going to have to use our own ground tackle a little bit more creatively in order to avoid this most vulnerable moment.

The Bahamian mooring

The Bahamian mooring is basically two anchors set in both directions of the tidal set and joined to the boat by a third piece of chain with a swivel attached at the boat end (Fig 34).

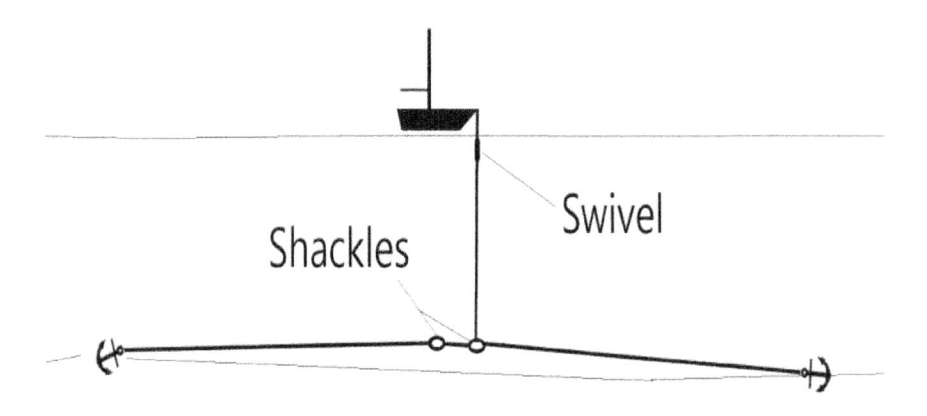

Figure 34: Bahamian mooring.

As the boat swings to the tide, neither anchor is rotated, thus we avoid the vulnerable moment where the anchor needs to re-bury itself. Fig 34 looks pretty simple, and it is, but it takes a little bit of organisation. In the following description, I will use a bow and a stern anchor, but it can just as easily be organised with two bow anchors if that is what you have.

Okay, let's get cracking. Firstly you will need:

- Two good anchors.[59]
- Two all-chain anchor rodes at least 5x the depth (at high tide) at your chosen spot.
- A third anchor chain of roughly the depth you intend to anchor.
- 3 shackles (or five, depending which method you choose).
- 1 Swivel.
- Two nylon rodes of about 3 meters (10 feet) each, appropriately sized for the weight of your boat. I use 2 x 18mm on *Calypso II* which weighs 10,000kg (11 US tons).
- A pleasing personality and preferably a reputation for helping your fellow sailors.
- A curly pipe (optional)

The good news is that you probably have most of this on board already (or you should have). So let's see how we lay it.

---

[59]Many people have Danforth anchors as stern anchors and are rightly suspicious of them as they don't have the best record. Fear not though as the research done by *Yachting Monthly* magazine clearly shows that the failures of Danforth anchors are due to their inability to re-bed themselves reliably when the boat swings. If the Danforth is not asked to do this, its holding figures are as good as (or better than) most anchors.

Firstly, before we approach our chosen spot, we need to prepare our nylon anchor rodes, swivel and third piece of chain as shown in Fig 35. Let's call this the 'mooring bridle' so as not to confuse it with the anchor chains.

There are many ways to do this. Some people like to make a rope to chain splice on the swivel, which is fine, but I like to splice my lines around a thimble and then shackle them to the swivel. Not only does this reduce chafe, but a couple of 3 meter lengths of thick nylon line spliced onto thimbles are insanely useful things to have on board anyway (Fig 36). If you don't have a bowsprit, you can use a single (thick!) nylon rode, but I prefer two regardless – one on the port bow cleat and one on the starboard – because I am a 'belt and braces' type of fella who values good sleep.

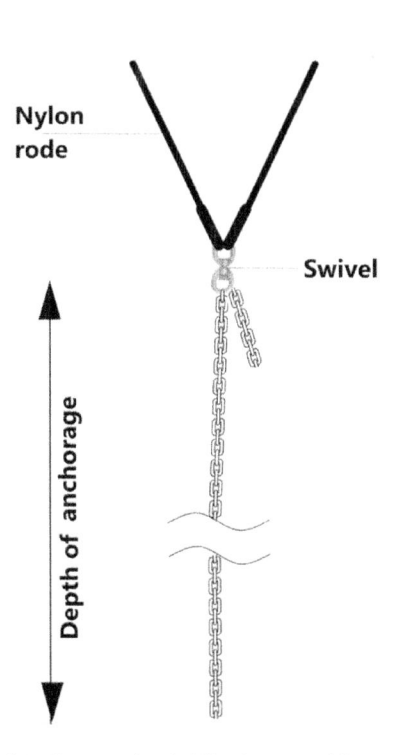

Figure 35: The mooring bridle. Prepare this before you enter the anchorage. You do not need to cut the chain to length, simply shackle it off at the correct depth for the anchorage at high tide and leave the tail hanging or cable tie it to the main chain.

271

Figure 36: Splicing directly to the swivel is okay, but I like to make an eye splice on a thimble like the one above and then shackle it to the swivel. If you don't know how to splice 3 strand nylon, then it's off to internet land for you! Learning this essential skill would make a good project and is something you can do on YouTube that is more practical than watching yet another episode of Sv La Vagabond.

Whatever system you use, you should end up with something like Fig 35.

Now, put all that bananas to one side for a moment and let's approach our chosen spot.

Anchor as normal and let out every scrap of your of main anchor rode.

Once you are happy that your bow anchor is dug in, launch your second anchor off the stern and tighten it up by winching in your excess bow rode whilst allowing your stern rode to feed out until you are more or less between the anchors (Fig37)[60]

Now, making sure that a cleat is taking the load of your anchor chains (and not you!) join the tails of the two chains together with a shackle (Fig 38).

---

[60] You can also anchor normally and then row a stern anchor out in the dinghy, but it is a bit more mucking about. Also if you have one of those nasty inflatables, you run the risk of puncturing one of its chubby love-handles with your anchor and rode.

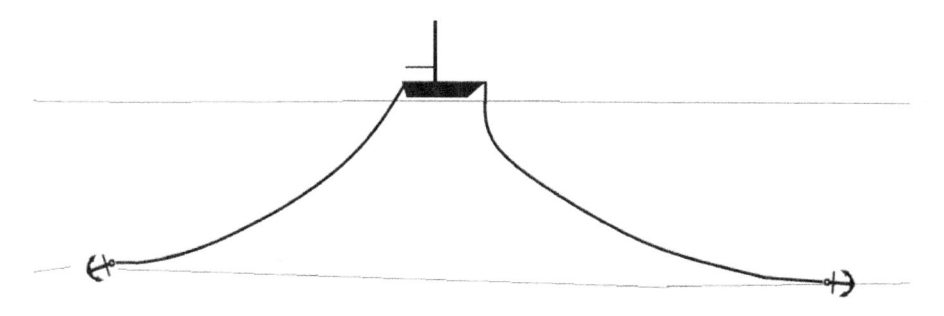

Figure 37: Hanging between to anchors

Figure 38: Shackle the two rodes together. Make sure that the bow and stern anchor rodes are secured on a cleat before you disconnect the bitter ends from the boat unless you want to re-create the feeling of the medieval rack or need extra-long arms to light your really curly pipe.

But before you uncleat the (now shackled) chains and launch the whole lot over the side, let's go grab the mooring bridle we made earlier in Fig 35. Connect your two x 3 meter nylon rodes to the port and starboard bow cleats and shackle the other end to the middle (more or less) of the newly joined anchor rodes.

TIP: Chose a link a little distance from the first shackle (the one you used to join the anchor rodes) to spread the load and avoid confusion as shown in Fig 34.

Drop the whole lot over the side and voila - you are now safely Bahamian moored without ever being out of control or having to rely upon muscle power.

All you need to do now is wait until the highest tide and snug (or loosen) the nylon rodes to make a perfect fit.

The advantages of this system are:

- Whenever the tide changes or the wind swings you the other way, the anchor does not pop out of the ground, thus avoiding the moment of greatest vulnerability.
- The angle described by the anchor rodes is smaller which simulates a rode of greater length to provide better holding.
- The swinging circle is greatly reduced.
- The swivel up by the bow ensures that the whole system doesn't twist up like a cat's cradle every time the boat turns to face the changing tide.
- The length (or lengths) of nylon are quite elastic and act like a snubber to reduce shock loading. The dual rode has built-in redundancy (which is why I like it).

Now you need to find somebody to keep an eye on your pride and joy while you goof off snowboarding in the desert or moshing at the Jimmy Buffet concert.

Making nautical mates

The good news is that making friends as a nautical nomad is easy. Because our friendships tend to be temporary, most cruising sailors are accustomed to creating close bonds rather quickly. All but the most misanthropic sailors (they are rare, but they do exist) are fairly accustomed to striking up good friendships in less time than their land-based counterparts. So once you have been somewhere for a while (and assuming you are not a total arse) you will have made some good friends and it is absolutely fine to ask them to keep an eye on your boat, check your lines for chafe, etc., while she is at anchor or on a mooring. Remember though that when somebody asks the same from you, the answer is always, "yes". This will keep your credit nicely topped up in the Sailors' Bank of Karma. (The Sailors' Bank of Karma is not a

Calypso II lies to her bridle which is shackled to a swivel, connected to a Bahamian mooring. Back in the day, I would use floating polypropylene line. I no longer do this as polypropylene may be cheap to buy, but has less UV resistance than Ed Sheeran. Please note the chafe guards on the bridle as it enters the fairleads.

vague, spiritual idea. Your name will quickly circulate if you never help anyone else).

Attitude to the rescue (again).

Of course, with the right attitude, this gets even easier. For example, if you are a couple, it might pay to have a vacation at different times – a little break from one another is healthy for a relationship. This removes the need to rely on a third party. Nor will you need marinas or mooring systems. However, if you are a single-hander or can't stand to be parted from your squeeze, I would suggest the following: Instead of deciding you simply *must* have a break and then looking for somewhere to leave your boat, everything gets much easier if you abandon the immediate gratification model in favour of one more in tune with reality and opportunity. For example: On your sailing journey you will naturally find yourself in great places to leave your boat. When you find yourself in such a place, and have made some friends in the normal course of your watery wanderings, let that situation trigger the thought that *this* would be a good time to have a break – rather than waiting until our weird minds decide they feel like a break and then running around like headless chickens trying to get everything together and desperately attempting to make friends.

So, when you feel like you might be coming up for a break, don't wait until crisis point. Make that mooring bridle, be patient and the right anchorage and people will show up soon enough. Or just come and find me when I am anchored somewhere secure and I will be more than happy to keep an eye on your boat – but only if you have a copy of both my books aboard. Now *there*'s a challenge! Consider the gauntlet officially thrown. ☺

CHAPTER EIGHTEEN

Staying Solo: The Joys of Single-handing
(Sisters are doin' it for themselves)

I have sailed with a partner and I have sailed with a crew and I have sailed single-handed. All have their benefits, but despite being a popular thing to claim, I certainly do not find them equal. In fact, I would say that there is a very definite hierarchy as far as happiness is concerned, and it is probably not what you think it is.

As you may have guessed, before any rational look at single-handing can be attempted, there is a little 'getting real' to do.

This comes mainly in the form of not letting images of perfection squat the spaces in our minds where reality ought to be not just living, but well ensconced on the couch and flicking through the channels. As previously discussed, chucking out the often media-based ideas of what should be happening and replacing them with a healthy dose of reality can help you not just keep your expectations in check, but avoid the inevitable disappointment that descends when your reality is nothing like that portrayed by the magazines or the pretty young trust-funders on YouTube.[61]

Living this dream is a wonderful experience, but it is nothing like the marketing image of gleaming white plastic gliding over a flat sea, while a

---

[61] I have nothing against the YouTube vloggers, but just bear in mind that many of the most popular sites sell the rich dream, not the budget reality. I highly recommend the YouTube site "wind hippy" for a good dose of sea-gypsy reality.

chic and strangely saucy (though not overly young – these people know their market!) French woman relaxes in white jeans and a Breton shirt (cashmere sweater tossed casually over the shoulders) on the forward deck drinking a glass of chilled Chardonnay. Perhaps there really is "always something special aboard a Beneteau" as their advertising claims, but the barnacles will outnumber her 1000 to 1. In short, it is certainly not necessary to be in a relationship to enjoy this lifestyle, despite how many images seem to imply it.

In fact, while having a partner can be a great way to enjoy this life, it can also be the thing that ruins it. I will talk about romance on board later on, but first let me share with you some things I have noticed about happy nomads: They all seem fairly satisfied, but some seem happier than others. Generally, I have found those in good relationships are the most content, with single-handers either equal or a very close second. Those in bad relationships (or in relationships with somebody who is less than 100% committed to the lifestyle) are significantly less content. In fact, I would say that league table of contentment looks a bit like this:

Nautical nomads in order of general contentment.

- Sailing with the right partner is in first place, but joint first or a very close second is...
- Single-handing, picking up contributing crew as needed/wanted.
- Sailing with Darth Vader as crew, recurring haemorrhoids, living off uncooked birds and listening to Coldplay B-sides on permanent loop.
- Sailing with the wrong partner or a partner that is not fully committed to the lifestyle.

So, if you are solo and think you would rather have a partner, go for it! But never believe the hype to the point that you actually feel you *need* a partner to enjoy this life. Not only is it categorically untrue, but if you adopt this erroneous belief, you run the risk of creating a living hell with the wrong one. I am happy if you have a nice squeeze, but whatever your gender, you simply don't need a partner to enjoy this lifestyle. Glad we cleared that up.

Even if you are in a relationship, you should still read this chapter because being able to single-hand your boat is also an important skill for couples. When your partner is off watch, this is essentially what you will be doing anyway, if your squeeze stands any chance of getting a little uninterrupted shut-eye. It is also very confidence-building to know that if your partner is incapacitated, or just in a huff again (because you simply had to take *someone* and made the wrong choice) that you can sail, dock and navigate your little floating domestic hell-hole by yourself.

A single hander's mind

Sorry to sound like a stuck record, but attitude is, as always, the secret. The techniques we will get to in a moment, but attitude of mind is still the most important single-handing technique of all. The two most important attitudinal attributes I have noticed in happy single-handers (including myself) are foresight and capacity for drill.

Foresight

The last thing you need as a single-hander (particularly in your early days when you have less confidence and might be feeling your nerves a bit) is to be blindsided by something unexpected. Single-handed journeys are easy when everything goes as planned! Of course, sailing being what it is, there will always be surprises, but as a single-hander it will take longer to deal with them because you cannot drag the bleary-eyed, off-watch partner out on deck in his tartan pyjamas to give you a hand. The best way to avoid being blind-sided is to try and think ahead to predict what might occur and do something about it before you leave. This will keep surprises to a minimum, as big problems can easily be the result of a lot of little problems all holding hands.

In terms of boat preparation, this can mean identifying where you need to put handholds, practicing moving around the deck whilst clipped on and generally performing all those tasks that you have normally relied on your crew to assist you with.

Every boat is different and you will have to mentally imagine all the likely tasks she may present you with at sea and try to use your foresight to predict what is going to be problematic in advance. But pay special attention to reefing and the poling arrangements for headsails as they can create a few surprises for the new solo sailor or the sailor accustomed to having crew.

It will of course pay to be so on top of your boat maintenance that you never have equipment failures, but that is not possible. One habit that can certainly move you at least a little closer to that impossible dream (and something I have finally disciplined myself to do since returning to single-handing) is the immediate fitting of spare parts.

There is a tendency amongst sailors (including myself) to buy a spare part, stow it away and immediately start to bask in the warm, fuzzy smugness of being well prepared. While this is better than not having the spare part at all, it is still not ideal and here's why:

When you have crew and your impellor splits into pieces whilst motoring in a busy channel, you can raise some sail, hand the helm over to your squeeze and dive below with a smug look on your face to fit the spare part you so cunningly stowed away for such an emergency. All well and good.

This is usually the moment you find out that you have been supplied with the wrong part and now you have to re-think your strategy. Not the end of the world, but it is a whole different bucket of clams doing this on your own, where the need to steer/keep a lookout and the need to stick your head in the bilge tend to compromise one another. Cue the stress levels.

So, what I have disciplined myself to do (and I strongly recommend this to all single-handers) is whatever spare part I buy, I fit it immediately (whilst at anchor or at the dock) and keep the existing part as the spare. This has six real-world advantages:

- You immediately know if you have been given the right part and banish any future nasty surprises.
- If the part is wrong, then you can return it for an exchange or refund while you are still in the neighbourhood where you bought it.
- Any fitting disasters (seized nuts, broken studs, etc.) can be dealt with in a safe, calm environment with your favourite music on and a glass of rum on the go.

- You can identify any other fitting problems at that time too such as the need for special tools or human assistance.
- Best of all, should an emergency occur in the future, you absolutely know for sure that the spare part you have taken out, is the right one, is 100% fit for purpose and that you know how to fit it.
- You also reduce the likelihood of such emergencies because the new spare you have fitted will be less prone to failure than the older part that it replaces.

There is no down-side to developing this habit, yet somehow, on the occasions when I have been sailing with partners, I found it very difficult to discipline myself to do this. However, you only need a couple of scary and embarrassing 'doofus' moments as a single-hander to force you to get real and start accepting that, although it takes a little discipline, fitting spares as you get them and stowing the existing part is hugely preferential to swearing like a celebrity chef at the wrong part while being rolled around like seaweed in a sushi bar and trying not to get run down in a busy channel.

Once you have used up all your foresight, fitted all your spare parts and done everything you can to avoid future surprises to the point your head is hurting, this would be a good time to remember that as a single-hander you have your own exclusive extra problem to manage.

Fatigue.
However much you have tried to predict and simplify every scenario (and it may all look straight forward now standing on your deck in the

harbour), they will look like as confusing as a Rubik's cube to a Phys Ed teacher after a few days of sleep deprivation.

To that end, it pays to make the day-to-day operations and the emergency procedures of the boat as close to second nature as possible. And that means only one thing.

Drill.

Most day-to-day operations on your wee boat should be (and probably already are) known to you by now. However, we tend to forget how much we rely on a well-rested brain to make good decisions and if you are preparing for your first ever solo sail, you need to perform all the basic operations on a calm day a hundred times. Do them at night too, with a head torch on, until you can perform them without thinking (or sinking). If you ask your tired brain to problem-solve, you run the risk of a mutiny, as one of the first casualties of fatigue is the ability (and desire) to tackle complicated problems. It is far easier to get your tired mind to perform a routine task and this is why it is increasingly important for the single-hander to make everything as automatic and uncomplicated as possible.

Deserving of special attention here is your reefing protocol as even well-rested crew can often be slow to order a reef because it can be tiresome if the process is difficult or conditions are worsening (which of course, they will be). What looks tiresome to a well-rested crew can look truly daunting to a fatigued mind and can often encourage the tired sailor to leave the boat's sail trim right on the edge of vulnerable – somewhere you really don't want to be as a single hander! (Can you see all the little problems starting to hold hands?).

My technique to avoid this is quite simple. I use a philosophy of 'non-negotiation'.

The moment the thought of a reef comes into mind, I reef. I absolutely refuse to indulge in wishful thinking and the inevitable self-negotiation that it spawns, such as:

> "It's probably only a gust" or,
> "That squall is probably going to miss me"

If you think you might need a reef, then reef. And do it now. It is that simple.

You might be able to push it with a crew, but as a single hander, do not negotiate with yourself. Drill this into your head.[62]

Speaking of drill, many single-handers lead all their lines aft so they can perform their sail operations from the relative safety of the cockpit. There is a lot to be said for this, not just from a safety point of view, but from a drill point of view. Accident and disaster studies around the world clearly show that if a drill is easy to follow, it is more *likely* to be followed by those without military training (military training is all about applying complex drill under pressure and they are much better at it than us civilians). If your reefing procedure can

---

[62] I am not sure I should tell you this because it sounds a bit nuts, but I call the part of my brain that tries to be lazy and negotiate not reefing, my 'terrorist'. It is always there telling my tired mind that it will be okay not to reef, not to check my lines, to sleep another hour, not plot my position on paper or any of the other practices of good seamanship that make a real sailor. When it rears its ugly head at sea, I slap it down with the phrase, "Sorry, this captain does not negotiate with terrorists" and get on with what I know I should be doing. This helps me enormously. (See, I told you it sounds nuts).

be followed easily from the relative comfort of your cockpit, it will be much more likely that you will be able to follow my advice of 'not negotiating with yourself'.

However, there are some drawbacks to this approach too. If you can do everything from the comfort of your cockpit, there is a danger that you will start to lose your ability to move around on deck. I know several sailors who consider the deck as some kind of minefield to be avoided and treat it as if only instant death awaits those foolhardy enough to venture there.

I don't have all my lines led aft so I have to go to the mast to perform most tasks - and I like it this way because when my bow anchor looks loose or my dinghy lashings are coming undone, I am already well versed in the art of moving around on deck (albeit on all fours sometimes – I am not proud!) and the prospect of shimmying forward like a slug in a life jacket holds no particular fear for me. Often while I am out there securing the dinghy I notice something else that needs a stitch in time to prevent a larger problem somewhere down the line.

Perhaps the best compromise would be to have all the lines led aft and then also make a complete circuit of the deck a few times a day to stay current and check for problems, but do you have the discipline to do it? Only you can answer that.

In either case, if reefing is quick, easy and automatic, a well disciplined single-hander will be able to follow his own, pre-drilled method in a timely and seamanlike manner – even when sleep deprived and a bit nervous. Having a well-drilled standard operating procedure (SOP) saves a lot of brain power at the exact moment it is in very short supply.

Reefing is not the only system that needs its own SOP. Just about everything you do regularly on the boat needs to have the deliberation and thought rinsed out of it and replaced with drill. But start with reefing as it is such a largely overlooked safety issue (although whoever said, "there is never too much wind, just too much sail" has been extremely fortunate with weather and has never had my Goan fish curry).

Setting the pole for downwind sailing often catches single-handers out too, but as this is not a safety feature (plenty of sailors are happy to bear off a bit and just sail a slightly longer route without the pole) it can be left until you have mastered reefing, launching your life raft, making emergency calls, locating bungs for broken through-hulls, etc. But be warned: setting the pole needs a good, well-drilled SOP to ensure that you are safe throughout the whole process and not weaving around on deck like a drunk tight-rope walker).

Once you have a fairly good arsenal of SOPs, you can deal with more complex problems as they arise because what little sense your sleep-deprived brain has left is not being over-loaded with the need to re-invent the wheel every time the wind picks up or the jib needs poling out.

Two very important issues for single-handers

You may not have thought it possible that I could become more vocal on the importance of having a boat that can heave-to properly, but you would be wrong. I am not sure what language I can use to convey how important it is for a single-hander to have a boat that heaves-to well. Having already used the word, 'essential' I have already shot my bolt a bit as, 'more essential' makes very little sense. But you get the point.

Something that seems to surprise many people is the relentless nature of the sea. The sea is totally indifferent to how exhausted we are or how many of our little problems have all started holding hands. The waves will just keep on coming – hour after hour, day after day. That can be quite mentally demanding. Even if you get beaten up by a gang of ruthless thugs, they will eventually grow tired of kicking you once your body has gone limp and you can no longer fight back. No such mercy from the sea! She will keep on pounding you with total indifference and your only safety valve as a single-hander is having a boat that heaves-to well. I won't bang on any more about this (you can re-read chapter twelve again for more info on heaving-to) but you get the point.

The other issue I wanted to bring up for the single-hander, is parking. Docking your longer-keeled boat with crew is fairly straight forward once you have mastered the techniques in chapter three, but how do you do it when you are on your own? You will be pleased to know there is a fairly simple technique that works on most boats, but to understand it, we have to briefly get technical for a minute and talk about something called the Centre of Lateral Resistance (CLR).

Have a look at Fig 39 below. As you can see, when pushing the pencil from the left, the left swings out. When pushed from the right, the right swings out. When pushed from somewhere around the centre, the pencil moves straight back. This point is called the Centre of

Lateral Resistance. For symmetrical objects, this is usually the actual centre, but for this pencil the CLR is slightly to the right (because it has an eraser at the end and is therefore not symmetrical).

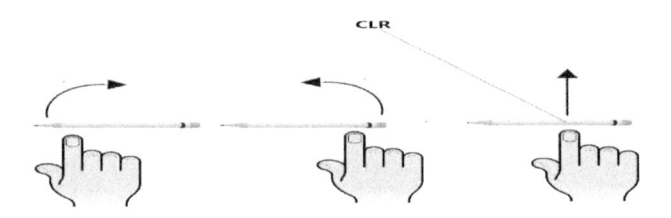

Figure 39: Determining the Centre of Lateral Resistance

Your boat is certainly not symmetrical, so you cannot assume the CLR is in the middle and must find this point is by experiment. You can do this easily at the dock on a calm day by slackening the lines a bit, taking a guess and pushing the side of your boat. If the bow swings out, you need to try again further back. If the stern swings out, then try further forward. Eventually you will find the point where the bow and the stern move evenly away from the dock. This is your CLR. Mark it on both sides of the boat.[63]

So now we know where the CLR is, we will need to grab some lines and set up our boat as in Fig 40:

From your bow cleat, set up a line back to where you have marked your CLR and tie a bowline (a). From your furthest aft winch in the

---

[63] This is another super-power of the longer keeled boat. The longer keel provides quite a generous CLR, so if you get it slightly wrong, it will be more forgiving. On a thin fin boat, the CLR is far smaller, more critical and can be really easy to mess up. Just sayin'.

cockpit, pass another line through the bowline (a) and tie another bowline in that (b). Keep it nice and slack and accessible as you approach the dock because you will have to drop this over a cleat ashore (this is fairly easy to do from a small boat. If you have insisted on buying a large one, then you might need a boat hook).

As you approach the dock, drop bowline (b) over a cleat in the centre of the dock. Now, start winching. As you are applying force from your CLR, your boat will be drawn flat to the dock. Produce curly pipe.

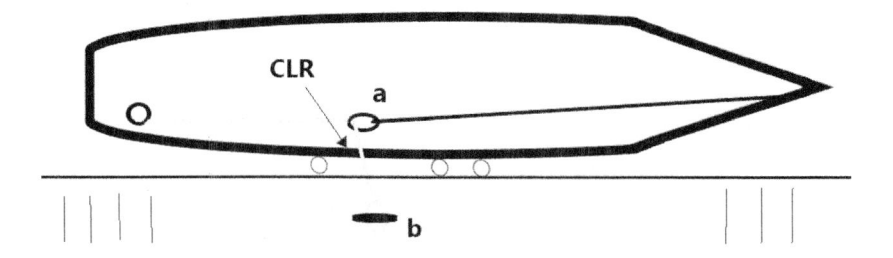

Figure 40: Shows the boat happily secured to a cleat from a point at its CLR. If you set this up right, she will lie quietly. If the bow is swinging out, then move your CLR forward. If the stern is swinging out.... well, you get it. Once you have your CLR sorted, consider making a permanent pennant with a snatch block for line (a), as this works even better and saves a lot of faffing around. Also consider tying a lariat instead of a bowline for (b) as that will tighten around the cleat as you winch the line in.

Obviously, it pays to practice this on an empty dock, but it has consistently worked for me on three different boats. I also prepare a separate bow and stern line and lead those amidships too so that, once the boat is secured in the manner described, I can step off, lift the lines off the deck and quickly secure the bow and stern on their own lines whilst affecting an air of faux nonchalance – after all, you never know when a gust or a surge is going to scupper your plans and, having already lit your curly pipe, you don't then want to be caught celebrating early.

Now, all of the above single-handing techniques become that much easier if you can get good rest. Your ability to function (and both your confidence and morale) will increase proportionally if you are well rested, so let us have a peek at how the single-hander can get a bit of kip.

Getting rest.
The regulations governing collision avoidance at sea (COLREGS) state that all vessels must keep a human watch 24 hours a day, thereby pretty much guaranteeing that single-handed sailors are breaking maritime law (you certainly won't be able to get insurance for any passages over 24 hours as a single-hander). Yet strangely, nobody ever seems to get prosecuted for this - probably due to the legal difficulty of proving somebody was asleep at any particular time without witnesses.

Nevertheless, you will have to get used to cat-napping if you stand any chance of keeping a half-way decent watch. The best time to become accustomed to this is at anchor. When you have a lot of work to do on the boat or on the computer, instead of sleeping your usual hours, catnap for 23 minutes at a time. Do this for a couple of days, catnapping when you feel tired. You may feel a bit spacey, at first, but you will soon get used to it and it will give you some valuable insight into how the brain reacts to this odd sleep pattern. It is such a great skill to have that I now use it anytime I have a lot of work to do, so it is also transferrable. I almost prefer it now.

Obviously, I cannot encourage people to break the law in print, but I can tell you that I know a couple of single-handers that sleep a full eight hours when offshore and away from the shipping lanes. One heaves-to (thereby reducing the likelihood of colliding with debris or whales) while the other slows down a bit, but keeps going.

The former obviously has the advantage of giving you a better sleep and I have done it myself when I was injured forty miles off Wallis and Futuna. The latter takes a bit of nerve and is far riskier. It would result (for me anyway) in a very troubled sleep and that would rather defeat the object. Learn the art of the 23 minute power-nap and you never have to take that kind of risk.

In a moment, I will talk about some little electronic gadgets that can help you (with the usual caveats you will have come to expect by now). But first I think I should explain why I consider 23 minutes as a good length for a power nap:

Somewhere, over the rainbow

To calculate how far away the horizon is, is simple. All you need to know is how high your eyes are above sea level. So if you are six feet tall and standing on the deck of *Calypso II* (which has a freeboard of about 4.2 feet) then your eye level is about 10 feet above sea level. Now, all you have to do is plug that number into the following formula and you will know how far the horizon is:

**Distance to the horizon in nautical miles =
1.17 times the square root of the height of your eye (in feet).**

This gives you: 1.17 x 3.162

= 3.7 miles[64]

3.7 miles! I bet that surprised a few people. So a ship travelling at about 15 knots, can be on you in 15 minutes from being hidden over the horizon. Fortunately, this is only half the story. The typical bulk carrier is about 100 feet high, so her bridge (or steaming light) will be seen while the hull of the ship is still hidden below the horizon. How do we work out what difference that makes? Another easy sum:

You simply do the same calculation again for the height of the ship and add the two results together.

However, as many commercial vessels are not as high as container ships, let's take a more conservative figure of 60 feet, just to be safe. So, assuming the ship's bridge or steaming light is 60 feet above sea level:

The distance from which you will see her = 1.17 x square root of 60 plus the total of the previous sum.

1.17 x 7.75 = 9.07 Nautical Miles

+ 3.7 (from out previous calculation)

= 12.77 Nautical Miles.

---

[64] If you don't know how to find the square root of ten, just press the √ button on your calculator or cheat and Google it.

So, from seeing a clear horizon all round, a bulk carrier travelling at 15 knots can be on you in just over 51 minutes if you are standing still.

But what if you are not standing still, but moving towards the ship at 5 knots? Then the total collision speed is 20 knots. So, if you are sailing towards it, the ship can be on you from a clear horizon in a shade over 38 minutes.

Power naps of 23 minutes give me 15 minutes to take evasive action if the worst comes to the worst and that is why I choose that particular time frame.

Coincidentally, it also happens to be the length of an episode of *The Big Bang Theory* if I can't sleep.[65]

Of course, I sometimes don't stick to that if in open waters, but it pays to know what the likely worst-case scenario is so you know by how much you are pushing the envelope.

TIP: Get yourself a cheap mechanical kitchen timer. Setting an electronic alarm is too prone to human error when tired, plus you don't really want to fully wake yourself up. To get the most out of short power naps you need to be able to fall asleep quickly again. In good weather, I like to take my naps on the cockpit sole. This means that I don't have to climb out of bed and fully wake myself up. The whole process looks like this:

---

[65] Some container ships regularly steam at 20 knots, so 23 minute cat naps may sometimes be too long if you suspect you are in an area of heavier traffic. The new Maersk container ship is said to have a top speed of nearly 30 knots. However, to get a bulk carrier to go twice as fast, uses eight times as much fuel, so most cargo ships tend to keep their speed down. Having said that, if you are in a shipping lane, nothing less than 100% awareness is acceptable until you can exit it again.

- Alarm goes off.
- Stand up
- Scan horizon
- Glance at compass
- Twist alarm
- Back to sleep

This way I can avoid the much riskier practice of sparking out for 8 hours and letting the devil do his worst.

Now we have dealt with the good seamanship practices, let's talk about the gadgets.

Automatic identification system (AIS)

As with all electronic devices, they should only be considered aids to, not replacements for, good seamanship. The AIS transceiver is a wee gadget that emits a signal from your boat showing your details, heading, speed and position, and receives the same signal from other boats. AIS can provide early warning of ships in your path (and warn other ships of your presence), but it only sees other ships that are broadcasting an AIS signal. It does not see ships without AIS, fishing boats that are running blind (that have their AIS switched off so as not to alert their competitors as to where the good fish are) whales, reefs, squalls or land. AIS *does* give you the name of the vessels it detects, which may sound immaterial, but if you have the name of a vessel and call them on the radio, they are far more likely to respond. Large ships seldom respond to calls that begin, "large vessel heading east off my starboard bow, this is *Calypso"* which is your only option if you don't have her name. Calling by name usually produces a response.You can then clarify that that they have seen you and make clear their intentions.

A further advantage of AIS in these strange times is that some countries allow you to take time at sea against quarantine time. For example, on my recent passage to Australia from Fiji, I was only required to quarantine for one day of the statutory fourteen as the coast guard could see from my AIS signal that I had been at sea for 13 days continuously and had not stopped anywhere.

The cost of these little units has fallen dramatically over the last few years and can be had for the price of a really good night out, which makes them almost a no-brainer for the single-hander (particularly if heading to South East Asia where they are compulsory in many countries).

Watchmate

Watchmate is a function of the radar. Few small boats have the reserve electricity at night to keep the radar on permanently. Watchmate is a little program installed on many radars (sometimes under a different proprietary name) that you can program so that the radar switches itself on every 23 minutes (or whatever) and has a look around. If it sees nothing, it switches itself off. If it sees something, it sets off an alarm so you can leap out of bed, smack your head on the dodger, run in nine directions at once, fall down, get up again and eventually take evasive action. Radar sees most boats, big squalls and land that is significantly above sea level (i.e., not reefs that are awash or low-lying atolls) so it can be very useful.

Now, if all that sounds tiresome and you are beginning to think that single-handing sounds as much fun as being slapped with a mackerel whilst undergoing modest amounts of dental torture, then I must offer my apologies. It is something of the nature of a book like this to dwell on the negatives in order to improve safety, but that does not mean that single-handing is all struggle and no rewards.

In fact, the opposite is true.

For me, there is nothing quite like being alone at sea. I enjoy my own company and the satisfaction of self-sufficiency. I also enjoy not having to worry about anybody else.

When I have crew and the weather gets up, I can feel their nerves and their worries. Their sea-sickness is a bit of a bore too. Quite often I end up single-handing *and* dealing with sick/frightened people at the same time, which makes simply 'single-handing' much the easier and more enjoyable option as it is less trouble and does not spoil my equanimity with the need to be falsely empathetic towards people who think a little seasickness is a reason not to stand their watch.

Ahhh, the pure joy of solitude and the sound of the water gurgling against the hull under a night full of stars as your gallant little ship points her nose towards another new place full of promise, new friends, experiences, tastes and smells! I wonder what this landfall will bring? What great nights out, interesting foods? Will there be any old friends to catch up with or romances to be re-kindled? I hope Roger and Pam on *SV Serenity* are there – I could really use some of his home brewed craft beer and a decent game of chess. Whatever happens, I will have my lovely, cosy, wee home to come back to at the end of the day – my books, instruments, music, movies and imaginary curly pipe. I really must get a ship's cat.

How marvellous it is to sit in your snug, safe cockpit musing about the next great adventure without even the pressure of concepts like, 'bedtime' having the remotest effect on your inner calendar, or the dictates or needs of others ordering your actions even in the tiniest way, while little phosphorescent waves slip past your quarters and whatever consciousness not consumed by this dream is lightly focussed on the magical interplay of wind, canvas and water. What joy indeed! Well worth a bit of drill and foresight - and possibly the pinnacle of the sailing experience.

Yet every now and then we all need a bit of human contact – whether it is for help on a particularly difficult passage or just that your joy of being alone (awesome!) has started to drift into the murkier waters of loneliness (not good). So let us now have a quick look at a good way to sort the pearls from the weevils and get some good, honest and hearty shipmates.

CHAPTER NINETEEN

Staying Social and Finding Good Crew

"Which is more important" asked Big Panda, *"the journey or the destination"?*

"The company" said Tiny Dragon

Big Panda and Tiny Dragon
by James Norbury

Pretty much everybody believes these three things about themselves:

1. They are good drivers.
2. They are good in bed.
3. They are good judges of character.

Obviously this can't be true for everybody as there is no shortage of terrible drivers or selfish lovers, and dishonest salesmen make great money virtually everywhere that sells teeth whitener. The most common of these misconceptions (and the one we need to focus on here) is the idea that you are a good judge of character.

You are not.

Research shows that practically nobody is. There are literally mountains of evidence that show that we humans are bloody awful at judging character and that we can be easily fooled by even the most modestly talented of charlatans or twinkly-eyed frauds. However, as with all self-knowledge, once you know this and learn to distrust your own judgement, you can put yourself in a position of enormous strength. Just as the person who (rightly) mistrusts his own sense of direction is likely to check the chart more thoroughly and therefore become a better navigator, the person who accepts that we are all shocking judges of character is more likely to use extra measures to decide with whom they want to lock themselves in a small boat, sprinkle with stress, shake well, stand back and observe.

Perhaps the biggest own-goal you can score by trusting your largely fictional, awesome powers of character judgement, is hubris. Confident that you have picked the perfect crew, you let down your guard and become 'matey' with your ideal choices, when you should be keeping a little bit of distance and establishing yourself as Captain, not friend. This is a shame because, while experienced crew are comparatively difficult to find (without payment), there are literally thousands of people who, if treated with a little friendly discipline at first, can be moulded into first class crew and excellent company.

If you are prepared to put in a bit of patient, but firm, training, the world is full of eager travellers looking for adventure with their own unique story to tell, who would make perfectly good watch-keepers and sailing buddies. This type of potentially good crew are easier to find than Wally in the Arctic and can make your sailing life quite wonderful as well as providing a link to sanity for even the most dedicated, salt-encrusted single-hander. But you must have some kind of framework and structure for them to follow if you don't want a boat full of bored crew playing Candy Crush Saga on their phones and complaining about the speed of the internet while the dishes pile up in the sink.

Before I started my peripatetic perambulations of the prodigious puddles of the planet, I worked in the horse business and dealt regularly with volunteer/intern equestrian crew and pretty much the same applies. Whether raising a mainsail or shovelling horseshit, the whole process of dealing with volunteer crew can be made quite pleasant for all parties with a few simple techniques.

Get comfortable single-handing your boat.

If you are on your own and need to find crew every time you want to cast off the dock lines, you will be dependent on those crew and they will sense that and run rings around you. They may never have been to sea before or hold any nautical qualifications, but they will be telling you how to do things within weeks if your reliance on them is obvious.

Your reliance on them will also make you hesitant to leave behind the ones you are suspicious of - despite the fact they may already be displaying signs of problematic behaviour- and that can lead to having a toxic presence onboard, which is way harder than single-handing and will fill your boat with tension and bad atmospherics quicker than a flatulent dog in a diving bell.

On the other hand, if you don't *need* crew, then their purpose changes from 'essential help' to, 'enhancing your life' and you become free to throw anyone out who is not actually contributing to the quality of life aboard, making the whole experience far more agreeable to everyone else and allowing the joy to flood back into your existence and remind you why you chose this lifestyle in the first place. Believe me, the wrong crew can really make you forget.

Learning to be confident single-handing will also have benefits for your chosen crew. The skipper who is lost without help is easily stressed by a less than stellar crew member, as he needs that crew member to perform well. A good single-hander does not require anything from the slightly imperfect crew member (which is most novice backpackers) and can find them a task that is more appropriate to the skills they have.

When I met Jasna, she was backpacking around Australia and her only experience sailing was in dinghies in flat conditions, but as I was already a confident single-hander I was able to make her experience on my boat *Marutji* agreeable enough to court her (although her first day out on the real ocean nearly sent her packing!). So becoming confident sailing your boat on your own is likely to improve your romantic life too, as an un-stressed, confident single-hander is much more likely to be capable of calmly explaining what a crew member is doing wrong (and thereby make that crew member feel comfortable and valued) than the red-faced Captain Bligh in full panic mode because his essential source of help is being a bit of a doofus[66].

Many captains make the mistake of arriving at their port of departure and *then* looking for crew for an ocean passage. This is a mistake. It is much better to pick them up several stops before an ocean crossing

---

[66] I would like to point out that I am not prejudiced against doofuses. I am a doofus myself and some of my best friends are doofuses. I bow to nobody in my need to have seemingly obvious things explained to me several times.

is planned so that you can get an idea of who they are before you are stuck with them. There are endless stories on the internet and around the dock about captains who pick up nice, smiley crew and set off across the Atlantic only to find they have a psychotic bully on board or someone who is so lazy/sea-sick or generally useless that they are a constant burden and would be better replaced with a cheap backscratcher or laminated Beaufort Scale. Even an inoffensive millennial screen-gazer can be annoying if he treats you like Voldemort when you suggest an early departure or acts like you are harassing him every time you ask him to drag himself away from his vlog long enough to perform his duties. (Also, be ready to have his opinion of you immediately disseminated on Instagram with an unflattering picture of your head transposed on to the body of Anthony Hopkins' otherwise amazing portrayal of Captain Bligh).

Really, you are better off single-handing. If you find that you are always making the coffee in the morning, dragging people out of bed (or the other side of the coin, suggesting they get sufficient rest so they can be alert for their watch), constantly reminding them of the safety rules and generally jollying them along, then drop them off at the next port and save yourself the bother. Your boat should be a happy place, full of people who are happy to be doing what they are doing and keen to do it better every day – or it should be a haven of peace for you alone. No compromise.

Let everyone know what to expect

We all like to be liked, but remember that whoever you invite aboard is first and foremost, crew. If you can be friends later, that is a bonus. But it must be a friendship based upon your position as Captain and their position as crew. I have had several crew applicants who have said they are happy to follow orders "only if I respect and understand them". You don't want this person. Boats are not a democracy. Your position as Captain is not negotiable based upon the understanding of somebody who may not have stepped on a boat before or thinks that a boom is something that has a microphone on the end of it. Your relationship is firstly hierarchical and only then if personalities permit, as friends.

I have been crew on many boats and have never had a problem with this. I have been captain on many boats and never had any problem with this, so don't let anybody tell you that it cannot be done.

You are the boss

To establish yourself as Captain is more about being clear and consistent than throwing your weight around like Donald Trump in *The Apprentice* (which often has quite the opposite effect). Clearly state what is expected of your crew and why. Also (kindly) explain what will happen if they do not comply with those expectations. For example:

I run a dry boat on passage - anchor up to anchor down. Things can get weird too quickly at sea without having a drunk crew to deal with as well. If anyone breaks that rule they will be left at the next port, wherever it is. No appeals will be heard, no quarter given. Drink and you are off.

For minor offences like not turning the gas off after use, everybody gets to put a beer on that person's tab (to be consumed at anchor of course) as he has endangered us all equally. Next time they forget, it is two beers, etc. If it gets past that, then a little talk about the dangers of LPG gas on board might accompany said beers.

You will no doubt make up your own rules that suit your type of sailing, but the important thing is to make them clear, talk them through and give everyone a chance to ask questions. Print them out and give everybody a copy so nobody is in doubt or can claim ignorance of the rules. Strangely, if you are crystal clear about the rules, you hardly ever have to enforce them, which suggests that the problem of finding good crew is less the standard of applicants (as is often heard muttered by sailors) than the clarity of the Captain. If you would like a copy of what I give my crew, then drop me a line on sailingcalypso@gmail.com.

In the event that you have a continual law breaker, you need to let him go quickly as they only get worse (this again is where you need to be happy sailing on your own or short-handed, as your rules will have no authority at all if they don't have teeth). Incidentally, some of my best crew have been last minute replacements for unsuitable people I have let go – and I would never have met them if I wasn't not only prepared, but happy, to make the journey alone. If your law-breaker is one of a larger crew, then letting him go will be good for morale as well as sending a strong signal as to the gravity of ignoring the safety rules.

Explain the difference between a crew position and a yacht charter.

Much has been written about the difference between travellers and tourists, with just about every person with a backpack fervently claiming membership to the former category. In reality, most belong to the latter category. The difference between a traveller and a tourist is time. A traveller is on an adventure where the lack of need to be somewhere allows him to be open to new ideas and experiences. A tourist has a schedule. Any person who puts you under pressure to leave at a certain time or visit a certain place because they have a hair appointment or a flight to catch is trying to bend adventure (and weather) to fit their plan, rather than adapt to the adventure and embrace it. In other words, a tourist.

Being poor does not make you a traveller, it just makes you a broke tourist. Being time flexible enough to embrace new opportunities and respond to the world as it is, rather than how you would like it to be, makes you a traveller.

But as most potential crew you meet will be tourists masquerading as travellers, it is best not to ignore them, but learn to deal with them.

I do this financially. I have always run my boats as non-profit entities. All my crew are required to contribute towards some (but by no means all) of the expenses of running a sailboat in order to be part of a working crew. They are expected to work, stand their watches and generally pitch in with the general running and maintenance of a sailboat. At the time of writing, that contribution is US$35 a day which includes tuition, food, water, accommodation, bedding, marina fees, mooring , diesel, harbour fees etc, - basically everything except personal expenses and alcohol. For a pure charter I charge $300 a day per person. If any of my crew do not want to pitch in or do as I ask, I politely offer them the opportunity to change to the charter tariff. That seems to get the message across and make the point I want to make which is this: The cost of being on my boat and learning about the sea gypsy life is $0. The $35 per day is just a contribution towards *some* expenses and they should not be patting themselves on the back because they have discovered the stupidest charter captain in the world, but get a scraper in their hand and clean the barnacles off the prop to justify their position. (NOTE: This is a complete bluff on my part as I am not actually licensed for charter. The law governing the line between contributing crew and paying charter guests is important, with the latter requiring a whole bunch of paperwork and other conditions to be met. This line varies wildly around the world, so check out the bylaws in your area).

Manage expectations

There is a degree of overlap between this subject and the one above. Many new crew think that their life will be gentle day-sailing between one idyllic anchorage and another, sipping cocktails at the end of each day while you entertain them with sea stories or let them stream endless YouTube videos on your expensive internet connection. So, you will need to nip that idea in the bud and the best way to do that is with some kind of schedule.

While you are on passage, the watch schedule will make this easy as it will determine when your crew are on duty and that is easily explained. At anchor though, you will still need a similar schedule or your entire crew will become indolent and mutinous.

So, unless we have a particular trip organised that takes the whole day, my crew need to give at least three hours per day at anchor to the boat. That means sanding, stitching, cooking, varnishing, polishing, scrubbing the decks, cleaning the prop, hull diving, sail cleaning, locker cleaning, dinghy scrubbing, provisioning or any of the millions of things a voyaging boat asks of you. This not only keeps your boat in Bristol condition, but reminds the crew what they are here for and that they haven't simply found a captain who is so out of touch that he doesn't know how much a charter trip costs.

This approach also leads to a happy crew. As the French philosopher Blaise Pascal (he of the famous 'Pascal's Wager') so famously said;

"All of humanity's problems stem from man's inability to sit quietly in a room alone,"

This is certainly true for many backpackers who, while often lacking the motivation to work, will be a lot happier and get a lot more out of their time on board when they do. It is very much a win/win situation for all concerned.

Drugs and alcohol.

To paraphrase the late Bill Hicks, not all drugs are good - some are excellent! Seriously though, whatever your view on drugs, it makes sense to have none on board that you don't know about because, as the master of the vessel, it is you who will take the fall.

Alcohol (although by no means the safest available drug) has the distinct advantage of being legal in most places, so best to stick to that one and let your crew know there is a zero tolerance policy on other drugs. (If I suspect somebody of carrying something they should not, I usually scare them by telling them that the customs people will be bringing a dog onboard before we leave).

Do not include alcohol in your daily charge. While most crew are responsible, there is always one who will try and drink $35 worth of alcohol a day in order to get his 'money's worth'. Instead, stock up with beer and run a non-profit bar. Put a bar book on the fridge and ask everyone to write down whatever they take. When there is no beer left (or someone is leaving the boat) have a look at what you spent and divide that by the *amount written in the book* not the amount you bought. This makes sure that the cost of unrecorded alcohol is shared amongst the group (rather than going directly on your tab) and this sets the tone in the clearest way possible that everybody needs to play their part and that the action of a shirker effects us all. In this case, the only repercussion is a slight rise in the beer price, but the message is there and the group tend to get it and start policing themselves a bit more by having a wary eye for any shirkers in other aspects of their collective duties. This kind of group culture is the secret to building a good team.

Now, if all that sounds a bit impossible or just plain tiresome, fear not. Much of what you hear about bad crew is actually the captain's fault.

If you are a captain, this is not an attack on you, but actually quite a positive thing because if it is our fault, we can do something about it. If the problem was just 'kids today' or 'you just can't get the crew these days' (as I often hear bandied about the docks) there would be nothing we could do about it at all. So I am pleased to say that there is a great deal we can do it about it and most people can have happy, disciplined and active crew if they follow the guidelines above.

Another word about the best crew

Never forget that the best, most reliable, economical, crew you can ever have is a mechanical wind vane self-steering system for all the reasons given in *Get Real, Get Gone*. A good windvane will serve you tirelessly and accurately without answering back, consuming resources or putting hip-hop on your sound system.

Finally, I would like to warn new captains: If you pick up an attractive crew of your preferred gender and find yourself short of breath and not being able to think straight, check your gas fittings. Gas poisoning and being in love have identical symptoms, so test all your connections before you decide to hand over the keys to your soul to somebody whose main motivation is to impress the folks back home or pad out their Instagram profile on your dime.

CHAPTER TWENTY

Not Staying Gone: Exit strategies

The only way to make a million out of a yacht is to start with two million and work your way down.

Me.
(Adapted from the Aga Kahn's comments on horses).

One of the blessings of the surprise success of my first book is that I get to vicariously accompany many other people on their own epic journey to nautical nomadhood. In the six years since publication, thousands of people have contacted me to say 'hi' or to ask for advice. Hundreds of those have made the jump and are loving it.

But not all.

Something I did not previously address is the best way to return to a shore-based life if you decide the sea is not for you, or once you have had enough of watery wandering and feel other adventures are calling you.

If your life takes an unpredicted turn, if your partner becomes pregnant with octuplets, or you decide that life as a sea gypsy is simply not your cup of tea/bowl of seaweed/ basket of weevils/ the pearl farm you thought it might be, or if you simply fancy a crack at another way of enjoying this short free-fall, then you will need to sell your boat and realise some cash.[67]

Again, this is where you will not regret buying a small, simple sea boat as she will be fairly easy to sell without taking too much of a hit compared to a brand new yoghurt pot with all the bleepy things.

Exiting with your wallet intact

Many richer sailors will buy the boat they want brand new and specify everything down to the seat covers. They will then go on to lavish attention and money on her until she is 'just so'. Like buying a new car, this owner is going to take a massive hit when she sells as the depreciation curve is steepest in the first few years. As so many people do this and subsequently publish their story in books and media sites, it can often seem the only way to go and is partly responsible for the myth that sailing is only for the wealthy. If you are so financially blessed that losing significant chunks of capital every few years makes no difference in your life, I am happy for you, but my books concern themselves with the less financially fortunate. For us, we must try and preserve as much of our little nest-egg as possible for the next chapter in our lives.

Even if you have followed the advice laid out in the last book and bought the right boat at the right price, it is nearly impossible to

---

[67] No need to feel bad if it is not for you. There are no more bragging rights in 'years aboard' than there is in 'miles under the keel'. We are here for a good time, not necessarily a long time.

make money when you sell your boat, as the quote at the beginning of the chapter implies. This is mainly because the value of your improvements are only ever partially reflected in the value of the boat. For example, if your boat is worth $30k and you spend 12k and a whole bunch of your time fitting a new diesel, your boat will probably now be worth 38k and you will have lost some money and a lot of time. Almost everything you buy for your boat has that element of 'over capitalization' to it, so the best we can realistically hope for is getting our money back or not losing too much. There are, however, a few steps you can take and a few things you can buy that will increase the value of your boat significantly without costing too much.

The most cost effective improvement you can make to your boat.

Having just said that whatever you add to your boat will raise its value less than the cost of the addition, there is one huge exception to this. These things:

Clean is the new seaworthy

Presentation is absolutely everything. Cleaning products and elbow grease will give you the best bang for your buck in relation to the sale price of your boat than any other investment. Human nature being what it is, means that it will always

312

be easier to sell a Rolls Royce with a Ford engine than a Ford with a Rolls Royce engine. We humans are such magpies and no matter how well your boat is set up or how seaworthy she is, it is the gleaming clean one that will fetch the best price.

Remove the stuff that does not work

Remember that if you come to a deal with someone it will normally be 'subject to survey and test sail' (see chapter eight). Hopefully you will get a super-keen buyer who loves your well-maintained, gleaming boat and is not going to sweat the small stuff at the survey, but that is not always the case. Some buyers use the survey just to drive the price down because they are short of money - and that is okay. You can't blame somebody for trying to get the best deal they can, that is just good capitalism. However, if you have something on your boat that is not working, then either fix it (if it can be done cheaply) or remove it. If you have say, a wind direction indicator that is not working, then your buyer will use that to bargain the price down. If it is not there, he can't. So pull it out and replace it with a diagram of code flags (which is far more useful anyway).

I once had a buyer try to beat me up on the price because the immersion suits (that were not on the inventory and were being left as a gift) were a bit mouldy. If I had simply given them to my neighbour, that could not have happened and I would have made another nautical friend. So remove any non-functioning extras. This will also make your boat look more tidy.

Location, location, location

Due to currency fluctuations and market depth (the amount of people looking to buy/sell a boat) certain places are better for selling than buying and vice-versa.

Location can play a big part in the quest to protect our wee pile of cash, but it can also work against us.

Plenty of sailors head south from the US west coast to Mexico on the annual rally known as the 'Baja Ha Ha'. It is a lovely sail downwind and can be a bit of a hoot as the name suggests – but the bash back against the wind to the US can be bloody horrible and many sailors put their boat up for sale in Mexico (often under pressure from a partner they partially coerced to join them) rather than face the journey back or the spectre of divorce.

Similarly in Malaysia, the tax-free island of Langkawi has a heap of boats for sale, as many people end their sailing adventure there. If you have learnt to sail in Europe or the US, then goofed off in the Caribbean for a while, passed through the Panama canal and explored the delights of the Pacific for a season or two before heading to, Australia and on to Thailand/Malaysia, you will have had pretty wonderful trade wind sailing for a number of years.

Once in Malaysia though, you have to make the choice of bashing back against the trade winds or carrying on in a westerly direction across the Indian Ocean to Madagascar, the Cape of Good Hope, the South Atlantic, etc.

Many people take a hard look at themselves and their boat at this point and, quite understandably, decide to call it quits while the going is good. They put their boat up for sale and fly home with some great memories. Job done. No regrets.

In the Caribbean, there are a lot of boats for sale in the Rio Dulce delta in Guatemala for similar reasons. Heading east back to the central Caribbean and Bahamas means bashing against strong headwinds and steep seas. The other two alternatives are sailing with the wind through the Panama Canal and undertaking the 3000 mile journey to French Polynesia, or selling your boat where it is.

This can make these spots a good place to buy a boat cheaply, but not the best place to sell one. So, as soon as you think you might be coming to the end of your time afloat, it pays to start planning the geography of your exit strategy so that you don't end up in a place that is inundated with boats for sale.

Brokers and immediate gratification.

Remember that if you have to leave your boat and fly home, then you will need a broker to sell your boat. Brokers are generally quite professional and honest, but can cost you anywhere between 10% and 20% of the sale price. There are also some other costs to consider because a broker is not going to sit on your boat at anchor keeping her polished and airy-fresh until she is sold. Instead, he will require the boat to be stored somewhere it is convenient to show to clients – and that normally means a marina or a boatyard.

Also, as you will have learnt over the preceding years, boats tend to go off the boil very quickly if not maintained on a daily basis. If your boat is not sold in the first few weeks, then it will start to deteriorate (mould is a big problem in the tropics) and become less likely to be sold for anything near the asking price. The broker may then have to hire somebody to bring her back to something approaching presentable condition. On land these people are called 'cleaners' and can be hired for a reasonable price. As soon as you enter the marine world of course, they morph into professionals, rebrand themselves as 'detailers' and charge like orthodontists.

The broker may not even be prepared to do this for you and your boat will start sagging and developing the unmistakable smell of neglect, whilst collecting a layer of dust (or a mountain of pelican crap if on a mooring) in the corner of a forgotten boatyard, and racking up storage fees until some smug smart-arse like me (or one of my readers) sees the gem under all that neglect and makes a lowball offer.

Given the current appearance of the boat, the broker will recommend you accept that offer and, given the ongoing nature of storage fees and/or overpriced cleaners, you would be well-advised to accept it too. So the 80k you hoped to get for your boat is now significantly less. For example:

Offer of 60k accepted due to condition

Less 15% for the broker = 51k

Less 4 months of storage fees at a minimum of $500/month (very conservative estimate) = 49k

Add a few visits from an overpriced, re-branded cleaner and suddenly your hoped-for return is barrelling towards being half of what you were originally banking on.

I am not saying this is inevitable, but it happens to so many boats, it is worth trying to avoid this scenario by planning your exit more carefully. Again, our old friend 'attitude' is about to hove into view and save the day.

Exit attitude

Some sellers will be forced to sell quickly due to health or family emergencies, but the overwhelming majority of quick sellers I have encountered are simply those who want to move on and have the type of impatience that comes from years of becoming accustomed to immediate gratification. But there is a better way.

DIY and time

In this internet, peer-to-peer, twenty-first century world we find ourselves living in, there is absolutely no good reason to hand over thousands of dollars to a broker to sell your boat other than convenience. Increasingly, nautical nomads are taking control of their exit strategy in the same way they have been taking control of every other facet of their lives.

In many ways it is easier to sell your boat privately to another person than it is to comply with all the demands (and ultimately charges) of a broker. Plus of course, you only have one boat to recommend – and it happens to be the one that you are the world's biggest expert on. Expertise and product knowledge have been repeatedly shown to be very strong selling points (which is why so many companies send their salesmen on product training junkets) and the poor old broker can't be expected to know more about your boat than you do.

You also have a few other strengths that brokers do not have:

- **You can choose your location**
    While a broker tends to be fixed geographically, you are a watery wanderer rolling with the trade winds and can decide where you would like to sell your boat based on market demand and exchange rates. For example I sold *Marutji* in Australia because the market was as hot a Hades in 2012 and the Aussie Dollar ruled the world. I bought *Calypso* in USD, so she only cost me 93c on the dollar. I sold *Calypso* seven years later in USD in Fiji because the demand in Fiji was quite high and the American Dollar was back on top. I have just sailed *Calypso II* to Australia to be sold here because the market is red hot again due to Australians being banned from international travel due to Covid 19.[68]
    Demand and exchange rates change all the time, but there are always places that are better than others to sell your boat and exchange rates that are more favourable.
    You can take advantage of these changing conditions (usually by asking around on the sea-gypsy telegraph), whereas the broker is stuck with whatever situation prevails in his area.

- **Maintenance**
    As you will be staying on board your boat, you can keep her in tip-top condition for prospective buyers. Just like selling a house, a boat is more than simply a vessel and will be far more attractive to buyers if she is well aired and there are

---

[68] Details of 'project *Calypso III*' will be published on the website as soon as I have anything concrete to report.

happy people on board enjoying the aquatic life, mixing drinks and having fun. You certainly won't need 'detailers' to relieve you of your hard-earned cash as if cleaning a boat was rocket science.

- **Storage**
As mentioned above, storage fees can eat a large chunk into your ultimate payout. Some brokers have free or discounted berths for boats on their books, but these tend to be reserved for the high net-worth boats that they can see a decent payday in. Believe it or not, many brokers do not see making 10k out of you for putting your boat online and showing a few people around it, much of a payday. If you decide to sell your boat privately and have identified on the scuttlebutt the best place that is within your sailing abilities, then put your ad on Yachthub (or wherever is relevant in your area) and let people know when you will be arriving. This will stir up interest before you even get there and hopefully generate a few leads. It is worth taking some time here and making a detailed ad with links to videos and great photos of a TIDY boat (you would be surprised how many people photograph their boats with a sink full of washing up unmade beds and skanky-looking laundry all over the place). Stage your boat properly – with place settings, wine bottles etc and use the same types of photos that high-end brokers use.
When the weather is right, set sail and go and enjoy a few months cruising in your new area whilst selling your boat.

This will not only keep your boat current and free of mould, funny smells and the unmistakeable air of abandonment, but will also avoid the storage fees associated with brokers as you will be living at anchor and enjoying your cruising as usual. Relax, stay happy and enjoy your long goodbye.

- **Negotiation**

    It is so much easier to negotiate a favourable price if you are enjoying your cruising life and about as desperate to sell as people holding Pfizer shares in the next pandemic. It is also much easier to come to an agreement that the buyer is happy with when you know that there is no broker to relieve you of another 10% or 20%.

However, if all the above sets your impatience circuits into overload and you feel that you will simply go nuts if you spend another couple of months leisurely cruising a small area, then firstly I would suggest that you have a little break, a cup of really good tea and try and calm yourself down. The difference in price will be worth it and if you can resist the need for instant gratification, the money you will save will effectively mean you are being paid to cruise your boat – and that is a rare thing indeed! This is certainly the best way to go, but if you are prevented from choosing that option by time constraints, unavailability of tea or general temperament, all is not lost. If you really must arrive at the end of a downwind run, step off your boat and onto a plane, the right attitude can still help you.

The right attitude for people with the wrong attitude

In the end, there is no such thing as something for nothing and if you want something from the world (in this case, the convenience of handing your boat over to a broker in a place that favours the buyer) then usually, you have to give something back. The trick is to try and limit the amount.

Make your boat as presentable as possible, price it attractively and get her sold quickly. Remember, every month you wait is more storage fees, more glorified cleaners, more insurance premiums and more deterioration. Selling quickly at the end points of great sea journeys means you probably won't get top dollar, so it is important to not kid yourself. If you get a 'close enough' offer, take it and don't sweat the last few thousand. You really want to avoid the situation that befalls so many who stubbornly wait for the price they want while their boat is deteriorating and therefore increasingly less likely to achieve that price - whilst the bills continue to rack up on a daily basis. This can end up eating a huge part of your little nest-egg as well as adding an unnecessarily bitter end-note to your wonderful journey.

Taking a massive hit on your capital may also make buying another boat more difficult once you have been on land with the muggles for six months and have realised what a ghastly mistake you have made.

A final word about over-capitalizing.

Earlier in the chapter, I warned about over-capitalizing when you sell a boat, but many people do their over-capitalizing when they buy, rather than when they sell.

I know it is hard to believe, but here we are drifting towards the end of my second book and I am still banging on about not buying fancy, shiny boats with everything aboard except a decent rudder and keel. But, if you have gone ahead anyway and spent US$400,000 on a new Frenchy Ocean 45 footer and a few years later you decide to exit the lifestyle (probably because you are tired of the enormous bills and dock fees or you have, quite understandably, scared yourself to death when your spade rudder fell off) you will take at least a 30% knock on the new price when you sell her (more if you are in the wrong place). Add the brokers' commission, storage fees and 'detailers' etc., and you can easily be staring at a capital loss of over US$200,000 and a future sitting in the corner of the yacht club bar, echoing the chorus of, 'boats are a money pit' with the rest of the terminally disillusioned.

On the other hand, take a look at Tina and Oyvan – the two plucky Norwegians I spoke of in the last book. They bought their tough, seaworthy, little Bayfield 29 with her encapsulated full keel and properly supported rudder (in a place that favoured the buyer) for US$17,000 and were sailing after a month in the boatyard checking all the important things.

If they now decide to sell their boat and go back to Norway (and I truly hope they don't) they could sail to somewhere boats are in demand and sell her for pretty much what they bought her for – even possibly make a small profit. Actually, they could give their boat away for free to a local fishing co-op in Thailand, hop on a plane and be back in Norway knowing they have done something wonderful in this world and still be showing a capital loss of only 1/12th of that of

Mr Frenchy Ocean 45.

Be smart. Be like Tina and Oyvan.

CHAPTER 21

Staying Strong:
Ignoring the trolls and doubters.

If you wrestle with a pig, you both get covered in shit, but the pig enjoys the process.

Latvian proverb

There have been many improvements and much to celebrate in the world of communications since my last book, but the meteoric rise of uninformed trolling and 'post-truth' denialism is not amongst them. Increased connectivity is helping many people (including me) achieve the dream of a nomadic lifestyle and I am extremely grateful for it.

However, it seems that the price we must all pay for this wonderful portal is that to get to the good stuff, we are forced to wade through the boggy marshes of ignorance and listen to the petty voicings of unkind sentiment. Despite having more to say for themselves than their intellect or experience could possibly justify, people with vile and hateful opinions (who would have previously had the good sense to keep them to themselves through fear of never being invited to another dinner party), are now 'linked to' similar people and emboldened by the group anonymity that has always been the refuge of the cowardly and the bitter. The constant white noise of this random ugliness increases the moment you start following your own path. As John Lennon famously said, "the more real you get, the more unreal others around you become".

So do your best to ignore the furious keyboard warriors – they are on their own journey (although the destination is something of a mystery) and you are on yours. This could be the greatest adventure of your life, or a bloody disaster if you let them into your head.

This is extremely easy to do when things are going your way. When you are gliding across a rolling ocean under full sail or spear-fishing in a coral lagoon, it is unlikely that anyone can get to you. However, when things aren't going so well, this can provide the chink in the armour that the trolls are always looking to exploit. So when things are bleak, uncomfortable, scary or all three, try to keep the following in mind:

It is perfectly normal that there will be times in your sailing life when you would rather be anywhere else than on that damn boat!

Perhaps you are into your third day of bad weather or have had a row with your squeeze, but there will be times when you would happily kill the world's last panda and skin its tubby monochrome hide to be practically anywhere else on earth than on that damn boat.

When we feel like this on land, it just gets chalked off to 'life'. When you feel like this on a boat, all the unkind words of the trolls and doubters emerge from your subconscious to say:

"See, I told you it was a dumb idea!"

"You've really bitten off more than you can chew this time you doofus!"

"This is what happens if you please yourself or don't hang around in case your grand kids need bigger toys/ more free babysitting, etc, etc"

"Who the hell do you think you are anyway?"

As with all things on the path to watery wonderfulness, the way to send this self-recrimination sailing back into the bleachers is to use the right attitude and preparation.

Accept in advance that these moments are part and parcel of this (and any) change of lifestyle and be prepared for them. This is one of the many reasons I stress (perhaps overstress) the importance of not buying into the Jimmy Buffet/Mark Twain nonsense of, "buy a boat, cast off the docklines and sail over the horizon to margarita paradise". If you have bought that idea, then the inevitable arrival of the odd difficult period can create a crack that the voices of the trolls can easily slip into and exploit.

So my briny brothers and salty sisters, I reiterate that this wonderful dream is practical and achievable by anybody and on a modest sum, but go into your wonderful new adventure with the knowledge that the odd period will seriously suck and when it arrives, you will see it for what it is – just one of those days that the doofus on *Calypso* was banging on about for 600 pages – and not evidence that the trolls and doubters were even close to being right.

Let it pass and soon the sun, salt water and rhythms of the ocean will work their magic and the trolls will settle back into the primordial sludge from whence they came. [69]

As always, the right attitude will be your greatest ally. So keep dreaming, but install a mental firewall to help you stay real by keeping the nastier elements of connectivity in the shadows where they belong. Keep moving forward and you will find it will all fall into place soon enough.

⚓

So as we produce our curly pipe for the last time, put our feet up on the gunnels and point our bowsprit towards the cosy anchorage at the end of my second (and probably last) book on the subject of personal transformation through simple living afloat, I hope I have successfully made the point that whatever form your adventure takes – from coastal hopping to ocean bashing - it is important to stay loyal to those things that bring enduring happiness, rather than constantly chasing the empty and transient buzz of novelty that often wears its clothes. Cut out the white noise of the marketing and the A-type

---

[69] A message to trolls: No opinion, however strongly held, survives contact with the reality of the ocean. You just can't argue with physics, no matter what you have read on the internet, so stop raining on everyone's parade because nobody cares. However, if you still find that you have been offended by any of the information in this book, feel free to express your uninformed 'reckon' by logging on to www.sailingcalypso.com and simply banging the keyboard with your hairy fists or enormous Cro Magnon forehead.

personalities who think speed, boat size or 'miles under the keel' have any other value than as signals of their own neurosis, and sail the way that makes you chuckle quietly to yourself. Do it safely and in your own time and don't set yourself ridiculous or arbitrary goals - because whatever form your current dream takes, it is not worth giving up all future dreams for.

Whether you stay with this lifestyle or just do it for a while, whether you are young, old, retired, rich, poor or just plain nuts, there really is no downside to buying a small, seaworthy, well laid-up boat with a properly attached keel and supported rudder, keeping your life simple and joining us happy sea gypsies out here on the big blue wobbly thing where the plankton play and there is no address for the junk mail to find.

Good luck and fair winds to everyone!

Captain Rick "well-fishy" Page
Somewhere on the east coast of Australia
2021

www.sailingcalypso.com
FB: Sailing Calypso
Email:sailingcalypso@gmail.com

Afterword

I am fevered with the sunset,
I am fretful with the bay,
For the wander-thirst is on me
And my soul is in Cathay.

There's a schooner in the offing,
With her topsails shot with fire,
And my heart has gone aboard her
For the Islands of Desire.

I must go forth again to-morrow!
With the sunset I must be
Hull down on the trail of rapture
In the wonder of the sea.

The Sea Gypsy
Richard Hovey 1869-1900

Thanks again for buying my second book. I enjoyed writing it and I hope you found something in it that will help you stay afloat and enjoy this wonderful lifestyle on the wobbly stuff.

As always, I am available on email if you have any questions or just want to say 'hi'. I have not been at this sailing lark so long that I have forgotten what it is like to be just starting out, so no question is too obvious or too personal. Ask away! I am always happy to help new nautical nomads.

Good luck everyone! In a few dozen years, none of this will really matter - your fulfilment or mine will count for nought. But today, when these things can actually make a difference in our short free-fall, I hope you can find the will to get gone and stay gone. I look forward to seeing you all out here and maybe we can free-fall together over a beer for a while. Until then, stay safe and last one left on land, turn off the gas.

⚓

Recommended Reading

I read a lot and my list is constantly changing and evolving. To see the latest list, go to:

www.sailingcalypso.com/books.

About the author

Rick Page holds an honours degree in Disaster Engineering and Management and is a regular contributor to sailing magazines worldwide. He became a RYA qualified skipper in 2008 and has lived aboard since 2007 when he bought his first boat Marutji - a steel Van de Stadt 34. He first bought the idea of the Sea Gypsy life to a wider audience through the TV documentaries *New Lives in the Wild* and *New Lives in the Wild Revisited*[70] where he attacked the myth that you have to be rich, gifted or crazy to travel the world by sail.

The book, *Get Real, Get Gone* was released several months later in order to elaborate on the ideas and philosophies that were touched upon in the TV documentary and to answer the thousands of questions from budding (often completely inexperienced) sea gypsies who were inspired to follow his example and head out to tropical paradise on their own boat and limited budget. *Get Real, Get Gone* has since been translated into Spanish, Portuguese and German with more languages planned. There is also an audiobook published by Tantor available on Amazon read by BAFTA nominated narrator Liam Gerrard.

Rick is currently back where it all started on the Australian east coast and contemplating his next leap.

For more details see www.sailingcalypso.com

---

[70] This series is also known as Where the Wild Men Are in certain countries.

Printed in Great Britain
by Amazon